The New Method *of* Learning *and* Teaching Jurisprudence

According to the Principles of the Didactic Art
Premised in the General Part and in the Light of Experience

Gottfried Wilhelm Leibniz

The First Complete English Translation
of the 1667 *Frankfurt Edition* with Notes by
Carmelo Massimo de Iuliis

The New Method *of* Learning *and* Teaching Jurisprudence

According to the Principles of the Didactic Art
Premised in the General Part and in the Light of Experience

Gottfried Wilhelm Leibniz

The First Complete English Translation
of the 1667 *Frankfurt Edition* with Notes by
Carmelo Massimo de Iuliis

TALBOT
PUBLISHING
Clark, New Jersey

ISBN 978-1-61619-547-2

TALBOT PUBLISHING

AN IMPRINT OF

THE LAWBOOK EXCHANGE, LTD.

33 Terminal Avenue

Clark, New Jersey 07066-1321

Please see our website for a selection of our other publications and fine facsimile reprints of classic works of legal history: www.lawbookexchange.com

Library of Congress Cataloging-in-Publication Data

Names: Leibniz, Gottfried Wilhelm, Freiherr von, 1646-1716. | De Iuliis, Carmelo Massimo, translator. | Butler, William Elliott, 1939- , writer of preface.

Title: The new method of learning and teaching jurisprudence according to the principles of the didactic art premised in the general part and in the light of experience : a translation of the 1667 Frankfurt edition with notes by Carmelo Massimo de Iuliis / by Gottfried Wilhelm Leibniz.

Other titles: Nova methodus discendae docendaeque iurisprudentiae. English

Description: Clark, NJ : Talbot Publishing, an imprint of The Lawbook Exchange, Ltd., 2017. | Includes bibliographical references and index.

Identifiers: LCCN 2016057978| ISBN 9781616195472 (hardcover : alk. paper) | ISBN 1616195479 (hardcover : alk. paper)

Subjects: LCSH: Law--Study and teaching--Early works to 1800.

Classification: LCC K100 .L45313 2017 | DDC 340.071--dc23

LC record available at https://lccn.loc.gov/2016057978

Table of Contents

Preface vii
William E. Butler
Acknowledgments xi
Introduction xiii
Leibniz and Legal Science **between** *Topics and Dogmatics*
Translations of the *Nova Methodus* lxxi
Abbeviations and Notice to the Reader lxxiii

Epigraph lxxvii
Dedication lxxix
Preface to the Reader lxxxiii

Part I 1
The new method for learning and teaching jurisprudence, general and common to all other intellectual abilities. The plan of studies in general.

Part II 31
Special, solely restricted to the Jurisprudence

Index 211

PREFACE

Gottfried Wilhelm Leibniz (1646–1716) is secure in his place among the true polymaths of the seventeenth century. His contributions to the advancement of learning extend to philosophy, logic, mathematics, physics, technology, philology, theology, history, library science, and others. As his immense correspondence and repository of scholarly papers are gradually published, we have come to appreciate even more the quality of his mind. Continental scholars have enjoyed better access to his thinking than the English-speaking world; Leibniz wrote principally in Latin, French, and German.

Although his renown lies principally in what used to be called the exact sciences, he earned his keep as a jurist and diplomat. His contributions to the law of nations and to the science of jurisprudence are underappreciated not least because they have been linguistically inaccessible. An excellent reason to welcome the translation of the present work, which illuminates Leibniz's thinking on legal education and, in passing, comparative jurisprudence.

Proficient in Latin at a young age, a facility in language attributed to the access he enjoyed to his late father's private library, Leibniz matriculated as a fifteen-year old at the University of Leipzig and some months later completed a first degree in philosophy in December 1662. By February 1664 he was awarded the degree of magister, having defended a dissertation that explored the theoretical and pedagogical relationship between law and philosophy. He then turned to the study of law; the degree of baccalaureate of law was conferred on 28 September 1665 for a dissertation devoted to "conditions". After defending a habilitation thesis in philosophy in March 1666 at Leipzig, Leibniz returned to the study of law and determined to secure a license and a doctorate.

The University of Leipzig rejected Leibniz's application for a doctorate, possibly because of his youth and his haste (law was usually a three-year course of study). Leibniz promptly enrolled at the University of Altdorf and submitted a dissertation that presumably he had commenced while at Leipzig; it was devoted to perplexing legal cases. By November 1666 Leibniz had received his license in law and his doctorate.

Few individuals with Leibniz's range of interests were as accomplished in law and diplomacy. The present work on jurisprudence attracted the attention of Prince-Bishop Johann Philipp von Schönborn (1605–1673), Elector of Mainz, among the most influential personalities in the Holy Roman Empire. Following several years in service to the Elector, Leibniz traveled to Paris, where he remained until 1676, with a side visit to London, where he was elected to the Royal Society in 1673. Unsuccessful in obtaining diplomatic assignments to which he aspired, Leibniz removed to the electorate of Hanover, where he remained for the rest of his life. As a recognized historian, librarian, and judge and sometime traveler about Europe, he dedicated himself to a number of causes, not least the reunification of Christendom. Among his services to the science of law was his compilation and publication of the *Codex Iuris Gentium* (1693), an enduring contribution to the law of treaties and evidence of State practice.

The present translation of Leibniz by Carmelo Massimo de Iuliis makes available at long last the full text of one of Leibniz's key early works, a work that launched Leibniz towards becoming "… one of the half-dozen greatest philosophers of the seventeenth century".[1] Composed at the age of twenty-one while journeying about Germany without a library at hand, this volume addressed universal jurisprudence as an object of learning and recommended that law be approached from four perspectives: didactic, historical, exegetic, and polemical. For each approach he suggested what materials should be studied and how they should be used. Wigmore believed that Leibniz anticipated the great reform movements of the following two centuries — national codification or systematization of law and the historical school of the late 1700s and 1800s. His Justinian Rearranged was pursued by Robert Joseph Pothier (1699–1772) in France a century later; the polemical moots that Leibniz suggested, in Wigmore's view, may have been precursors of Caspar Rudolf Ritter von Jhering's (1818–1892) practical exercises.[2]

Passages of Leibniz's work herein presage the prospects for comparative legal studies, especially his contemplated "Theatrum Legale". Leibniz has recently been rediscovered in the post-Soviet world. The present work was excluded from the multi-volume Soviet edition of Leibniz and is unknown to Russian, Ukrainian, and other post-Soviet jurists.[3] Until now even in English the work has been available only in excerpts.

William E. Butler

---

[1] Patrick Riley, *Leibniz' Universal Jurisprudence: Justice as the Charity of the Wise* (1996), p. 11.

[2] J. Wigmore, "Nova Methodus Discendae Docendaeque Jurisprudentiae", *Harvard Law Review*, XXX (1916/1917), p. 813.

[3] See O. V. Kresin, «К вопросу о сравнительном подходе к познанию права и идее «театра права» в трудах Лейбница» [On the Question of a Comparative Approach to the Cognition of Law and the Idea of a 'Theatre of Law' in the Works of Leibniz], in V. Gamurari (ed.), Ştiinţa juridică universitară în contextul promovării valorilor europene (Kishinev, 2013), pp. 378–382.

ACKNOWLEDGMENTS

I wish to thank for their encouragement to the publication of my essay and translation of Leibniz's *Nova Methodus*, the following professors of the Università Cattolica del Sacro Cuore, Milan: firstly Carlo Castronovo, full professor of Civil Law; Antonio Albanese, full professor of Civil law; Alessandro D'Adda, Director of the Department of Public and Private Economy Law, full professor of Private law; Stefano Solimano, Director of the Department of Legal Sciences, full professor of History of Medieval and Modern Law; Gianluca Varraso, full professor of Criminal Procedure.

A special thanks also to Dr. Mattia Luigi Pozzi who gave me useful advices in preparing the indexes.

Introduction

Leibniz and Legal Science **between** *Topics and Dogmatics*

1. *Biographical sketch of Leibniz.* 2. *Editions and translations of Nova methodus discendae docendaeque jurisprudentiae.* 3. *Current ideas about Leibniz, Logic and Nova Methodus.* 4. *On the general method of study.* 5. *Mnemonics and didactics.* 6. *Recommendations for life.* 7. *What is jurisprudence.* 8. *Historical jurisprudence and the historical training of the jurist.* 9. *Exegetical jurisprudence.* 10. *Logic and rhetoric.* 11. *Logic as functional for systematic reconstruction of the legal system.* 12. *Leibniz and logic.*

1. *Biographical sketch of Leibniz to date of publication of Nova Methodus (1667).*

Gottfried Wilhelm Leibniz[1] was born at Leipzig in 1646,[2] the son of Frederic Leibniz, Professor of Moral Philosophy in the University, and Catharine, the daughter of Wilhelm Schmuck, Doctor and Professor of Law in the University of the same town. The sister of his mother had been married to Johann Strauch, secretary of the town of Brunswick and prominent jurist.

The same Leibniz in his *Vita Leibnitii a se ipso breviter delineata*[3] relates that he lost the father at the age of six and that his primary education was based on home schooling. A powerful attraction to the Latin historians, in particular Livy, played an important role in his education; then he discovered Cicero, Quintilian, Seneca,

---

[1] Leipzig, 1 [N. S.] (3?) July, 21 [O.S] June 1646–Hannover, 14 November 1716.

[2] Maria Rosa Antognazza (2009), *Leibniz*. Cambridge: Cambridge University Press, 27: "two years after marrying Friedrich Leubnitz, Catarina Schmuck, mother of Leibniz, gave birth to her first child on 1 July 1646". As the nearly fifty-year old father recordered the event in a now lost family chronicle, 'On Sunday 21 June [O.S.] my son Gottfried Wilhelm was born at 6.54 P.M.'". The dates differ because of the calendar system. According to the New (Gregorian) Style [N.S.], the birth date of Leibniz corresponds to the 1st of July: "The so-called Gregorian calendar was introduced in 1582 in Catholic countries following a papal bull issued by Pope Gregory XVIII. In February 1700 the Gregorian style was introduced into the Protestant States of Germany: after 18 February ten days were cancelled to make the following date the 1st of March. Great Britain and her colonies did not adopt the new calendar until 1752. Because 1700 was a leap year in the old (Julian) calendar, after 29 February 1700 (O.S.) the difference between the two systems became eleven days" (Antognazza, XV).

[3] Alexandre Foucher de Careil [1826–1891] (ed.) (1857), *Nouvelle lettres et opuscules inédits de Leibniz*. Paris, 379, "Natus sum illi jam quinquennario et vix sexenni amisi patrem" ; hereinafter : *Vita Leibnitii.*

Pliny, Herodotus, Xenophon, Plato and the historians of the Augustean era[4] in his father's library.

Biographers stress that

> the chronology of this programme of home schooling also remains unclear: much of this advanced reading in the sources must have taken place (if at all) in Leibniz's university years. Not entirely clear is how much of this material was in his father's library, or precisely if why it might have been there.
>
> What is immediately evident, however, is that this understructured program of avid, independent, and wide ranging reading informed Leibniz's approach to learning from the very outset of his schooling and played the crucial role in producing his extraordinary educational results.
>
> Its first consequence was to accelerate his mastery of the subject still foundational to all higher learning: by the age of twelve he was proficient in the Latin language.[5]
>
> In fact, he was able to write 300 verses in hexameter, publicly praised by the preceptors.[6]

Fascinated by mathematics and logic, he claimed to have read Jacopo Zabarella [1533–1539], a major Aristotelian philosopher and logician in the University of Padua; and, above all, prominent Jesuit thinkers: Antonio Rubio [1548–1615], Pedro de Fonseca [1528–1599], Francisco Suarez [1548–1617];[7] these are the only names of the favorite thinkers from his youth which Leibniz

---

[4] *Vita Leibnitii*, 381.

[5] Antognazza, see note 2, 37.

[6] "versus 300 hexametros praeceptores laudatos, et quod affectaveram, sine ulla elisione, quos publice stata die pronuntiavi", *Vita Leibnitii*, 382.

[7] "Rubio et Zabarella interea in Fonseca et aliisque scholasticis non minori, quam antea in Historicis voluptate versabar et eiusque profeceram, ut Suaresium non minore facilitatem legerem, quam Milesias fabulas solemus, quas vulgo Romanos vocant", *Vita Leibnitii*, 382.

mentioned expressly in his above-quoted autobiography, together with those of the Latin writers, already mentioned, and few other jurists of his time.

The young Leibniz began his studies at the University of Leipzig in April 1661, some months before his fifth birthday. Here, he said, "I had the good fortune to have as teacher the famous Jacob Thomasius [1622–1684]".[8] The influence of the latter was decisive on the formation of the young Leibniz because he treasured the method of direct reading of the philosophers, especially Aristotle, in order to acquire direct knowledge of the great thinker's works and gain an opinion wholly different from that provided by his scholastic interpreters. On 2 December 1662, he took a bachelor's degree in philosophy; six months later he defended his *Disputatio metaphisica de principio individui* (*Metaphisical Disputation on the Principle of Individuation*)[9] under the presidency of the same Thomasius.

Ten days after the defense of this dissertation, on 20 June 1663, Leibniz enrolled for the summer semester at the University of Jena. The lectures on mathematics given there by Erhard Weigel [1625–1699] were the principal attraction. Weigel had written the *Analysis of Aristotle according the geometrical demostration of Euclid*[10] under the influence of the recent rediscovery of the *Elements* by Euclid reprinted in the famous critical edition by Isaac Barrow [1630–1677] in 1655.[11] In the culture of those

---

[8] Leibniz's note (1660s?) in Alexandre Foucher de Careil (ed.) (1905), *Mémoire sur la philosophie de Leibniz*. Paris: F.R. de Rudeval, Part I, 6.

[9] Leibniz (1663), *Disputatio metphisica de principio individui*, in AA VI, 1, 3.

[10] Erhard Weigel (1658), *Analysis Aristotelica ex Euclide Restituta*. Jenae: apud Grosium.

[11] Euclid, *Elementa*, in Isaac Barrow (ed.) (1655), *Euclides Elementorum libri XV*. Cantabrigiae.

years Euclid's Elements became almost a myth. All thinkers tried to reread every field of knowledge through the Euclidean geometrical demonstrations.

This "geometrization" of knowledge, *i.e.* applying in every field of knowledge the Euclidean method to reach a mathematically consistent certitude of every conclusion, seems to have greatly influenced Leibniz. He tried to make good use of this scheme of thinking in the most uncertain and unreliable human science: the science of right. We find evidence of this undoubted cultural influence in *Specimen quaestionum philosophicarum ex iure callectarum* (*An essay of collected philosophical problems of right*), written for the master's degree in philosophy at the University of Leipzig, conferred in February 1664, and in *De conditionibus* (*On Conditions*) for the bachelor's degree in law, granted in the same University in September 1665. Above all, in the dissertation *De arte combinatoria (On Combinatorial Art),* [12] which Leibniz wrote for his habilitation in Faculty of Philosophy of the University of Leipzig in March 1666. In this booklet Leibniz tries to build a system

---

[12] See for the premises of the operation, Leibniz, *Dissertatio de arte combinatoria,* AA VI, 1, Prob. II, VIII *usus*, 40, 189.

> *Jurisprudentia cum in aliis Geometriae similis est, tum in hoc quod utraque habet Elementa, Utraque casus. Elementa sunt simplicia, in Geometria figurae triangulis, circulus etc., in Jurisprudentia actus promissio alienatio etc.. Casus: complexiones horum* [...]. *Termini quorum Complicatione oritur in Jure diversitas casuum, sunt: Personae, Res, Actus, Jura.* (Jurisprudence, just as geometry in several aspects, as [is similar] in this, because each of them has elements, each of them has cases. The simple elements in geometry are the figures of the triangle, circle etc., etc., in jurisprudence act, alienation, promise etc. Cases are the complex of them [...]. The terms from which derive the diversity of cases in law are: persons, things, rights.). [ed. transl.].

> based on the Ramon Lull's [c. 1233–1315] *Ars magna* (1305), whose basic idea was to resolve complex ideas into their component simple concepts, then to combine them, through some mechanism, to generate complex concepts or propositions—possibly even ones that had not previously been thought of, as Leibniz suggests. By choosing an appropriate mechanism, moreover, one could combine concepts into valid arguments, thus generating all propositions that express true and certain knowledge[13].

However, in his legal doctoral dissertation *De casibus perplexis in jure* (*On puzzling legal cases*) defended in the University of Altdorf in 1666, Leibniz already was aware that mathematical or geometrical proofs in law are not always possible and wrote in this book that algebra can merely make order, but does not provide solutions for every case: in puzzling cases such proofs can only tell us that the case is impossible to solve

> … and the impossible problems in perplexing cases, in which the solution consists in remarking upon and demonstrating the impossibility, is the thing that is achieved through algebra.[14]

It is still a "mystery" why Leibniz took his law doctorate in Altdorf University rather than at Leipzig. Leibniz's "truth" is the following:

---

[13] Richard T. W. Arthur (2014), *Leibniz*. Cambridge MA: Polity, 30, who points out that the Lull's proposal that a true proposition could be delivered by combinatorial means had been taken up by the Herborn scholars: Johann Heinrich Alsted [1588–1638] who, along with his students Johann Heinrich Bisterfeld [c. 1605–1655] and Jan Amos Comenius [1592–1670], was Leibniz's immediate source of inspiration (see 12).

[14] Leibniz (1664), *De casibus perplexis in jure*, in AA VI, 1, 235, "*….et impossibilia casibus perplexis, in quibus pro solutione est advertere et demonstrare impossibilitatem, quod Algebra praestat.*".

> The law faculty of the University of Leipzig is formed of twelve assessors (assistants), which are quite different from professors. *Assessores* deal with advice and opinions about cases, rather than lessons and reasoned discussions on controversial topics. All the Doctors Juris are allowed in the faculty, according to the doctorate order, just that a place is vacant, for the death of one of them. I was aware that if I soon would have become a Doctor I would be among the first and that fate was protecting me; but then, by chance, there was a great dispute, for certain people wanted to be appointed as the only Doctors, excluding the younger candidates and postponing them to another promotion. Many members of the faculty had agreed. As soon as I perceived the deception of the emulators, I changed my mind, took the decision to travel abroad, thought it unworthy that a young man remained hammered as a nail in a certain place: for the mind wanted to get greater glory and knowledge of foreign states and the mathematical disciplines. (…) Shortly after I graduated as a Doctor in the University of Altdorf with the highest praise. [ed. transl.]. [15]

---

[15] *Vita Leibnitii*, 383:

> Facultas juridica Lipsiensis constat duodecim Assessoribus, qui a professoribus sunt diversi. Hi vacant responsis potius atque consultationibus, quam lectionibus atque disputationibus. In eam recipiuntur omnes doctors juris Lipiseinsis, ordine doctoratus, ubi primum vacuus ipsis locus fit, alterius decessu. Ego videbam, si mature doctor crearer, me inter primos fore fortunamque in tuto collocaturum; sed tum forte ingens orta erat disputatio, cum quidam soli doctors creari vellent, aliis junioribus exclusis et in aliam promotionem dilatis. Illis favebant plurimi ex facultate. Ego animadverso artificio aemulorum, mutato consilio ad peregrinations animum applicavi, indignum ratus, juvenem velut clavo affigi certain loco: nam diu ardebat animus ad majorem gloriam studiorum et cognitionemexterorumet disciplinas mathemathicas. (…) Paulo post in Academia Norica Doctoris gradum sums ianno aetatis vigesimo primo, maximo omnium applausu.".

In any case, this is not a convincing version of events because Leibniz could boast many protections (his maternal grandfather was the great jurist, Wilhelm Smuck, and his uncle, Johann Strauch, was a prominent jurist) and had a network of friends in academia.[16] The first biography[17] of his life, printed twenty years after his death, reported no more than gossip about M[onsieur] Bernard le Bovier de

---

[16] Indeed, in *Vita Leibnitii*, 383, he wrote:

> "Erat mihi amicus … provincdis Lipsiensis, quam vocant, die hofgerichte consiliarius assessor. Is et me secum ducebat saepeat acta legenda dabat, et qua ratione concipienda esse sententiae, exemplis docebat. Ita ego maturein hujuus scientiae intima penetrabam; judicis enim munere delectabar, advocatorum aversabar, eamque ob rationem numquam causas orare volui, tametsi omnium consensu valide satis atque apte germanica quoque lingua scriberem ["Was friend of mine … an assistant adviser of the Court of Leipzig Province, which they call *Hofgerichte*. He used to bring me with him and gave me legal acts to read and to teach me with examples on what ground the judgments had to be pronounced. Thus I soon penetrated the secrets of this science; I was indeed attracted by the work as a Judge, abhorred the malices of the attorneys and for this reason I would never do harangues in court, although for the unanimous opinion I wrote quite vigorously and appropriately in German" [ed. transl.].

[17] M. L. de Neufville (1734), *Histoire de la Vie et des Ouvrages de Mr. Leibnitz*. Amsterdam: chez François Changuion. Gottschalk Eduard Guhrauer [1809–1854] (1842), *Gottfried Wilhelm Freiherr von Leibnitz: Eine Biographie*. Breslau, Vorrede, X, informs us that according to what "Remond von Montmort, the younger, wrote from Paris on 26th December 1738 to the President Bouhier 'Mr. le Marquis de Joucourt m'emmena hier un frère nouvellement reconnu par sa famille et rendu à sa patrie. Il s'est toujours appelleé en Hollande Neuville et j'ai vû de lui la vie de Mr. de Leibnitz. C'est un garçon aussi amiable par son charactère et par son esprit, que laid de figure. Ses connoissances sont justes et étendues'. (From the handwritten correspondence of the President Bouhier in the Royal Library of Paris)" [ed. transl.].

Fontenelle [1657–1757],[18] contained excellent memories, and rejected the cause of this refusal being only due to the Dean of the Law Faculty of Leipzig. His wife, annoyed with M.[onsieur] Leibniz, easily persuaded her husband to postpone it [i.e. the date of Doctorate] under the pretext of his [of Leibniz] young age. Whatever the reason for the bad mood of this woman, which could not be unravelled, for the character of his genius it is always certain that Mr. Leibniz was very sensitive to rejection of that light grace, and for this reason he took the decision to abandon his homeland, where people knew so little of his value and where the same people could have taken advantage of his talents [ed. transl.][19].

Having earned his doctorate in law, Leibniz wrote the *Nova methodus discendae docendaeque jurisprudentiae* (1667), during a journey from Mainz to Frankfurt, "afflicted by the uncertainties of the journey, clatter of the inns and the lack of books".[20] His aim of this book was to enter the employ of Johann Philipp von Schönborn [1605–1673], Elector and Prince-Archibishop of Mainz, to help reform the judicial body. This book would prove to be a milestone, as we will see *infra*, in philosophical legal thought, especially in civil law countries, because it con-

---

[18] French author and influential member of three academies of the *Institut de France*, noted especially for his accessible treatments of scientific topics.

[19] De Neufville, see note 17, 20,

> M. de Fontanelle qui paroît avoir eu d'excellens Mémoires, rejecte uniquement la cause de ce refuse sur le Doyen del la Facultè de Droit. La Femme irritée contre M. Leibniz, obtint aisèment de son Epoux qu'il le renvoyât sous prétexte de sa jeuness. Quelle que soit la cause de la mauvaise humeur de cette femme, ce qu'on ne pourroit bien dèmêler qu'en connoissant le caractere de son génie, ilest toujours certain que M. Leibniz fut fort sensible au refus de cette legere grace, et que cela lui fit prendre la resolution dìabansoner une Patrie, où l'on connoissoit si peu ce qu'il valoit, et ce qu'on pouvoit fe promettre de ses talens.

[20] Nova Methodus, *Dedication*.

tains the first idea of a new conception of a Body of Right in comparison to the Digest of Justinian.

2. *Editions and translations of Nova methodus discendae docendaeque jurisprudentiae*.

> This book, small in size, but considerable if we consider the aim which Leibniz pursued, became an extraordinary rarity. It would have been useless movements to seek it in bookshops, or at friends, if the case would not have dropped it in my hands in an unforeseen way. [e. transl.].[21]

Indeed, after the first issue at Frankfurt in 1667, published under the initials of the author, [22] the *Nova Methodus* was reprinted only in 1748 with a short preface by Christian Wolf (or Wolff, 1679–1754)[23]. This edition was reissued twenty years later by Luis Dutens[24] in the first critical publication of Leibniz's works.

---

[21] De Neufville, see note 17, 25,

> Ce Livre, petit par rapport à sa grosseur, mais considerable si l'on examine le but que s'y propose M. Leibnitz, est devenu d'une rareté extraordinaire. Je me serois sons doute donné des mouvemens inutiles pour le trouver dans des boutiques de Libraires, ou chez des amis, si le hazard ne l'eût fait tomberentre mes mains d'une maniere imprévuë.

[22] Autore G.[ottfredo G.[uilielmo] L.[eibnuzio] L.[ipsiensi] (1667), *Nova Methodus Discendae Docendaeque Iurisprudentiae.* Francofurti: impensis Johannis Davidis Zunneri.

[23] Christian Wolf (ed.) (1748), *Leibnitz, Nova Methodus Discendae Docendaeque Iurisprudentiae.* Lipsiae et Halae: Ex Officina Krugiana.

[24] Luis Dutens [1730–1812] (ed.) (1768) *Leibnitii Opera Omnia,* II vol., T. 4, Genevae: Apud Fratres De Tournes.

At the end of the seventeenth century, Leibniz added the so-called note "D"[25], now printed in the footnotes to the critical edition of *Nova Methodus* by Paul Ritter [1872–1954], Willy Kabitz [1876–1942], and Heinrich Schepers of the German Academy of Science.[26]

As for translations of *Nova Methodus* in modern languages,[27] to my knowledge the only complete one is mine in Italian[28] and here in English. I have tried to give the most comprehensive framework of the juridical thought of Leibniz not only in a philosophical sense, but also in a juridical technical sense, which is the most important in this book, being specifically devoted to the Right.

The other translations into modern languages contain selected passages and pursue different aims, so that a judgment about them cannot be expressed, except that in some cases they inaccurately translate juridical terms, for they are made by philosophers not by jurists, and this is unacceptable for a legal book.

We have in the *First Part*, devoted to education in general:

- in English, selected passages, in Leroy Earl Loemker [1900–1985] (ed. and transl.) (1989),

---

[25] Gaston Grua [1903–1955] (ed.) (1948), *G.W. Leibniz, Textes inedits*, Paris, II, 704.

[26] Paul Ritter, Willy Kabitz, Heinrich Schepers (eds.) (reprs. 2006, 1990, 1st 1930), *Leibniz, Philosophische Schriften*, in short title AA VI, 1; AA VI, 2, the *Nova Methodus* is in the AA VI, 1.

[27] Italo Birocchi (2002), *Alla ricerca dell'ordine. Fonti e cultura giuridica nell'età moderna*. Torino, 211, n. 300, points out very well this gap.

[28] Carmelo Massimo de Iuliis (ed. and transl.) (2012), *Leibniz, Il nuovo metodo di apprendere ed insegnare la giurisprudenza*. Milano: Giuffrè.

Leibniz, Philosophical Papers and Letters. Dordrecht: Kluwer.

- in Italian, in Mario di Dario (ed. and transl.) (1965), *Leibniz, Il metodo Generale degli Studi.* Napoli: Nuovi Orientamenti.

As for the *Second Part*, devoted expressly to the education of the jurist, we have:

- in English, only §§1 to 22 and 69 to 76 by Christopher Johns (2013), *The Science of Right in Leibniz's Moral and Political Philosophy.* London, New York: Bloomsbury, but the topic indicated in the title is not useful for the jurist;
- the same can be said for the translation into German, selected passages, by Hans Zimmermann, Hubertus Busche (eds. and transl.) (2003), *Leibniz, Frühe Schriften zum Naturrecht.* Hamburg: Meiner;
- an old French version, with omission of the §§91 to 100, by G. L. Maurin (transl.) (1830), *Leibniz, Nouvelle méthode pour apprendre et einsegner la jurisprudence.* Paris. This is the only translation made by a lawyer, but notwithstanding, it is not satisfactory as for the explanations of technical juridical words used by Leibniz.

3. *Current ideas about Leibniz, Logic, and Nova Methodus.*

Leibniz today is seen as a true supporter of logical *calculus* (one may mention Bertand Russell,[29] among others),[30] intended to meet a compelling need for order, for convincing arguments and for a restatement of legal reasoning based on unquestioned axioms, from which to derive solutions *de proposito casu.* This should be achieved through a process of deductive calculation, as certain as a mathematical proof. It was probably this intellectual restlessness that ultimately led him, through the mediation of his thought by Christian Wolf and his disciples (Johann Ulrich von Cramer, 1706–1772; Daniel Nettelbladt, 1719–1791, etc.), to continental legal science in the nineteenth century and prompted his development of the concept of *dogma.*[31]

---

[29] Bertrand Russell [1872–1970] (1937), *A Critical Exposition of the Philosophy of Leibniz.* London.

[30] See Roger Berkovitz (2005), *The Gift of Science: Leibniz and Modern Legal Tradition.* Cambridge MA: Harvard University Press; in Italian literature, Umberto Vincenti (2008), *Metodologia Giuridica.* Padova, 64–67; Cesare Vasoli [1924–2013] (1973): "Enciclopedismo, pansofia e riforma 'metodica' del diritto della 'Nova methodus'". *Quaderni Fiorentini per la storia del pensiero giuridico moderno*, II, 39; according to this Vasoli, *NM* should be reread: "with the specific intent to analyze the methodological doctrine that is expounded and the route followed by Leibniz to provide law with an epistemological status that is as certain and indisputable as thát of the mathematical sciences." [ed. transl.]; and in the same meaning, already Bruno Leoni [1916–1967] (1947): "Probabilità e diritto nel pensiero di Leibniz". *Rivista di filosofia*, 74.

[31] Maximilian Herberger (1981), *Dogmatyk.* Frankfurt a. M., 4, but especially the chapters 7 and 8; Tullio Ascarelli [1903–1959] (1960), "Hobbes e Leibniz e la dogmatica giuridica", in *Testi per la storia del pensiero giuridico.* I, Milano, 161, n. 182. In Italian literature, on the concept of legal dogma, Luigi Mengoni [1922–2001] (1996), "Dogmatica giuridica", in *Ermeneutica e dogmatica giuridica.* Milan, 46:

In the early phase of his legal studies, Leibniz expresses the belief that it is necessary to clearly identify and sort the rules in force,[32] stripping law of every predicament and exception, because

> For the function of a rule is to calm the mind, which draws confidence from the certainty that the predicate maintains its validity for all subjects. But, if the rules have exceptions, or are misleading, then they cannot be trusted (*NM*, II, § 24).

Therefore lawmakers and jurists should encourage the certainty of legal relations by applying to the subject own suggestions, which are contained, in particular, among his

---

> "The first service of legal dogmatics is, therefore, in reducing the variety of legal matters to a unitary form, through which there is shared not rhapsodic knowledge, stored in repertoires of adages or in catalogs of *topoi*, but systematic knowledge, qualified by 'mastery of the subject through logic concepts'" [ed. transl.];

Id. (1985), "Ancora sul metodo giuridico", in by the same, *Diritto e valori*. Bologna, 99, n. 65,

> In our language, the word 'dogma' has lost its original meaning, similar to that which is proper in theology and ideological doctrines of political parties. However, the legal dogmas cannot entirely inappropriately continue to be called by that word because they perform a task of (relative) stabilization of value judgments (evaluations undertaken by the legal system in a given historical moment) *by turning them into cognitive concepts, which provide fixed points of reference for the understanding of the case to be decided.* [italics added; ed. transl.].

[32] On the constant search for order in the law, which has covered the legal and philosophical speculation of the past *millennium*, see Birocchi, note 27, 209 ff.; *adde* for the different concept of *ordo juris* in the Middle Ages, which is based not on positive legal basis, but on the *ordo universalis* "secret, key [which] belongs to the nature of society and consequential his innermost bones, the right", Paolo Grossi (2006), *L'ordine giuridico medievale.* Roma, Bari, 80–85 [ed. transl.].

other writings of the time[33] and in the essay analyzed here. Thus, logic is listed in *NM* among the predominant means of investigation with which a jurisconsult should be thoroughly acquainted. Several paragraphs of the text describe the partitions of this discipline, with references for further information to another work by Leibniz, the *Combinatorial Art,*[34] which deals with logic in general[35] and which, with regard to its applications in law, focuses specifically on the *Ars casus formandi Jurisprudentiae.*[36] Only in *NM* do we find a complete description of what Leibniz seems to indicate as the key operational requirement for the effective utilization of logic itself in law, that is, the need to arrange the rules in force in order to reconstruct, without contradiction, if possible, the entire discipline of the institutes surveyed, variously located in the *Corpus Juris*. Thus the book presents an early example[37] of what is now called the "systematization" of Roman law (*NM*, II, §§. 56, 57, 58). This is, according to Leibniz, an indispensable preliminary step for identifying deductive premises that are certain and therefore "true", free from the personal opinion of the interpreter.[38]

---

[33] Leibniz (July 1665), *Disputatio Juridica (prior) de Conditionibus*; id, (August 1665), *Disputatio Juridica (posterior) de Conditionibus*; id, (1666), *De casibus perplexibus in jure*, in AA, VI, 1; id, (June 1668), *Ratio Corporis Juris Reconcinnandi*, in AA VI, 2.

[34] See note 12.

[35] There reformulated *ex Arithmeticae fundamentis* as a cognitive system, effective per *universum scientiarum orbem.*

[36] See note 12. The process of identifying the *elementa simplicia* in law, described in this passage quoted in note 12, suggests that it is one of the most exemplary among those that express, in the legal works of Leibniz, the theoretical premises for the subsequent founding of the Dogmatics by the Pandectists in the XIX sec. (see above note 31).

[37] As shown in the first version of this essay published (2010) in *Europa e Diritto privato,* 3.

[38] Already in *Dissertatio de arte combinatorial,* note 12, Prob. II, 39, 189

If the initial certainty of Leibniz on the effectiveness of the *calculus ratiocinator* in solving legal disputes can be considered a safe harbor of historiography,[39] it does not exhaust the entire speculative parable of our author because it merely grazes the surface of his later further reflections on the subject, put forward in *Noveaux essays sur l'humain entendement* (1704) (up to now, only *Noveaux Essais*)[40].

Worried, not without reason, about highlighting solely the decisive influence that the *Nova Methodus* and the other juvenile works[41] were to have on the method of the

---

> *Ut taceam, rem judiciariam* in *qualibet republica hoc constitutum esse melius, quo minus est* in arbitrio *judicis* (...). Such as I shall conceal that the administration of justice in any state is better ruled, when it is not left to the will of the judge. [ed. transl.]

[39] Since the dissertation which Leibniz defended at Altdorf in 1666, the idea that dubious cases can be resolved by logical calculus has been of crucial importance; also, Leibniz, *De casibus perplexis in jure*, see note 14, XI:

> *Nos speramus* ex mero iure *decidi omnes casus posse*, *Gloss. Landrecht. I. n. 33 2* (*wenn es ist kein Sache, do thu das recht zu,, als die Ertznen zu der Seuche, id est nullam essem causam, cui jure occurri non possit, uti nullus sit morbus qui omnem prorsus medicinam respuat)* (We *hope* that all cases can be decided on grounds of mere law, as stated in the Gloss to the Landrecht, I. 33, note 2 (*Wenn es ist kein Sache, do thu das recht zu, als die Ertznen zu der Geuche*", i.e., "There is no lawsuit to which law cannot be applied, as there is no disease that rejects absolutely every medicine"), [e. transl. italics added].

[40] But posthumous: the *Noveaux essays sur l'entendement* humain were published by Rudolf Erich Raspe [1736–1794] (1765), *Leibniz, Oeuvres philosophiques latines & Francois*. Amsterdam, Leipzig; now in a critical edition by André Robinet and Heinrich Schepers (1962, 1990, 2006), AA VI, 6; for the standard English translation, see Peter Remnant and Jonathan Bennet (eds. and transl.). (2000, reprint of 1996 version), *Leibniz, New Essays on Human Understanding*. Cambridge, from which I will quote.

[41] V. *supra* notes 33 and 12.

jurists,[42] both philosophical [43] and legal historiography[44] no account of the German philosopher's afterthought can be traced in his mature works, where he questioned the effectiveness of logic alone as a means to recognize the best choice to make in all cases where "no absolute decision can be made". That is to say, he felt that mere logic was inadequate in all cases in which we do not have sufficient data for the solution of a problem (for instance, the difficulty of gaps in the laws,[45] antinomy in legal rules and sentences, antithetical doctrinal opinions).[46] The merit of having accurately and promptly emphasized this change in Leibniz' thought belongs, as far as I know, to Luigi Mengoni [1922–2001] in Italian juridical literature.[47] We will

---

[42] V. *supra* note 31.

[43] See, among others, Gabriel Nuchelmans (2003), "Deductive Reasoning", in Daniel Garber, Michael Ayers (eds.), *The Cambridge History of Seventeenth-century Philosophy*. Cambridge, I, 133.

[44] Among others, Damiano Canale, Paolo Grossi, Hasso Hoffmann (eds.) (2009), *A History of the Philosophy of Law in the Civil Law World 1600-1900*. Volume 9 Treatise of Legal History and General Jurisprudence, ed. in chief Enrico Pattaro. Dordrecht: Springer, 76 ff.

[45] In general, in the legal systems of civil law there is a clear preference for self-integration (this means that the judge first must derive the rule from the rules in force by inference; his intervention in "creating" law as if he were the lawmaker comes in the last instance; see, for example, Article 1, Swiss Civil Code; Article 12, 2d limb, *Provisions on the Law in General* of the Italian Civil Code, which does not give any power to the judge to create rules), whereas the common law calls upon the judge to fill the gap by creating a new rule. In the latter, however, the standard created by the court to settle the case may become part of the legal system under the principle of *stare decisis.* See Kent Greenawalt (2012), *Statutory and Common Law Interpretation*. Oxford, 96.

[46] Leroy Earl Loemker (ed.) (1989), *Leibniz, Philosophical Papers and Selected Letters*. Dordrecht Boston London, 462, *Leibniz to Gabriel Wagner* (1696); *Noveaux Essais*, see note 40, IV, 2, §. 14, 353–355.

[47] In various writings, collected in the volumes of Mengoni quoted in note 31 above.

return to this topic later (see *infra*, n. 9), but this initial mention will be helpful in order to provide the reader with a less incomplete introduction to the following brief guide on the structure and contents of the *NM*.

4. *On the general method of study*. The *incipit* of the booklet (*Studiorum ratio*) bears a striking similarity (the terms are merely reversed) to the concise locution (*Ratio Studiorum*) of a famous and well-known pedagogical treatise drawn up by the Jesuits at the end of the sixteenth century.[48] By this reversal of terms, Leibniz sought to juxtapose his plan of studies to that proposed by Ignatian pedagogy, which enjoyed considerable prestige even in the environment of the Reformation that had shaped Leibniz' background.[49] Although the latter work is never mentioned, the first part of the *NM* reveals some pedagogical suggestions derived from the Catholic *ratio*. The following elements coincide with Jesuit didactics: the technique of periodical *ruminationes* (*NM*, I, §§12 and 15)[50], the reward of honor and social status granted to deserving pupils (*NM*, I, §7). However, Leibniz departs from Ignatian pedagogy in the passage where he points out the need, for the teacher, to include *jocunditas* (*NM*, I, §§19, 20) in teaching, whereas there is no explicit reference to this suggestion in the Jesuit method. Furthermore, the *NM* never talks about corporal punishment (and the Catholic *ratio* also seems to abhor it), except for the question of

---

[48] (1599), *Ratio atque institutio studiorum*. Romae: In Collegio Societatis Jesu; see English transl. in Allan P. Farrell, S.J. (1970), *The Jesuit* Ratio Studiorum *of 1599*. Washington D. C.: Conference of Major Superiors of Jesuits, in www.bc.edu/sites/libraries/ratio/ratio 1599 [accessed 4 May 2015].

[49] Leibniz himself testified to the influence of Jesuit thinkers in his education. See note 7 above.

[50] See note 48, n. 26.

fasting in the boarding schools, which Leibniz mentions without expressing any condemnation (*NM*, I, §6).

At the beginning of the treatment, the terms *ratio* and *methodus* are used synonymously, according to the tradition of the Renaissance writers,[51] but Leibniz gives priority to the second term, in the title of the book as well, using the connotation which Pierre de la Ramée [1515–1572] attributed to the word, namely:

> Méthode est dispositif par laquelle entre plusieurs choses la premiére des notices est disposée au premier lieu, la deuziesme au deuziesme la triziesme au triziesme et ainsi consequentemment. Ce nom signifie toute disciplines et disputes, néammoins communément east pris pour adresse et abrégement du chemin[52].

The reading of the *NM*, II expressly devoted to the education of the jurist, in particular §§7 and 11, confirm this. Nonetheless, we cannot affirm that "the justification for placing this reform through the *Nova Methodus* of legal education in an encyclopedic context, was essentially Ramist",[53] recalling that Leibniz, much later in a letter to Wilhelm Bierling of 7 July 1711 reviewing a *Lineamenta Methodi studiorum* by the latter, would have written that "his early methodology was 'not much different from the Ramist one'".[54] The Latin text of the letter regarding this topic recites precisely:

---

[51] Herberger, see note 31, 233, n. 87, who points out that for the writers of the Renaissance (Bacon, Budé, etc..) *ratio* means method (*ratio sive methodus*). Sometimes the two words were joined by hendiadys: one may recall the work of Matteo Gribaldi Mofa (1541), *De ratione ac methodo studendi*. Lugduni.

[52] Michel Dassoville [1927–2012] (ed.) (1964), *P. de la Ramée, Dialectique* (1555). Geneve, 144–145.

[53] By Antognazza, see note 2, 82.

[54] Leibniz, Letter to Wilhelm Bierling, 7 July 1711, in Carl Immanuel Gerhardt [1816–1899] (ed.) (1875–1890), *Leibniz, Die*

> *Etiam fuere in Ramistis digna non negligi. Memini me adulescentem his adjutum de materia quadam scribere, ut legentes amici mirarentur, unde mihi omnes considerationes suppetiisent: eas methodus dederat non plane dissidens a Ramea. Recte Methodos vel dispositiones regulis comparas (p. 35) quibus tremula puerorum manus dirigitur. Sed Mens nostra, etiam cum pueri esse desiimus, semper tremula esse solet, nisi methodo dirigatur* … (Also among Ramists, there are worthy indications that are not taken into account. I remember that when I was an adolescent I wrote about some topic, helped by these indications. Friends were amazed that there were all the observations: those were supplied by a method not completely discordant with the Ramist method. Let us compare in the right way the methods and dispositions with rules by which the shaky hands of the children are driven. However, our mind, even when we grow up, remains always shaky, unless driven by a method) [ed. transl.].

From this sentence we cannot conclude that Leibniz was substantially Ramist; nor can we say that:

> the key rule of the *methodus naturalis* proposed in this work for organizing knowledge in general (as opposed to the *methodus occasionalis* employed in specific disciplines) was little more than a restatement of the basic law of the Ramist method: 'If one thing can be know without a second, but the second cannot be known without the first, the first should be put before the second'.[55]

Although this is true, we cannot forget that actually as for the *methodus naturalis* in the same *Nova Methodus* our young Doctor Juris will write:

Philosophischen Schriften. 7 vols. Berlin: Weidmannsche Buchhandlung. Reprint, Hildesheim: Olms, 1960–1961, 7, 496.

[55] Antognazza, see note 2, 82–83.

> An innumerable multitude of others followed them Pierre de la Ramée and his disciples, but they did not fully attain the goal we desire, the method that I call natural. In fact, as the incomparable Bacon of Verulam rightly objected to Pierre de la Ramée and his followers (Ramists), the latter group of scholars devoted such scrupulous care in formulating the subdivisions that they ultimately achieved the result of delimiting rather than understanding the subject, which, meanwhile, escaped like an eel, or otherwise stated, left useless straws of subdivisions in place of the grain of the peculiarities"[56].

5. *Mnemonic and didactics*. It is interesting that Leibniz recalled the Renaissance *artes mnemorativae*, which rest on foundations of occultism and hermeticism,[57] of which there had been a copious production in the sixteenth and seventeenth centuries. Although the author indicated several titles,[58] here he described a quite common mnemonic system based on the frequency and intensity of repetition of the notions to be learnt, with an amusing reference to the method of learning nursery rhymes, popular and widespread even among the "sissies" (*NM*, I, §§12–15).

In addition to the "mnemonic" techniques, helpful during the school years, mention should be made of the methods of learning prescribed by the *emblemata* (em-

---

[56] *NM*, II, §. 7. In addition see Gustav Hartmann [1835–1894] (1892), "Leibniz als Jurist und Rechtsphilosoph", in *Festgabe für Rudolf von Jhering*. Tübingen (1979 repr. anast. Aalen), 20–21.

[57] Whose function was to help investigate the encyclopedia and the world in order to discover new knowledge [in this regard, of course, Francis Amelia Yates (1966), *The Art of Memory*. London and Paolo Rossi, *Clavis universalis*. Mnemonic arts and combinatorial logic from Lull to Leibniz (Bologna, 1983)]: among these, the exemplum of Giulio Camillo Delminio [1480–1544], in Lina Bolzoni (ed.) (1991), *G. Camillo Delminio (1550), L'Idea del Teatro*. Palermo.

[58] See, for example, *NM*, I, §23, Leibniz recalled the work of Johann H. Alsted (1621), *Thesaurus artis memorativae*. Francofurti.

blems) of Andrea Alciato [1492–1550],[59] Diego de Saavedra y Fajardo [1584–1648][60] (*NM*, I, §20), and, above all, by the tables contained in *Orbis sensualium pictus*[61] (*NM*, I, §40) by Jan Amos Comenius [1592–1670], who is considered the father of modern pedagogy.

Encouragement should be given to the use of the so-called marks (*notae*), the real foundation of Thomas Hobbes' [1588–1679] cognitive psychology (*NM*, I, §23). According to the English philosopher, such marks consist in "sensible things taken at pleasure, that, by the sense of them, such thoughts may be recalled to our mind as are like those thoughts for which we took them".[62] We would not expect the visualization of "recollections" to involve elements other than the notions to be acquired, but the marks or signs would be useful to create very personal connections with the knowledge to be held in one's mind. A theoretical treatment of this very same subject is found in the study on memory by one of the leading twentieth century scientists of the brain, Alexander Lurija [1902–1977]. In a famous essay on prodigious memory, Luria observed that all most tenacious memorization techniques start out from the ability to create an association between emotive elements, not bound by any connection with the information to be retained in the mind, and the complex notions to be learnt.[63]

---

[59] Andrea Alciato (1531), *Emblemata*. Augusta Vindelicorum.

[60] Diego de Saavedra y Fajardo (1640-1642), *Idea de un principe politico cristiano rapresentada en cien impresas*. En Monaco en Milan.

[61] Jan Amos Comenius (1658), *Orbis sensualium pictus*. Noribergae: sumtibus Michaelis et Joannis Friderici Endteri.

[62] Thomas Hobbes (1655), *Elementa Philosophiae* 1, *De corpore*. Londinium: Crook, chap. II, par. 1, English transl. London 1656, in William Molesworth [1810–1855] (ed. 1839), *The English Works of Thomas Hobbes of Malmesbury*. I, London: Bohn, 14.

[63] Alexander Lurija (1968), *The Mind of Mnemonist*. Cambridge MA: Harvard University Press; Rossi, see note 57, 5.

6. *Recommendations for life.* Of disarming realism is the "life advice" (*NM*, I, §§41–42) given to young people who, after their course of studies, embark on academic or professional careers. They are urged to travel, seek the company of powerful men, and, above all, gain the "protection" of a politician or of an influential person, for every time that a young scholar achieves something "new", he increases the body of acquired knowledge, or, on the contrary, whenever he demonstrates the fallacy of some idea, his accomplishment will be greeted with envy (*NM*, *Preface to the Reader*). Therefore, "protection" is essential in order to publish and disseminate one's own ideas, especially in the academic world. Such suggestions are dictated by personal life experiences.[64]

7. *What is jurisprudence.* The second part of *NM*, specifically dedicated to the method of legal studies,[65] does not enter immediately into *medias res*. The author prefers to dwell first on the object of jurisprudence itself and how it should be improved. According to Leibniz, "Jurisprudence is the science of the Law connected to a case or fact"[66] (NM, II, §1); and

---

[64] See above par. 1 and Antognazza, note 2, 65–66; Eric Aiton (1985), *Leibniz. A Biography*. Bristol, 30;
[65] "Nova Methodus", Birocchi points out, see note 27, 211 "is part of a problem—that of the teaching of the law and the training of the jurist—very much alive in the sixteenth-century humanist circles. [e. transl.]". See, for example, also quoted by Leibniz (*NM*, II, §13), Jean de Coras [1515–1572] (1560), *De iuris arte libellus*. Lugduni: Apud Antonium Vincentium; Matthias Stephani [1570–1646] (1630), *De arte iuris, et eius principiis*. Gryphiswaldae: Koep; Joachim Hoppers [1523–1576] (1590), *Seduardus*. Antuerpiae: In Officina Plantiniana, apud viduam et Ioannem Moretum.
[66] On philosophical aspects of the definition of jurisprudence in *NM*, see above par. 2, Christopher Johns, 7–12.

> Jurisprudence is the science of the actions, insofar they are called just or injust. Just and unjust is defined as whatever is publicly useful or harmful. Publicly, that is, first for the world, or for God who is its rector, and second for mankind, and finally for the state: with this subordination, in case of conflict the will or the utility of God, if it be permitted to speak thus, is to be preferred to the utility of humankind and this to the utility of the state, and this to one's own utility. Hence, one may speak of divine, human, and civil jurisprudence. To talk about one's own utility, however, is a topic of politics not of jurisprudence. (*NM*, II, §. 14).

Leibniz believes that the *modus ratiocinandi* in the decisions of the courts is the same as that of theology:[67] just as theology is based on reason and Scripture, jurisprudence is based on reason and positive law, especially that contained in the *Corpus Juris*. Jurisprudence, just as theology, cannot be compared to medicine, mathematics, and philosophy (*i.e.* to science, considered "exact") because in the human and divine laws "the will stands in the place of reason"[68] (*NM*, II, §4). The conditions necessary for jurisprudence are not naturalistic, but voluntaristic, because jurisprudence deals with rules which need the human will to impose themselves (*NM*, II, §4): they are not able to impose on their own *rerum natura, unlike* the laws of the physics.

---

[67] Also in *On Combantorial Art*, AA VI, 1, Prob II, VIII usus, 47, 190 "Par in Theologia terminorum ratio est, quae est quasi Jurisprudentia quaedam specialis, sed eadem fundamentalis ratione caeterarum". This inseparability between theology and law, was to remain a constant pivotal idea in the late works of Leibniz (Birocchi, see note 27, 211, n. 303).

[68] It is a quotation from Juvenal (c. 50–after 127), *Saturae*. 6, 223, *Hoc volo, sic iubeo, sit pro ratione voluntas* (This I will, thus I command, let my will be in place of a reason), [ed. transl.].

Jurisprudence is divided into two practical parts: a) didactic, and b) polemical (*NM*, II, §3).

a) The didactic part consists in the collection of undisputed legal principles, which, similarly to the fundamental geometric notions, as in Euclid, are called *Elements* (*NM*, II, §6).[69] The elements fulfill two functions: that of giving definitions (*NM*, II, §§7 and 24) and that of "processing" precepts (*NM*, II, §§24–28).

b) The polemical part (*NM*, II, §69) is inherent in the collection of the principles of decision-making and the collection of decisions. "The principles of decision-making are reason based on natural law and similarity based on certain civil law" (*NM*, II, §70). Leibniz thus proceeds to analyze the foundations of natural law according to the ancient philosophers (*NM*, II, §71), modern scholars (*NM*, II, §72) and Leibniz himself (*NM*, II, §§73–76); this is followed by treatment of the correct method for compiling the collections of decisions (*NM*, II, §§77–99). It is therefore hardly surprising that a large number of paragraphs is devoted to natural law, one of the most controversial chapters in legal, political and philosophical speculation since ancient times, both as far as its definition is concerned, and also the search for its foundations.

---

[69] See notes 11 and 12.

The break with the conception of the ancient world[70] in this respect came about, as is known, in the second half of the sixteenth century, when an attempt was made to incorporate in positive law the principles that are intuitively common to all men ("all precepts which are well-known from natural law itself and from sound principles of reason, or that even a peasant would be able to understand after having grasped the basic learned terms (which therefore we have premised in the definitions)", *NM*, II, §23). So widely accepted are such principles that not even the *imperium* supporting *the status quo* can violate them in any way: indeed, the use of violence is legitimate to resist to their violation.

The problem was, however, the identification of those principles[71] and their foundations. Thus Leibniz "opposes

---

[70] But this is a modern conquest, because for the Romans, as we know (1 Ulp., Inst. D.1.1.1.3):

> The natural law is that which nature taught to all of the living beings, therefore this right is not characteristic of mankind but is common to all of the animals that are born on earth and sea and to the birds. Thence derives the union of male and female, which we call marriage, thence follows the procreation of children and their education. Thus we observe that all of the other animals, even wild ones, are deemed capable of knowing this right. (Generoso Melillo (2007), "*Persona, Status* e *Condicio* nell'esperienza romana. La dogmatica moderna", in *Studia et documenta historiae et iuris*, 89-90) [ed. transl.].

[71] Very historically relative, in truth: for Leibniz, as for any man of his time, torture was still *in naturalibus*, so that in another context of the work (*NM*, II, §26), he said:

> Similarly, on matter of torture I conceive this general rule: *only who would be condemned,* rebus sic stantibus,[71] *if the proceedings were civil, the same is to be tortured in criminal trial.* Because in a criminal trial nobody is to be sentenced, unless they confessed. Therefore, he has to be compelled to the confession, who has been demonstrated guilty of a crime. It follows that he is to be tortured even who cannot prove his exception, *sondern muss er sie auf der Tortur er-*

the laicization of natural law, of which he continues to claim a divine foundation [*NM*, II, §§75, e. n.]. This set him at odds with the jusnaturalism of Hugo Grotius [1583–1645], Gabriel Pufendorf [1632–1694], and Jacob Thomasius [1622–1684]".[72]

In an attempt to reconcile the speculative results of Grotius and Hobbes, particularly in what Leibniz called the third degree of natural law, namely rigid right (the other two are equity and piety, *NM*, II, §73),[73] he reconstructs organically the principles of the latter, driven in this operation by a disenchanted pragmatism regarding the verification of primitive human instincts (aggression and self-defense), which support such principles. Here, let us give the floor to the author:

> The rigid or pure law derives from the intrinsic, the definition of the terms, and if assessed, it can be seen to be nothing other than the law of war and peace. In fact, between person and person the law of peace is in force, as long as the other does not begin the war, or engage in harmful conduct. Between person and thing, however, there is a perpetual law of war, because a thing has no intelligence. And it is lawful for a lion to tear a man and for a mountain to crush a man by a landslide; equally, it is lawful for a man to restrain a lion, break down a mountain. But the victory of a person over a thing and the captivity of the thing is called possession. Thus, possession endows the person with a right over the thing, by law of war, provided that the thing belongs to no-one. If, however, the thing belongs to someone, then no man is allowed to damage it or to

---

halten. Because in civil proceedings whosoever cannot prove an exception has to be condemned. This is the only rule equivalent to many about sufficient evidence for torture, which commonly are applied.

[72] Birocchi, see note 27, [ed. transl.], 215; Vincenti, see note 30, 52.
[73] On which Johns, par. 2, 12-16; Birocchi, note 27, 214--215, and diffusely, Hubert Busche, par. 2.

> appropriate it, any more than he is allowed to kill the slaves of others or give shelter to fugitives. Therefore, if one damages another either in his person or in his things, this gives him the same right as that which he has over a thing, namely, the right of war. And even malicious deception is counted among the species of damage, because the damage is inflicted on the mind, from which there derives the need for keeping promises. It is therefore clear that the only true precept of natural law is: never injure, hurt, or damage anyone (*neminem laedere*); in this manner you will ensure that no person can claim the right of war against you. To this belongs commutative justice, and the right that Grotius calls faculty. (*NM*, II, §73).

It is noteworthy that among the authors quoted by Leibniz on the topic there is no mention of one of the fathers, together with Grotius, Pufendorf and Thomasius, of jusnaturalism. The allusion here is to the figure of Johann Althusius [1563–1638], which is recalled by Leibniz, but on other grounds, that is, not as a theorist of jusnaturalism, but of the legal method (*NM*, II, §13).[74]

The learning of the practical parts (didactical and polemical) of jurisprudence does not complete the jurist's education, because such training will merely enable him to discover which rule should be applied to the case at issue, but not to argue against those who claim the opposite. Strictly speaking, a jurist who only identifies the rule to be applied could not even be called a jurist, but only a practitioner: the real jurist is one who not only possesses knowledge of didactical and polemical jurisprudence, but

---

[74] Only the *Dicaeologia* is quoted (Johann Althusius) (1618), *Dicaeologia.* Prostant Frankfurti: Apud Christophorum Corvinum, and not the important Id. (1603), *Politica, methodice digesta.* Herbornae Nassoviorum: Ex off. Christophori Corvini, which is among the fundamental texts on the modern foundations of natural law.

can also speak authoritatively on the i) historical[75] and ii) exegetical aspects, that is, on the means of aid proper of jurisprudence (*NM*, II, §3).

8. *Historical jurisprudence and the historical training of the jurist.* i) Historical jurisprudence is internal or external (*NM*, II, §28). Internal jurisprudence concerns the different laws among the various peoples; in contrast, external jurisprudence deals with Roman, ecclesiastical, medieval and contemporary history, (*NM*, II, §30). From §§30 to 41, Leibniz gives a wide range of bibliographic information, a true *silva silvarum*[76] for each of the historical periods indicated; such information is not only important for the historian of philosophy (in order to have extensive knowledge of the training texts for a philosopher), but also decisive as a methodological indication for jurists of all times. In particular, mastery of Greek and

---

[75] According to Guido Aceti [1929–1988] (1957), "Sulla *Nova Methodus discendae decendaeque jurisprudentiae* di Goffredo Guglielmo Leibniz". *Jus*, 7, n. 9, it is clear what is meant by Leibniz: "*philosophia* [of which in *NM*, II, §2, e. n.] means "adequate cognition" including historical knowledge of the law, which does not stop at the "rough empiricism" given by the simple identification of the rule to be applied to the case raised. The Leibnizian distinction of the study of the Right in didactic, polemical, historical, and exegetical Jurisprudence was transposed in political terms in Europe, only (so it seems) by Vincenzo Cuoco [(1770–1823), adviser of Joachim Murat (1767–1815), King of Naples from 1808 to 1815], in his (1809) *Progetto per 'l'Ordinamento della Pubblica Istruzione nel Regno di Napoli* ("Project for the Legal System of Public Education in the Kingdom of Naples"), which can be read in Walter Cariddi (1981), *Il pensiero politico e pedagogico di Vincenzo Cuoco.* Lecce, 381 ff., in particular 469–470.

[76] The sentence belongs to Roberto Palaia (2000), "Unità metodologica e molteplicità disciplinare nella *Nova Methodus*", in Antonio Lamarra and Roberto Palaia (eds.), *Unità è molteplicità nel pensiero filosofico e scientifico di Leibniz.* Firenze, 143.

Roman history is important for an understanding of civil law, competence in contemporary history for deciphering German public law, and knowledge of the history of the church for penetrating canon law, which was still dominant in the institutions of family law. This vast range of bibliographical information overwhelms the reader, who is left with the feeling well described by the original title of Umberto Eco's book: *The Vertigo of List.*[77] The erudition of the young *Juris Doctor* is boundless. But, these are details that underlie the invitation to acquire, among others, an attitude that will prove to be of great help in the identification of regulatory rationales: the contextualization of the historical moment in which the rule was enacted. Even today, this is an aspect of education that is unfortunately overlooked in law schools.

9. *Exegetical jurisprudence.*

> ii) From historical jurisprudence, we turn to the exegetical. Although the exegetical is in some way historical, it describes what actually is likely to have been the idea of the law-maker, and because as large amount has been produced, it is rightly treated separately. There are two strands: one from the text, the other on the text. The former is derived from various texts simultaneously, not according to the order of the texts, but by combining one with the other, whereas the latter, namely the strand based directly on the text, is applied κατά πόδα [in Greek in the text, word for word, e. n.] to the texts themselves. The former belongs to the Philology of right in imitation of the

---

[77] Umberto Eco (2006), *La vertigine della lista*. Milano (English transl. by Alastair McEwen (2009), *The Infinity of List*. Milan): vertigo might indeed be the real sensation of the reader deriving from the immense bibliographical references given by Leibniz.

Sacred Philology by Salomon Glass [1593–1656];[78] the latter is in imitation of the Commentaries of Law (*NM*, II, §41).

The philology of right (*NM*, II, §42) consists in the application of specific disciplines to jurisprudence; it is divided into: legal grammar (*NM*, II, §43), legal lexicon (*NM*, II, §44), legal orthography (*NM*, II, §45), didactics (*NM*, II, §47), rhetoric (*NM*, II, §46), history (*NM*, II, §48), ethical-political and forensic medicine (*NM*, II, §49), logic and metaphysics (*NM*, II, §50), reconciliation of the antinomies (*NM*, II, §51).

10. *Logic and Rhetoric*. One should expect to find that the *NM* offers indications on method that are different and innovative in comparison with classical logic. However, in this booklet the rules of legal logic refer, in essence, to Aristotelian syllogisms[79] and to Quintilian "topics" (*loci*).[80] Leibniz speaks of logic and metaphysics

---

[78] Salomon Glass (1623), *Philologia sacra*. Jenae.

[79] In *NM*, I §22, Leibniz states, in compliance with the scheme of the Aristotle's *Organon*, that "topics and analytics are included in the single lemma of logic".

[80] For example, the general forms of argument employed in probable reasoning; see Quintilian, in Donald A. Russel (ed.) (2001), *Quintilian, The Orator's Education*. Cambridge MA, London: Harvard University Press, 5, 10, 20,

> Let us now investigate the Places where Arguments are found, though some hold that these are identical with the topics I have just been discussing. By 'Places' I do not mean what are nowadays commonly meant by *loci*, namely set pieces against luxury, adultery and the like, but the areas in which Arguments lurk and from which they have to be drawn.

Harold. E. Butler (ed.) (1927), *The Institutio Oratoria of Quintilian*. London, New York, 213," (...) in the sense of the secret places where arguments reside and from which they must be drawn forth".

(*NM*, II, §50), reconciliation of the antinomies (*NM*, II, §51) and "interpretation of the law" (§52), but he *does not deal specifically or at length with these topics*. He provides the reader with nothing more than a bibliography on the subject, warning that the authors recalled François Hotman [1524–1590], Johann Thomas Freige [1543–1583], and especially Martin Schickard [1579–1636] deal with "certain philosophical rules that are to be respected in right, but which commonly are inappropriately mixed with the rules of right" (*NM*, II, §50). Moreover, in the *Preface to the Reader* he invites the reader to:

> bear in mind that the arguments we will set forth concerning the things that must be done and learned are by no means a meritorious reflection of things we ourselves have done or said—let such presumption be far

---

Heinrich Lausberg [1912–1992], in David E. Orton, R. Dean Anderson (eds.) (1998), *Handbook of Literary Rhetoric: A Foundation for Literary Study*. Leiden, 171,

> [*loci*] the formal analysis and classification of the *argumenta* presupposes the content of the arguments. It is precisely the task of rhetorical *invention*, however, to provide instructions for the discovery of ideas that correspond with the issue and the party, that is, for the discovery of the content.

Leibniz points out, *NM*, I, §24, that:

> The foundation of the topics, or the art of invention, are the dialectical arguments, that is the transcendent relations, such as the whole, the cause, the matter, the similar, etc. And, as we have diffusely explained in our *Dissertation about Combinatorial Art*, propositions grow out from things connected by any such relations by means of the combinatorial art. Nor are to be despised the contributions that *Raimond Lul* gave on this matter in several works and Johann Heinrich Bisterfeld in the *Epitome of Art of Meditation*.

And on this, see Leibniz, AA VI, 1, especially the whole of Probl. II, *Dato numero complexiones simpliciter invenire*.

from our minds—, because long ago we had no knowledge of these topics[81].

Although in the *Disputatio Juridica* (*prior*) *de Conditionibus* (1665) the German philosopher sought to reduce to "very certain and almost mathematical demonstrations"[82] most of "the argumentative patterns the Roman juriconsults use, when they have to interpret the meaning of a statement in which a person claims to create a new

---

[81] In the argument, George Kalinowski [1929–2000] (1977), "La Logique juridique de Leibniz". *Studia Leibnitiana*, Band IX/2, 187, points out that in *NM*, as well as in other early legal works, "Leibniz n'a pas illustré sa théorie des inferences juridiques par des exemples" and nevertheless he believes that:

> Si l'on laisse de côté le einseignement d'Aristote sur le syllogisme practique, einsegnement plutôt philosophique que Logique, et quelques idées de détails touchant directement ou indirectement à la Logique des normes qu'on trouve chez de certains auteurs du l'antiquitè et du moyen âge, Leibniz apparaît, à la lumière de nos connaissance historique actuelle (...), comme l'auteur d'une premier ébauche de la logique des normes, ébauche assez avancée puisque comportant deux parties: la théorie de l'opposition des normes et le modèles aléthiques, comme on les appelle depuis *An essay in modal logic* de G. H. von Wright, Amsterdam 1951.

And see also George Kalinowski and Jean-Louis Gardies [1925–2004] (1974), "A logicien déontique avant la lettre Gottfried Wilhelm Leibniz". *Archiv für Rechts und Sozialphilosophie* 60, 79 ff.

[82] Leibniz, AA VI, 1, 101

> *Hic illud saltem praeterire non possum, tanto ingenio tantaque profunditate in reddendo jure versatos esse Juris Consultos veteres, ut in certissimas ac pene mathematicas demonstrations eorum responsa redigendi laboris potius sit in digerendo, quam in supplendo ingenii*...(Here I cannot conceal that the ancient jurists made justice with such insight born and so profoundly that I have only to give to their advices the shape of the most certain and almost mathematical demonstrations, rather than to integrate them of ingenuity...) [ed. transl.].

right by transferring one of his rights to another person",[83] nevertheless "Leibniz's legal theory of conditions *has obvious legal results*".[84] But in the subsequent *De Casibus Perplexis in Jure* he showed his awareness that "(…) et impossibilia casibus perplexis, *in quibus pro solutione est advertere et demonstrare impossibilitatem, quod algebra praestat*"[85], and, finally, here in *NM* (II, §4) he states that "Euclidi non creditur quia dicit, sed quia probat, quod secus est in legibus divinis humanisque, ubi stat pro ratione voluntas".[86] Thus, on this basis, as demonstrated in 2010,[87] Leibniz regarded formal logic, as merely a tool to axiomatize law, in order to make clear the rule that was to be applied to the case raised.

---

[83] Alexandre Thiercelin (2008), "On Two Argumentative Uses of the Notion of Uncertainty in Law in Leibniz's Juridical Dissertations about Conditions", in: Marcelo Dascal (ed.): *Leibniz: What Kind of Rationalist?*, Dordrecht/Heidelberg/London/New York, 251.

[84] Alexandre Thiercelin (2010), "Epistemic and practical Aspects of Conditionals in Leibniz's Legal Theory of Conditions" in Dov M. Gabbay, Patrice Canivez, Shahid Rahman, Alexander Thiercelin (eds.), *Approaches to legal Rationality*. Dordrecht/Heidelberg/London /New York, 211, [italics added]:

> Leibniz's legal theory of conditions *has obvious legal results* [italics added]. Based upon the logical theory of conditionals, it provides many answers given by the Roman jurisconsults with 'very certain and almost mathematical demonstrations' *insofar as it provides them with general and systematic reasons* [italics added]. To put it more directly, Leibniz's logical approach to the law enables him to make it notably more explicit.

[85] See note 14.

[86] See note 68.

[87] In my essay, De Iuliis (2010), see note 37, 711–748; Scott Brewer (2013), "Law, Logic, and Leibniz. A Contemporary Perspective", in Alberto Artosi and others (eds.), *Leibniz: Logico-Philosophical questions and Perplexing Cases in Law*, Dordrecht 2013, 206, comes to the same conclusions: "[…] And this is vastly more true of Leibniz: he regarded axiomatization of law (whether deductive or not) as a tool for clarification, organization, investigation […]".

11. *Logic as functional to systematic reconstruction of the legal system.* Functional to this aim is the philology of right and its branches (legal grammar, legal lexicon, legal orthography, didactics, rhetoric, history, ethical-political logic and metaphysics, reconciliation of the antinomies), as mentioned above, to which are specifically devoted §§52 to 68. Among the latter, it is of interest to highlight the §§ 56 to 58 as a wonderful example of the systematic reconstruction of regulations inferred from the rules scattered throughout the *Corpus Juris*, on the procurator, on abolishing lapses (escheats), and on monks. Leibniz argues: "We, by abstracting the universals, summed up them, so that by means of our rules one may deduce all the laws of the title" (*NM*, II §56).[88] By this reconstruction of the code, Leibniz not only indicates the "way through which" (the method, *metà odòs*, namely) it is possible to infer the implicit rules in the *Corpus Juris*, but he also indicates how knowledge has to be organized in the legal ambit, in line, it would seem, with the epistemological pattern of the Spanish Jesuit Francisco Suarez, whose work was extensively studied by Leibniz in his youth.[89] According to Suarez the system[90] is the means for putting together

---

[88] Already in his doctoral dissertation (*De casibus perplexis in jure*, see note 14) it is evident in Leibniz's thought that the doubtful cases can be resolved, first, through the "logical calculus" of the written rules and in the *Dissertatio de arte combinatoria*. See note 12, Prob. II, 40, where he states that: "Elementa juris in eius corpore continentur"; in his letter of 1696 to Gabriel Wagner, see note 21, 496, the philosopher also insists that, "By logic I mean the art of using the intellect, not only to judge what is proposed, *but also to discover what is hidden*" [italics added].

[89] For the influence of Suarez on the formation of Leibniz, see Roger Ariew (2012) in Benjamin Hill, Henrik Lagerlund (eds.), *The Philosophy of Francisco Suarez*. Oxford, 46 ff.

[90] Hans-Georg Gadamer [1900–2002] (2000) teaches:

what is discrepant in appearance, but is in any case governed by common principles.

However, the reference to Suarez, also quoted in some passages of the essay, does not preclude the assumption that Leibniz had knowledge of the similar concept of "system" that was taking shape in the natural sciences, especially in medicine. One need only think of the pioneering, and opposed at the time, studies on the circulation of blood by William Harvey [1578–1657],[91] whose work

---

The concept of system appeared for the first time in the seventeenth century, and it became further disseminated in the next century. The term "system" also derives from a Greek word, derived from the world of music and astronomy (which according to the Greeks were always closely connected) and *has precisely the meaning of composing together what is dissimilar* [italics added]. (...) "System" then, suddenly becomes a, philosophical expression (...) The consequence of this new situation is precisely the reconciliation of the irreconcilable. [ed. transl.], (*Descartes, Leibniz und die Aufklärung* [*Videoaufzeichnung*] Interview mit Hans-Georg Gadamer–Roma: Rai Educational, 2000. - 1 Videokassette (VHS) (49 Min.) (Der Weg der Philosophie; 12: Von der Aufklärung zur Romantik, in emsf.rai.it/gadamer/interviste/12_cartesio. htm (accessed 6 May 2015), "the notion of system slowly matured during the Counter-Reformation, in response to the needs of the Catholic Church to oppose to the motions of the division of the Reformation, and to demonstrate how each element in the doctrine of the Catholic Church, was in agreement with all others. The first who made an attempt in this direction was *Suarez* [italics added], a Spanish counter-reformer, who introduced Aristotle according to an absolutely new model, that is, as a great systematics. If in our investigations on ancient philosophy we were to be satisfied with this, it would be evident that an absolutely false concept is used, to which unfortunately people still have recourse today, uncritically, in the history of philosophy. The world of Greek philosophy in the first place was dominated by rhetoric (the only way of communication was the spoken word, as silent reading did not yet exist). Suarez was the first to give to the Aristotelian philosophy a systematic structure; a result not even Thomas had achieved. (*Descartes, Leibniz und die Aufklärung, see above in this note*).

[91] William Harvey (1628), *Exercitatio Anatomica de Motu Cordis et Sanguinis in Animalibus*. Francofurti, sumptibus Guilielmi Fitzeri, Engl. Transl. by Chauncey D. Leake, V ed., Charles C. Thomas Pub. Ltd, locus, 1978.

appears in the cultural background of our young Philosopher (see *NM, Preface to the Reader*).

> What does a system mean for the anatomist?—wonders Eugenio d'Ors [1881–1954], and answers that it means a synthesis which, founded on the unity of distant elements, shows, on the contrary, the diversity of neighbouring and even contiguous elements. The unity of the nervous system, for example, includes both the brain, housed in the skull, and the nerve endings in the fingertip; whereas, in such a limited area as the latter, the muscle element forming the fleshy part, i.e. the vascular element, is discriminated, even though it irrigates the nervous element, which there is woven into a minuscule network. Moreover, following certain analytical investigations, it appears that there can be insulation of nerve fibers with the function of pain, including those adapted to the sensations of weight, heat or cold.[92].

Accordingly, just as the anatomist rebuilds the nervous system by identifying the elements which are common to the parts that compose it, although they are variously located in the human body, likewise Leibniz seems to urge recovery in the *Corpus Juris* of all the elements common to an institute scattered throughout the Justinian compilation. In this respect, he speaks disparagingly of the famous critical edition by Denis Godefroy [1549–1622] in 1583, [93] as "superfluous and

---

[92] Eugenio D'Ors (1935), *Du Baroque*. Paris, Spanish edition by A. d'Ors and A. García Navarro (2002) *Lo barroco*. Madrid, 64, from which I quote and translate into English.

[93] Denys Godefroy (1583), *Corpvs ivris civilis in IIII. partes distinctvm: qvarvm prima, dn. sacratissimi principis Iustiniani Institutionum lib. IIII.: Digestorum seu Pandectarum lib. L. continentur: Quae reliquis partibus includantur, auersa docebit pagina.: His accesserunt Commentarij, quibus inter caetera variae lectiones,*

disorderly, inasmuch as the title claims to examine the series of the laws, and flawed insofar as it considers only single terms, not the whole proposition" (*NM*, II, §55).

The work ends (*NM*, II, §§91–100) with advice on teaching related to the three courses in the study of jurisprudence: elementary, exegetical, and polemical. Even in this respect, there is no indication that goes beyond common sense (gradualness, and constant repetition of the concepts learned). Among the suggestions, however, what should be seriously reconsidered in teaching law in the universities is the exercise of practice by providing the student with experience through simulated trials[94] under the guidance of the teacher.

12. *Leibniz and logic*. Rightly, legal historians believe the *NM* to be one of the first attempts[95] to impose systematic order on Roman law;[96] furthermore, it testifies above all

---

leges similes, contrariae, abrogatae: verborum, legumq; difficilium interpretationes atque compendia, anni singulis Codicis legibus additi continentur: Praeter Institutionum nouam epitomen, accessit & alia Nouellarum Iustiniani, ad ordinem Edicti perpetui adcommodata. Lugduni, in officina Barthol. Vincentij: excudebat Iacobus Stoer.

[94] It is not a new suggestion, but it revives a tradition that "constituted a fundamental part of the work of Glossators". See Antonio Padoa-Schioppa (2005), *Il diritto nella storia d'Europa.* Padova, 337 [ed. transl.].

[95] Birocchi, see note 27, 211 ff.

[96] In that era this was in force with *consensus omnium* (with the consent/agreement of all) in almost the whole of continental Europe. See Leibniz, *Ratio corporis iuris reconcinnandi*, note 33.

> §. 1. Ius Romanus vocamus tam quod a Iustiniano Romano Imperatore, quam quod a Romanis Pontificibus profectum est; illud Iustinianeum dicitur, hoc Pontificium. §. 2. *Utrumque habet per Europam fere totam, spontanea quidam receptione vim Iuris Communis*, et quasi Iuris Gentium Christianorum; ut valeat quatenus ei speciali Regni, Regionis, Provinciae, Loci alicuius Lege, Statuto, vel Consuetudine non est derogatum. [italics added].

(together with other early contemporary works)[97] to the importance Leibniz ascribes to logic applied to the law[98] as a necessary tool for identifying solutions of perplexing cases. This belief, which he developed in the early years of his philosophical production, suffered, in the mature phase of his thought, inasmuch as he had a conspicuous change of heart, which led the philosopher to define[99] logic in the Letter to Gabriel Wagner [c. 1660–c. 1717], as "a bag full of good reminders". Leibniz points out, however, that:

> If logic is nothing but a bag full of good reminders, it is certainly not futile. I have no praise for the new logicians who condemn the old rather than improve it. *It is not always in our power to find the truth when not enough data are at hand*, but we can always guard against error if we have time to think about a matter and to discover everything possible from the data—if we bring logic to full perfection. I have brought matters so far with my infinitesimal calculus of differences and sums that many problems can now be solved in mathematical physics which one could not even venture to try before. *Even when data are lack-*

---

[97] See *supra* notes 35 and 12.

[98] The philosophical attitude towards this topic has not changed, "If a law is contradictory, it is also contradictory to everything that is done in relation to it - and it is also illegal *since the logic is the basis of the law* [emphasis added]". Thus in Emanuele Severino (2001), "Equivoci e rigore nei Patti Lateranensi". *Corriere della Sera*, 26 May 2001. It is hardly necessary to add that the term "illegal" used by the illustrious Italian philosopher does not appear in the proper sense. If illogical rules are present, unfortunately they do not thereby cease to have force.

[99] As pointed out by Mengoni, "Dogmatica giuridica", see note 6, 51, n. 68.

> *ing, we can at least observe what data we do need.*[100] [italics added].

Leibniz continues by stating that:

> If we had adequate practice in the true art of reason, it would also help us to thoughts which we must grasp on the spur of the moment, but for the time being we still lack most of such an art, and I have not had time to examine this point. I also admit that when a logician gives a rule without an example, it is like trying to learn to duel with mere verbal instructions.[101]

And in his more mature reflections on the subject, put forward in *Noveaux Essais*, he finally comes to the conclusion that the logic of his contemporaries (the logic of John Locke)[102] is "too narrow" and certainly not suitable for the solution of cases "when one cannot absolutely settle a question".[103]

In such circumstances the German philosopher believes it is necessary to seek help from the *logic of likelihood.*[104] The latter, based on the available data (*ex*

---

[100] See Loemker, note 46, 462; this is the original text of the first sentence, in Carl Immanuel Gherardt [1816–1899] (1931), *Die Philosophischen Schriften von Leibniz*. Leipzig, VII, 526, *Leibniz an Gabriel Wagner* (1696): "15. Ist die Logick ein sackh voll guther erinnerungen, so ist sie ja nicht vergeblich. […]".

[101] See Loemker, note 46, 462.

[102] John Locke [1632–1704] (1690), *An Essay Concerning Human Understanding*. London.

[103] Leibniz, *Noveaux Essais*, see note 40, IV, ii, §14, 372.

[104] Leibniz, *Noveaux Essais*, see note 40, IV, ii, §14, 373, "So there will be two sorts of knowledge, just as there are two sorts of proof: one results in certainty and the other leads only to probability", thereby anticipating by approximately forty years the thought of Gian Battista Vico [1688–1744], expounded in the inaugural lecture, (1709) *De nostris temporis studiorum ratione*. Neapoli [in Elio Gianturco (ed. and transl.) (1990), *Vico, On the Study Methods of*

datis), helps to determine and, therefore, judge which choice is reasonably more reliable.[105] This would lead to

---

Our Time. Ithaca: Cornell University Press, 1990], which the famous essay by Theodor Viehweg [1907–1988] (1953), *Topik und Jurisprudenz*. Frankfurt auf Main [in *W. Cole Durham* Jr. (ed. and transl.) (1993), *Viehweg, Topics and Law. A Contribution to Basic Research in Law*. Frankfurt am Main: Peter Lang, from which I will quote] reproposed to the attention of the jurists of the second half of the last century.

[105] Leibniz, *Noveaux Essais*, see note 40, IV, ii, §14, 372–373,

> In any case call it what you will, the study of the degrees of probability would be very valuable; we do not yet have such a study, and this a serious shortcoming in our logic text-books. For when one cannot definitively settle the question of whether P is the case or not, one could still establish how likely P is on the evidence, enabling one to form a reasonable opinion about which side—·P or not-P·—is the more plausible. And when our wisest moralists bring in the question of what is •safest as well as of what is •most probable, and even put safety ahead of probability thus *they are not really abandoning the most probable*. For here the question of safety is the question of the improbability of an impending evil. Moralists who are lax about this have gone wrong largely because they have had an inadequate and over-*narrow notion of probability*, which they have confused with Aristotle's *'acceptability'*: in his Topics Aristotle aimed only to conform to the opinions of other people, so that for him what is '*acceptable*' is ... *whatever is accepted by the greatest number of people or by the most authoritative people*. He *was wrong to restrict his Topics to that*; this approach meant that he only concerned himself there with accepted maxims, *most of them vague—as though he wanted to reason by means of nothing but old jokes and proverbs*! But *probability or likelihood is broader ·than that·: it must be drawn from the nature of things*; and the opinion of weighty authorities is one of the things that can contribute to the likelihood of an opinion, but it does not produce the entire likelihood by itself. At the time when Copernicus was almost alone in his opinion ·that the earth goes around the sun·, it was still incomparably more likely than the opinion of all the rest of the human race, namely that the sun goes around the earth. I suspect *that establishment of techniques for estimating likelihoods would be more useful than a good proportion of our demonstrative sciences, and I have more than once thought of trying it* [italics added].

The passage from Aristotle to which Leibniz refers, is the following, "ἔνδοξα δὲ τὰ δοκοῦντα πᾶσιν ἢ τοῖς πλείστοις ἢ τοῖς σοφοῖς, καὶ

a useful "*form of intermediate knowledge* between the demonstrative certainty and inductive probability (or *a posteriori* probability)", which, in turn, would establish "a new chapter of the logic just outlined by Leibniz, neglected also by Kant." [italics added][106].

The landing place is undoubtedly fascinating, but unfortunately, the cognitive tools to establish this new chapter of logic were not indicated by the philosopher,

---

τούτοις ἢ πᾶσιν ἢ τοῖς πλείστοις ἢ τοῖς μάλιστα γνωρίμοις καὶ ἐνδόξοις", on this, see Immanuel Bekker (ed.) (1831), *Aristoteles, Graece, ΤΟΠΙΚΩΝ Α.* I, Berolini: apud Reimerum, 100, the standard English translations are "Generally accepted opinions, on the other hand are those which commend themselves to all or to the majority or to the wise – that is, to all of the wise or to the majority or to the most famous and distinguished of them", by Edward Seymour Forster [1879–1950] (ed. and transl.) (1940), *Aristotle, Topica.* Cambridge MA, London, 100b 21–23, 273–275, from which I will quote; "On the other hand, those opinions are 'generally accepted' which are accepted by everyone or by the majority or by the philosophers-i.e. by all, or by the majority, or by the most notable and illustrious of them", by Arthur Wallace Pickard-Cambridge [1873–1952] (ed. and transl.) (1994–2009), *Aristotle, Topics* in http://classics.mit.edu/Aristotle/topics.html, [accessed 4 may 2015]; the Junctas edition of the *Topics* (1562–1574, anastatic repr. 1962, Frankfurt am Main: Minerva) in, *Aristotelis opera cum commentariis Averroes.* Venetiis: apud Junctas, I, Part. 2b u 3, fol. 3, translates the passage of Aristotle, which Leibniz cites: "*Probabilia* (italics added) autem sunt quae videntur omnibus, aut plurimis, aut sapientibus; & his vel omnibus, vel plurimis, vel maxime familiaribus, & probatis. Litigiosus autem est syllogismus ex eis, quae videntur probabilia non sunt autem". This, we can say, in adherence with the interpretation of the same passage given by Averroes (Ibn Rushd, 1126–1198) in his Comment, therein in the Latin translation by Jacob Mantinus (d. 1549), fol. 3, 4, "Generatim haec ars [the dialectics, e. n.] est qua cum nos argumentamus, possumus syllogismum efficere *ex propositionibus probabilibus ad destruendum omne problema* [italics added]".

106 Mengoni (1996), "Interpretazione e nuova dogmatica", in *Ermeneutica e Dogmatica Giuridica*, see note 6, 78, n. 26, which recalls the essay on the topic by Hartmut Schiedermair (1970), "Das Phänomen der Macht und die Idee des rechts bei G. W. Leibniz". *Studia Leibnitiana. Supplementa.* VII, 308, 335.

and his goal of developing the latter in the ambit of the *probable*[107] or *likelihood*, shown by the "nature of the things", remained *in votis*.

---

[107] Leoni (see notes 30, 89) believes that the concept of probability expressed in this regard by Leibniz is "as something objective, from which any arbitrary psychological intrusion, every appeal unrelated to logical principles must be expunged"; the pioneering concept in this sense, according to Leoni, is that of the concept of probability "as an objective logical relation between propositions, analogous to the relation of deductibility" [ed. & transl.], developed by von Kries, Waissmann and especially Keynes, ibid, 73; Mengoni, "Ancora sul metodo giuridico", see note 6, 84, n. 22, "'Probable' has here the meaning of probability in the rigid sense, i.e. *not empirical probability* [italics added], based *a priori* on rational arguments deduced *lege artis* from the nature of things" [ed. transl.].The latter concept, however, has never been clarified by Leibniz; Chaim Perelman [1912–1984, Lucie Olbrechts-Tyteca [1899–1987] (1958; 4th ed., 1983), *Traité de l'argumentation. La nouvelle rhéthorique.* Bruxelles, 348,

> Cela semble avoir éschappé à Leibniz loersqu'il a propose—le premier selon Keynes—que l'espérance mathémathique soit appliquée dals le problems de jurisprudence: si duex presonnes réclament une certain somme, on répartira celle-ci suivant les probabilités de leurs droits. Le raisonnement est fondeé sur une certaine conception de ce qui est equitable, laquelle est loin d'être admise nécessairement car habituellment on accordera toute la somme à celui don't les pretentions paraîtront le mieux fondées.

Points of contact with the Leibnizian logic of the *likelihood* or *probable* seem to be present in the thought of John of Salisbury [1120–1180], who in the twelfth century spoke of the dialectic *quae nec ad docentium aspirat gravitatem, nec nec undis civilibus mergitur nec seducit fallaciis, sed prompta et mediocri probabilitatem verum examinat* [in Clement Charles Julian Webb [1865–1954] (ed.) (1929), *John of Salisbury, Metalogicon.* Oxford, II, 3; "for dialectic neither aspires to the weighty authority of apodictical teaching, nor does it become the plaything of political currents. Neither does it seduce the unwary by fallacies. Rather it makes inquiry into the truth, using the ready instrument of the moderate probability", transl. by Daniel D. McGarry (1955), *The Metalogicon of John of Salisbury.* Berkeley and Los Angeles:

In fact, in the continuation of the latter passage *from the Noveaux Essais*, quoted above, it can be noted that, in the absence of a perfect art of evaluation of the likelihoods for the resolution of ambiguous cases, Leibniz believes that one should link "the safest with the most likely" because

> when our wisest moralists bring in the question of what is • safest as well as of what is • most probable, and even put safety ahead of probability, *they aren't really abandoning the most probable*. For here the question of safety is the question of the improbability of an impending evil.[108]

University of California Press, 79], referring specifically to the criterion of *experience*. On the basis of this criterion, John believed that what is to be considered probable is that which is *frequentissime*, and which has most probably never been found in a different way, and finally, the necessary is that which, according to our belief, cannot be otherwise than what it is: see *Metalogicon* quoted above in this note, III, 9,

> *Not est autem facile in singulis semper explorare rerum quam firmus sit nexus aut quanta dissensio, et ob hoc quid simpliciter necesse quidve magis probabile sit judicare, interdum difficilius est. Sed quod frequentissime sic, probabile quidem, quod numquam aliter, magis probabile; quod aliter esse non posse creditur, necessarii suscipit nomen.* (It is not always easy in particular cases to determine the precise sthenght of the connection between things, or the exact amount of their mutual repugnance. For the same reason, it is occasionally very difficult to judge what is absolutely necessary or what very probable), [transl., by McGarry, see above in this note, 188].

[108] Leibniz, *Noveaux Essais*, see note 103. The opinion of Leoni is not acceptable, see note 30, 89; obliterating this important cultural reference made by Leibniz himself, Leoni says in no uncertain terms: "No confusion must therefore be made between the Leibnizian concept of probability and the probability of theologians or casuists of the seventeenth century, founded on the authority or consent of most of doctors [e. n. transl.]". If this is true, the passage quoted in the text demonstrates, however, the intellectual stimulation that

In this passage, after the words "And when our wisest moralists…", the standard English translation of the Noveaux Essays[109] omits the following sentence, put in round brackets in the original French text: "(I allude to the wisest of them, like the current general of the Jesuits)". [110] the reference is to the Spaniard, Thyrso Gonzalez[111] [1624–1705], author of a (1694), *Fundamentum theologiae moralis id est Tractatus theologicus de recto usu opinionum probabilium.* Tyrnaviae,[112] almost thirty years after the *NM.*

Analyzing this work, one is surprised to discover that Leibniz in adulthood appeared to consider adequate the above cited *modus ratiocinandi*, together with some other reflections contained in this work, such as those on usurious contracts, where the authoritative religious view does not start in its reasoning from the nature of the things (*ex datis*, as Leibniz would like) in order to decide the controversial cases, but relies on conscience, not feeling obliged to share

---

Leibniz received on the topic from the debate on probabilism of theologians and casuists of the seventeenth century.

[109] See note 40.

[110] Leibniz, note 40, AA VI, 6, IV, ii, §14, 372, "Et lorsque nos moralistes (j'entend les plus sages, tel que le général moderne dés jésuites) …".

[111] See note 40, AA VI, 6, IV, ii, §14, 372, n. 17. Thyrso Gonzalez was elected, in 1687, the thirteenth Superior General of the Society of Jesus, until his death.

[112] This book is the last version of *Fundamentum theologiae moralis, id est tractatus theologicus de recto usu opinionum probabilium* (1676), which never received permission to be published; only later was Gonzalez, once elected superior general, and with the support of Pope Innocent XI, able to print secretly a work against probabilism (1691), *Tractatus succintus de recto usu opinionum probabilium.* Dilingae. Thanks to the opposition of theologians of the Society of Jesus, however, the work was not put into circulation. Gonzalez did not give up and, after obtaining the authorization of Innocent XII, printed his work under the title quoted in the text.

authoritative opinions to the contrary in this regard.[113]

---

[113] Here I quote from the Amsterdam edition of the 1697: T. Gonzalez (1697), *Synopsis Tractatus teologici de recto usu opinionum probabilium, cui accessit logistica probabilitatum*. Amstelodami, §XX, 83–85,

> *Si mercator a me roget, an sibi liceat talem contractum celebrare, non possum respondere: Licet: quia hoc ipso affirmarem, esse absolute licitum, quod absolute censeo esse usuram; et inducerem illum ad faciendum, quod iudico esse malum, et prohibitum: quae res est omnino illicita. Nec sufficit, quod detur sententia probabilis affirmans, illum contractum esse licitum; quia quamdiu illa sententia a me non approbatur, non possum secundum illam operari, et consilium dare. Sententiam contrariam esse probabilem, probat quidem, Suos Authores, et omnes, qui illam veram esse existimant, posse secundum illam operari et consilium dare; non autem eos, qui illam improbant, et ut falsam rejiciunt. In primis enim absolute affirmare exterius ut licitum, quod interius judico esse absolute illicitum est mendacium quod est intrinsece illicitum, utpote contrarium commercio et societati hominum. Deinde inducere ad faciendum, quod lege Dei est graviter prohibitum, est grave peccatum. Et quamvis ego non cognosca certo & evidenter talem legem existere, tamen prudenter judico existere, idque mihi persuasum habeo. [...] Quare in dicto casu, vel debeo absolute respondere, non esse licitum illum contractum, vel saltem dicere: Dantur quidem doctores affirmantes contractum istum esse licitum; caeterum ego illorum falsam esse existimo sententiam, ac proinde tibi absolute respondere ego non possum, esse licitum istum contractum; quia censeo illicitum. Tu alios doctiores consule; si illi affirmaverint esse licitum, & tu prudenter censeas, me potius quam illos decipi, eorum sententiam amplecti poteris* (If a merchant asks me whether it is permitted to enter into such a contract, I cannot answer it is permitted, because I would state that what I completely judge as usury is permitted; and I would induce him to do something that I judge to be evil and prohibited, which is entirely unlawful; because until that opinion is approved by me, I cannot act and give advice. In fact, it proves that the contrary opinion is probable, their authors and all of them who judge that opinion to be true and state that they are allowed to act according to it and give advice; not those who did not approve and rejected it as false. First, to classify externally as licit that which, in my inner self, I judge to be completely illicit, is lying, i.e. performing an action that is intrinsically illicit, inasmuch as contrary to trade and human society. Moreover, to induce someone into doing what is severely forbidden by the law of God, is a grave sin. And even if I do not

Moreover, the arguments of the Jesuit seem strikingly consonant with the methods of investigation of late Scholasticism, with those of St. Thomas and earlier writers, and with the Topics of Aristotle himself, which Leibniz felt to be totally inadequate for the resolution of disputes, because the "probable" for Aristotle, according to Leibniz, coincides with other people's arbitrary opinion.[114] But this is merely my impression on reading the *Synopsis,* which is here as an *obiter dictum* entirely negligible for the reader, in comparison to the originality of the cultural stimulus bequeathed by Leibniz through the project of a *logic of likelihood.* This is a legacy which, to date, legal and philosophical thought has not yet pursued because this new chapter of logic, to our knowledge, is still to be written.[115]

---

know with certainty and clearly that such a law exists, nevertheless prudently I judge that it exists and I am convinced. [...] therefore in such a case either I have the definitive answer that the contract in question is not licit, or at least I must say: just as there are, indeed, Doctors who state that this contract is licit, but I judge that the opinion of some of them is false, in the same manner I cannot answer you with certainty that this contract is licit, because I judge it to be forbidden. Let us consult other more learned men; if they affirm that it is licit and you prudently judge that I deceive myself rather than them, you will embrace their opinion.) [ed. transl.].

[114] See note 103. Enrico Berti (2004), "Il valore degli ἔνδοξα secondo Aristotele", in *Nuovi studi Aristotelici.* I, Brescia, 278–279, notes that according to Aristotle (Rhet. 1, 1335 a14–18) "because nature has endowed men with good ability to grasp the truth, most of them capture it, and the expression of this attitude is precisely the ἔνδοξα, shared by the majority of men and true in most cases." [ed. transl.]. Leibniz, however, as we have seen (note 74, 64), is not likely to share the generally accepted opinion because "the opinion of weighty authorities is one of the things that can contribute to the likelihood of an opinion, but it does not by itself produce the entire likelihood".

[115] In contemporary philosophy Edmund Husserl [1859–1938] (1900/1901), *Logische Untersuchungen.* Halle, English transl. by J. N. Findlay (2001), *Husserl, Logical Investigation.* London, New York, 1, 17–19 (from which I quote), summarizes the statements of Leibniz on the theme of probability and likelihood, but only to find that

If the logic of the probable (or of likelihood) remains a knowledge gap, Leibniz's early lesson on *calculus ratiocinator* by reducing right to *elementa simplicia*[116] seems to have been completed and to have achieved fruitful results. In effect, as highlighted by the best historians,[117] it seems to have greatly influenced modern legal thought, particularly in the elaboration of the Dogmatics, which basically pursues the same aim as the German philosopher, namely to resolve any legal case through a calculation of the norm. In this case, however, this is to be done by means of the use of cognitive concepts (*e. g.* legal transaction, act of disposal, etc.), inferred by the interpreter in the code through refined processes of abstraction.

But the Dogmatics too, as Mengoni[118] points out, is a "bag full of good reminders" because, like the *calculus ratiocinator*, it has proved inadequate to solve the so-called "question of the 'just'" to which, "the jurist must respond positively, that is: which one, among the possible

---

> The most perfect 'mark' of correctness is inward evidence, it counts as an immediate intimation of the truth itself. In the vast majority of cases, we lack such absolute knowledge of the truth, in whose place we make use—one need *only* think how memory functions in the above examples—of the inner evidence for a higher or lower degree of probability for our state or affairs, with which, if probability-levels become high enough, a firm judgment is usually associated. The inward evidence of probability of a state of affairs *A* will not serve to ground the inward evidence of its truth, but it will serve to ground those comparative, inwardly evident value-assessments, through which, in accordance with positive or negative probability-values, we can distinguish the reasonable from the unreasonable, the better-founded from the worse-founded assumptions, opinions and surmises. Ultimately, therefore, all genuine, and, in particular, all scientific knowledge, rests on inner evidence: as far as such evidence extends, the concepts of knowledge extends also.

Perelman, Olbrechts-Tyteca, see note 107, seem to have a reductive opinion with regard to Leibniz's logic of likelihood.

[116] See note 12.

[117] See note 31.

[118] Mengoni, "Dogmatica giuridica", see note 31, 51, n. 68.

solutions appropriate to decide, each consistent with the words or the frame of the law and the general logic of the legal system, comes close better to the justice, satisfies better the justice".[119]

In this sense a significant example can be derived from one of the most controversial central disputes in recent years in Italian civil law: that of the refundability of non-pecuniary damage, in cases where the law does not expressly so provide, as Article 2059, Italian Civil Code (now Article 2059 c.c.) requires.

Up to the mid-1980s, according to Article 185 of the Italian Criminal Code (now Article 185 c. p.), such cases were identified only in the criminal offenses from which only one known type of non-pecuniary damage could derive: mental suffering (so-called moral damage). There are, however, other "visible" injuries devoid of economic value, irreducible to the traditional notion of moral damage, and "justice" would require that they also be compensated (for example, the total disruption of peaceful family life, and the need to provide for the needs of a child permanently reduced to a vegetative condition due to negligent medical treatment). The courts, however, were denying compensation.

Instead the Bologna Court of Appeals on 22 February 2000 vacated a 1996 judgment of the Reggio Emilia Court, which had established that the vegetative state of a child was due to mistakes in diagnosis and to the negligent omission of a doctor employed by the national health service. The doctor and the national health service itself were ordered[120] to compensate the parents of the child through the payment of a sum for non-pecuniary

---

[119] Mengoni, "Interpretazione e nuova dogmatica" see note 106, 79–81, n. 27 [ed. transl.].

[120] In whose conduct was found negligent incompetence leading to a causal contribution quantified at 50%.

damages deriving both from "acute distress, but restricted only to the inner field", and from the frustrated expectations of the parents who had hoped to have "a normal family life devoted to the upbringing of the son, to a normal duration of life, to a serene old age". The judgment stated that the "moral damage from the harmful event considered in itself, was added to the damage consisting in the most total disruption of their normal habits and expectations, together with the need to provide for the needs of the child permanently reduced to almost exclusively vegetative condition".

The physician appealed to the Supreme Court, supporting the old argument under which in the Italian legal system it is not allowed to assume a *lata* sense of non-pecuniary damage beyond the usual concept of moral damage deriving only from criminal offences, because only the latter meaning can be derived from the rules of law under Articles 2059 c. c. and 185 c. p. Therefore, according to the applicant, since the Court of Appeal had included in the concept of non-pecuniary injuries certain injuries not consistent with the typical notion of non-pecuniary damage, it had in fact illegally duplicated the damage "items".

The Supreme Court dismissed the appeal with reasoning which, as we shall see, after starting from topical arguments—(*for authorities*, *for unpredictability of the identity* between non-pecuniary damage and transient mental suffering—*i. e.* so-called pecuniary damage—; *for reduction*, *i. e.* the need to choose between two values and ascertain which one is preeminent)—eventually established the systematic premise of positive/statute law for the solution of the problem.

The Court ruled:[121]

> In the sense of non-coincidence between the non-pecuniary damage as stated by art. 2059 c.c. and the subjective moral damages [moral damage deriving from criminal offence, e. n.], it should be recalled that this Supreme Court has considered compensable the non-pecuniary damage, obviously in a different sense from the subjective moral damages, also in favor of legal persons, i.e. of entities for which a psychological involvement in anxieties of mind is not configurable.

As already said, there is no definition of non-pecuniary damage in the Italian legal system, so there is no indisputable premise from which to start the deductive *sorites*; therefore, one has to resort to arguments based *on opinion* to reconstruct an acceptable premise of the reasoning. According to Aristotle:

> Generally accepted opinions, on the other hand are those which commend themselves to all or to the majority or to the wise—that is, to all of the wise or to the majority or to the most famous and distinguished of them.[122]

and it is clear from the extract taken from the ruling transcribed above that the Court has resorted to the argument *ab auctoritate*, or of the remarkable opinion, corroborated by the high number of rulings[123] that admit the compensation of non-pecuniary damage in favor of legal persons. Once the number of judgments has been recalled, this implies that the argument which supports them has also

---

[121] Cass., 31 maggio 2003, n. 8827, in *Danno e Responsabilità*, 2003, 8–9, 819 with a comment by F. D. Busnelli, G. Ponzanelli, and A. Procida Mirabello di Lauro.

[122] Aristotle, see note 105, 100b 21–23, 273–275.

[123] It should not be forgotten that the term *sentenza* (lat. "sententia"), in its etymological sense means precisely "highly qualified opinion".

been recalled, namely that although legal persons are legal creations, they are legal entities capable of legal relations similarly to an individual. Therefore, they cannot be excluded from the compensation of non-pecuniary damages, because the law does not state that such damages are necessarily to be configured in terms "ontologically" identical to the moral suffering, to the heartache of mind that only men and women, *rerum natura*, may suffer in consequence of a crime. Here we are in the ambit of the remarkable places of *the identical*, and in particular in the *topos* relative to the comparison between *the predicables*, according to which

> when (…) one is destroying a definition, it is enough to argue against a single point (for, if we have destroyed any one point whatsoever, we shall have destroyed the definition).[124]

Once we have demolished the "essence" of non-pecuniary damage as a form of mental concern or worry, by invoking the argument of the non-identity between the former and the latter:

> one can consider that the recognition of the *lata* extension of the notion of 'non-pecuniary damage' has been acquired in the positive legal system, and that it is understood as damage from injury related to the values involving the person, and no longer as moral subjective 'damage'.[125]

---

[124] Aristotle, see note 105, VII, 5, 35, 667.

[125] This conclusion is echoed by Cass., s.u., 11 November 2008, n. 26972, in *Riv. dir. civ.*, 2009, 1, 2, 97 with note by F. D. Busnelli; see where in the section on the reason for the decision n. 2.13 and, above all, n 4.8 "non-pecuniary damage under Article 2059, Civil Code [has to be identified] with the damage caused by the lesion of interest involving the person, such damage not being characterized by economic importance" [ed. transl.].

It remains, however, for the Court to resolve the key problem: whether the compensation of non-pecuniary damages is admissible outside of the cases provided by law, such cases being, at the time of the trial, restricted to crimes. So the Court reasons:

> Coming to the crucial question of the limits to which art. 2059 Civil Code of 1942 subjects non-pecuniary damages, through the legal reservation, originally explained only by art. 185 c.p. [criminal code, e. n.] (But see also art. 89 c.p.c. [civil procedure code, e. n.]), the Court believes that, taking into consideration personal values of constitutional significance, it must be ruled out that compensation for non-pecuniary damage occurring thereafter is subject to the limit resulting from the reserve of the law related to art. 185 c.p.

This is "a *topos* that is one of the most frequented in axiologically oriented legal argumentation, as it provides a reliable technique for rationalization of values: it is the *topos* of the *reduction*"[126] or of the choice between two values, whereby, when it is necessary to detect what route is preferable or better, the choice is to be made under that which is in itself more noble and valuable.[127]

---

[126] Mengoni, "Interpretazione e nuova dogmatica", see note 106, 85, which recalls Adalbert Podlech (1970), "Wertungen Werte und im Recht". *Arch off. Rechts*, 197–198, and the latter; on the topic, Aristotle, see note 105, III, 1 117, 140.

[127] So Aristotle, see note 105, III, 1, 117, 391, teaches,

> that which is in itself more noble and more valued and more praiseworthy is more worthy of choice; for example, friendship is more worthy of choice than wealth, and justice than strength. For the former in themselves are among things valued and praiseworthy, while the latter are valued and praiseworthy not in themselves but for some other reason; for no one values wealth for its own sake but for some other reason, but we value friendship for its own sake, even if we are not likely to get anything else from it.

In our system, which is a system of legal justice,[128] the value(s) which must be preferred in the judgment of preeminence is that/those recognized and guaranteed by the Constitution which, precisely because it is/they are positively provided by the Fundamental Law of the State (source of law superordinate to all others and parameter of the validity of all other laws), draw from their degree of superiority over other values from the latter and, therefore, is/are mandatory for the judge as a "benchmark" in the decision. From this assumption it is plausible to argue that if a constitutional value was affected, even in the absence of a specific provision for compensation of non-pecuniary damage arising from its violation (of the constitutional value), that value could not receive less protection than that accorded to the values protected by the ordinary law, for which, instead, such compensation is expressly provided. Indeed, according to the Court:

---

[128] Roberto Mangabeira Unger (1975), *Knowledge and Politics*. New York, 89:

> To understand the nature of adjudication one must distinguish two different ways of ordering human relations. One way is to establish rules to govern general categories of acts and persons, and then to decide particular disputes among persons on the basis of the established rules. This is the legal justice. The other way is to determine goals and then, quite independently of rules, to decide particular cases by a judgment of what decision is most likely to contribute to predetermined goals, a judgment of instrumental rationality. This is the substantive justice ...

> It follows from a constitutionally-oriented reading[129] that the limit [of the express provision of law, e. n.] should be considered inoperative if the injury has affected the values of the person guaranteed by the Constitution. Thus it must be considered that if the injury has affected a constitutionally protected interest, compensation by means of indemnity (...) is the minimal form of protection, and a minimum level of protection is not amenable to specific limits, as this it results in a refusal of protection of the excluded cases.

In a system of legal justice, such as Italian and continental civil law, the constitutional values mostly "do not carry a premise with deductive strength: their mode of application is not subsumption [130] 'but argumentation, which is precisely the *modus ratiocinandi* proper of the rhetorical 'places'".[131]

On the basis of this observation, it appears not overhasty to conclude that the the judge's manner of reaching a decision (the legal reasoning) cannot completely free itself from the lessons of rhetoric taught by Aristotle, Cicero, Quintilian, Lorenzo Valla, and Gian Battista Vico because there are no better cognitive tools to be used for

---

[129] Corte Cost., 21 aprile 1994, n. 149, est. Granata, in *Giust. civ.*, 1994, 1781,

> [...] When the judge [...] makes the reconnaissance of the normative content of the provision, he must always and constantly be guided by the need to respect the constitutional precepts; therefore, if an interpretation appears conflicting with some of the precepts, he must—especially in the absence of living law [i.e. of a previous case, e. n.]—adopt alternative readings which are closer to the otherwise violated constitutional parameter. [ed. transl.]

[130] Mengoni, "L'argomentazione nel Diritto costituzionale", in *Ermeneutica e dogmatica giuridica*, see note 31, 129.

[131] Mengoni, ibid., 124.

the solution of a case when pure analytical syllogism reveals itself unfit.

On the other hand, we run the risk of being ungenerous towards the Leibniz's effort to introduce the *calculus ratiocinator* in law if, with respect to its practical results, we reflected: "Supposing that the logic allows you to establish all of the interpretations logically consistent with the letter of a statutory rule, it does not teach how to choose the best". [132] The objection is certainly insurmountable, but it should not be misconstrued to mean that the use of analytics in the law plays a role, after all, albeit with a modest utility.

If this perspective were adopted, it would lead to the risk of losing sight of the most important (and constructive) contribution which Leibniz gave on the subject. Once he had demonstrated, with the *NM* and his other legal writings from the same period, that only through logic was it possible to achieve systematic organization of the rules on which to base the more certain deductive premises of the legal syllogism (in the sense of premises devoid of any arbitrary psychological intrusion of the interpreter, *i.e.* based on the pure letter of the rule), then, with the more mature reflections of the *Noveaux Essais*, he made it clear that logic is the only cognitive tool that is of aid in determining the moment in which the rules do not offer data by means of which logic itself can be used profitably; therefore this "legitimates" the judge in making use of dialectical arguments for solving the case.

---

[132] Mengoni, "Ancora sul metodo giuridico", see note 31, 84, n, 21. According to Hans Kelsen [1881–1973] (1934), *Reine Rechtslehre*. Leipzig, Engl. transl. by M. Knight (2005), *Kelsen, Pure Theory of Law*. Clark, NJ, 353 (from which I quote), "The question which of the possibilities within the frame of the law to be applied is the 'right' one is not a question of cognition directed toward positive law—we are not faced here with a problem of legal theory but of legal politics".

This happens, for example, as in the case just examined, when the legal system either fails to give univocal linguistic footholds in order to establish certain deductive premises, or the law itself deliberately does not wish to provide that element which often turns out to be important for the deductive argument: *the definition*, which in the Civil law, Romans teach, is dangerous[133] because "nothing will be more difficult and dangerous than to restrict and limit in strictly stable formulas the very concepts that should serve for the most disparate hypotheses of facts, times, peoples, and needs."[134]

It is at this moment, and only in this phase of the decision path, therefore, that the *opinio iudicis* can and must be recovered—that very *opinio*, which Leibniz hoped to subtract from the Aristotelian *topoi*: for such *topoi* were, in his view, necessarily arbitrary, inasmuch as they were based on the personal opinion of the judge. Rather, the latter should have recourse to this new logic of likelihood or of the probable, based on data "drawn from the nature of things".

Thereby Leibniz made it possible not only to identify the premises[135] of a decision which is based on a positive rule of

---

[133] *Omnis definitio in iure civili periculosa*, D.50.17.202.

[134] Thus, only *ad exemplum*, Trib. Napoli, 27 maggio 1908, D'Annunzio c. Scarpetta, in *Giur. it.*, 1909, II, 7–8, with comment by L. Ferrara *sr*.

[135] Dispatch by Ferdinando IV of Naples [1751–1825], 23 September 1774, in Gaetano Filangieri [1752–1825] (1774), *Riflessioni politiche sull'ultima legge del Sovrano che riguarda la riforma nell'amministrazione della Giustizia*, Napoli, XIII–XIV.

> And when there is no express law for the case in question, and one has to resort to interpretation or extension of the law, the King wants this to be done by the judge so that *the two premises of the argument are always based on expressed and literal laws*; and when the case is either completely new or totally open to doubt, so that it cannot be decided either by law, or by the argument of the

right,[136] but also those that are based (in the absence of any other possibility possible) on the personal *opinio judicis*, denuding it.[137] This is no small achievement.

But the circle is not closed; once logic, after the ordering of the rules, has shown the impossibility of starting from "certain" premises and has imposed the use of the *téchne rethoriché*, inevitably it comes back into play as the indispensable tool of verification of the inherent consistency of the arguments used to support the conclusions reached.[138]

Gamberale, Milano, Forte dei Marmi, August 2014-May 2015.

Carmelo Massimo de Iuliis

> law, then the King requires that you should refer to the H. M. to wait for the Sovereign Oracle. [italics added; ed. transl.].

For the judge, however, "The difficulty depends entirely on succeeding in establishing *those two premises*", Guido Calogero [1904–1986] (1964), *La logica del giudice e il suo controllo in Cassazione*. Padova, 51, [italics added; ed. transl.].

[136] It is hardly necessary to recall that civil law at the time of Leibniz consisted of the written rules of jus commune, namely the Corpus Juris and canon law, see note 96.

[137] *Opinio*, which does not change its nature, in our opinion, even when it rests on assumptions that are not arbitrary, but legal, such as the constitutional values (life, health, education etc.), because with the latter it is not possible to perform deductive chains, but only dialectical arguments, belonging to rhetoric (see Mengoni, "L'argomentazione nel diritto costituzionale", in *Ermeneutica e dogmatica giuridica*, see note 31, 124, 126); argumentations by their own nature amenable to counterarguments that may justify a different decision.

[138] Viehweg, see note 104, 9,

> On closer consideration of dialectical inferences, which as we have seen are the subject matter of Topics, we recognize the following: such as inferences cannot be differentiated from apodictic inferences in a formal sense (…). Dialectical inferences differ from the other types, rather—and this characterizes the entire way of thinking—according to the nature of their premises.

Translations of *Nova Methodus*

To our knowledge there has only been one full translation of *Nova methodus* into modern language published:

- in Italian, Carmelo Massimo de Iuliis (ed. and transl.) (2012), *Leibniz, Il nuovo metodo di apprendere ed insegnare la giurisprudenza*. Milan, Giuffrè.

These are the following translations of the *First Part*:

- in English, selected passages , in Leroy E. Loemker (ed. and transl.) (1989), *Leibniz, Philosophical Papers and Letters*. Dordrecht: Kluwer.
- In Italian, in M. di Dario (ed. and transl.) (1965), *Leibniz, Il metodo Generale degli Studi*. Napoli: Nuovi Orientamenti.

The second Part has been translated:

- in English, only the §§. from 1 to 22 and from 69 to 76 in C. Johns (2013), *The science of right in Leibniz's Moral and political Philosophy*. London, New York: Bloomsbury.
- in German, selected passages, in H. Zimmermann, H. Busche (eds. and transl.) (2003), *Leibniz, Frühe Schriften zum Naturrecht*. Hamburgh: Meiner.
- in French, with omission of the §§. from 91 to 100, in G. L. Maurin (transl.) (1830), *Leibniz, Nouvelle méthode pour apprendre et einsegner la jurisprudence*. Paris.

Abbreviations and Notice to the Reader

AA VI, 1: Academy of Science of Berlin (Paul Ritter [1872–1954], Willy Kabitz [1876–1942], Heinrich Schepers, eds.) (reprs. 2006, 1990, 1th 1930), *Leibniz, Philosophische Schriften*. Vol. 1, Berlin: Akademie Verlag, here the critical text of *Nova Methodus Discendae Docendaeque Iurisprudentiae* followed for the translation.

AA VI, 2: Academy of Science of Berlin (Paul Ritter [1872–1954], Willy Kabitz [1876–1942], Heinrich Schepers, eds.) (reprs. 2006, 1990, 1th 1930), *Leibniz, Philosophische Schriften*. Vol. 2, Berlin: Akademie Verlag.

AA VI, 6: Academy of Science of Berlin (André Robinet and Heinrich Schepers eds.) (1962, 1990, 2006), Leibniz, *Philosophische Schriften. Nouveaux Essais*. Vol. 6, Berlin: Akademie Verlag.

NM: *Nova Methodus*.

As for the dates of birth and death of the Authors quoted in the Introduction and in the text, I put them between [ ] when are an interpolation in the text or they precede the year of publication of the book quoted in footnotes.

In the footnotes, I reported the full text of the passages of the *Corpus Juris* by Justinian quoted by Leibniz: as for Digest in the translation by Alan Watson (ed. 1985, reprint 2011), *The Digest of Justinian*. 4 vols., Philadelphia PA: Philadelphia University Press; as for Code and

Novels in the translation by Fred H. Blume [1875–1971], *Annotated Justinian Code*, in http://www.uwyo.edu/law lib/blume-justinian/ajc-edition-1/book-6.htm [accessed on 30th May 2015].

The above mentioned passages of *Corpus Juris* as well as, obviously, the text of my translation, and the footnotes were subjected to a strict control during the re-reading of drafts, but the error of composition is always lurking, so that for any "oversights" I invoke the indulgence of the attentive reader, with the encouragement of Sebastiano Timpanaro [1923–2000], prominent Italian philologist, who wrote that after many re-readings

> "(…) we glanced at words as a whole we mentally 'integrate' them the rest of its letters. At least as far as alphabetical scripts are concerned, we tend to read them as if each word was unique 'design', an ideogram (This is the reason why misprints can so easily escape us we correct proof)", Id. (1976), *The Freudian Slip: Psychoanalysis and textual criticism*, transl. by Kate Soper, London: NLB, 22).

As for my translation of the *Nova Methodus*, I tried as far as possible to be faithful to the text.

Even in this case I invoke the indulgence of the cultured reader for any possible mistake, obviously without prejudice to the limit of decency, which I hope of having never exceeded, reminding him with a smile (as is well-known the susceptibility of the translators) that: "I know German all right. But as a language it's on par with Latin, nobody ever completely masters it. I suppose you've mastered Latin." (Guido Morselli [1912–1973] (1975), *Divertimento 1889*, transl. by H. Shankland (1986), London: Chatto & Windus, 117).

The New Method *of* Learning *and* Teaching Jurisprudence

According to the Principles of the Didactic Art
Premised in the General Part and in the Light of Experience

Gottfried Wilhelm Leibniz

The First Complete English Translation
of the 1667 *Frankfurt Edition* with Notes by
Carmelo Massimo de Iuliis

To the most reverend Prince and Lord
John Philip[*]
Archbishop of the Holy See of Mainz,
Archchancellor and Prince-Elector of the Holy Roman Empire for Germany,
Bishop of Herborn and Worms, Duke of *Francia Orientalis*,
His most merciful Lord:

The Author.

[*]Johann Philipp von Schönborn [1605–1673].

DEDICATION

Most Reverend Lord, the very topic itself, more than a passage of this book, prompted my mind to turn towards You, while I was wondering whom among my Patrons I should approach for such a small work, which is not to be envied in truth, yet nevertheless awakens envy (for all novelties are received in such a manner). It is befitting that everything which is devoted to the public good for Germany be presented to YOU: this is, for YOU, the objective of the counsels, to this cause YOU have directed all efforts and tasks for so many years. Neither the allurements of novelties, nor the sacred reverence for antiquity distract YOU from this goal. Germany owes peace To YOU, among distinguished men; the Church will be obliged to YOU, among the very few elect, if Heaven consents to such goals. Certainly it behooves us far more to appease pens than weapons; those pens which, I state, have poured blood on us instead of ink, but nothing is impossible to the minds of the princes who act in unison; they lack, however, an unswerving Guide and Leader. And as soon as virtue, but, in truth, first of all, fate, —that is to say, Providence—has positioned you in the appropriate place, continue to make use of your wisdom and strengths, which are destined to this office by the divine will. Let Heaven be propitious, let your actions be acclaimed by the best from both parts, the irreducible contrariness of others is an incitement for virtuous men. Incomparable men, in truth, have smoothed the way and relieved the sorrows of divisions through their moderate counsels.

Oh mihi tam longe maneat pars ultima vitae[1]

I eagerly await the moment when I will be allowed to see the healed wounds of Germany, and the concord of Princes rejoicing with mutual embraces. Then honor will return to the temples, charity to hearts, virtue to the people, terror to foreigners, prosperity to all of us: the whole of posterity will venerate your white hair and the poets of the future centuries will sing the *beautiful sources* of the bounty liberally bestowed on us by *Your Family*. And certainly with these lines, (which I am will seek to use use as my Creed):

Fata viam invenient aderitque vocatus Jova[2].

Meanwhile, neither do so many concerns divert you from less important things; nor is this Sun of the Empire ashamed of stooping to humble writings. Nor, indeed, are you unaware of how much of the tree is in the root, how much of the river is in the source, how much of the state is in the education. I will say nothing with regard to the seminars, which through your care have been preserved, increased and for the most part built up; nothing concerning temples, which are shining on account of your attention; nothing about ecclesiastical discipline, restored by virtue of your heedfulness. I cannot be silent about that which most properly concerns this topic, that is to say, how much has been achieved through your consideration in renewal of the University of Erfurt. There are

[1] Virgil [70 BC–19 BC], *Eclogues*, IV, 53, "I pray that the twilight of a long life may then be vouchsafed me", in Henry Rushton Fairclough [1862–1938] (ed. and transl.) (1916), *Virgil, Eclogues, Georgics, Aeneid 1–6.* Cambridge: Harvard University Press.

[2] Virgil [70 BC–19 BC], *Aeneid*, III, 395, "the Fates will find a way, and Apollo [not *Jova* such as in the text, e. n.] be present at your call", in Fairclough, see note 1.

two Julian Universities in Germany: one in Würzburgh, the other in Helmstedt, both bear this name [Julian] from their Founder[3]: who could doubt that the university of Erfurt, which through your bounty is now living for a second time now, must be called Philippine? The present name of your family befits this university: τῶν καλλιπήγων [in Greek in the text, of the beautiful sources[4], e. n.] such as the Hippocrene source[5]; no longer will it be named, because of its trickle, Gerana[6] in which another river has sprung from this *beautiful source*. To YOU, therefore, who are entrusted with these cares, I felt that it would not be inappropriate to express these reflections of mine, though in regard of the topic more than of the elaboration presented here, inasmuch as the latter, afflicted by the uncertainties of the journey, the clatter of the inns and the lack of books, has almost nothing to commend it. As I had not infrequently examined the common difficulties of learning and teaching, some noble young men, elevated above the inclination of the plebs, often entreated me to expound these considerations publicly. But I feared the hatred of those who believe that what is very ancient is the very essence of goodness, me thinks because they had the same experience with wine. Now, in truth, they too will be appeased by the name of such a Prince, and I will be defended: that sole hope gave

[3] The University of Würzburgh and Helmstedt were called Julian from the name of their founders: as for the former, Julius Echter von Mespelbrunn, [1545–1627], Prince-Bishop; as for latter, Julius Brunswick-Lünemburg (duke of), [1528–1589].

[4] Leibniz is playing with the meaning of the Bishop family name, Schönborn: it means in German, namely, "beautiful source".

[5] In the Greek mythology, the fountain on Mount Helicon sacred to the Muses and believed to be a source of poetic inspiration.

[6] The university of Erfurt was called Gerana from the river Gera, where once stood, see M. Bauer (2003), *Bürgerbuch der Stadt Erfurt 1761–1833*. Marburg an der Lahn, 17.

me the courage of manifesting my thoughts. And while other authors direct their discussion towards a variety of different disciplines, I myself often grieve over matters concerning law. I do not wish to imply that great men, who know and engage in more valid matters are lacking; but I grieve because they were crushed by the judgments of common people, and deprived of the possibility to introduce in public all the constructs prepared for few a small circle of students between private walls. Nor can hope survive unless, as if *ex machina,* extraordinary princes appear and demolish both the malice, and the idleness, and finally the envy of those whose actions are injurious. You, Prince truly born for the public good, have given the first stroke of the ax to extirpate the public evil. God offers chances only to the better decisions, and donates the additions of your years to the prayers of the Germany. The world will see YOU as Archchancellor of the Empire, with your own right to pre-establish the realization of every excellent thing. Then, in the matter of praise to be tribute to you for such great undertakings,

Non me carminibus vincet vel Thracius Orpfeus,
Vel Linus; huic mater quamvis, atque huic Pater adsit:
Orphei Calliopea, Lino formosus Apollo[7].

Meanwhile, Most Reverend Lord, receive from me these first offerings with a serene complexion; we desired to be useful to the public, and we will accomplish our aspiration if your protection is granted. And, if it flows unto us, we will surpass the heights of our talent. May GOD preserve YOU, Lord, to the country, the family, the subjects, and, if I may add, to me. Given in Mainz, in the year 1667.

---

[7] Virgil [70 BC–19 BC], *Eclogues*, IV., 56, "Then shall neither Thracian Orpheus nor Linus vanquish me in song, though mother give aid to the one and father to the other, Calliope to Orpheus, to Linus fair Apollo.", in Fairclough, see note 1.

PREFACE TO THE READER

I do not know if I owe You a preface, my Good Reader, because it seems that a small card in the guise of a preface is sufficient. But, nevertheless, custom must follow the public desire. Why then, you say, do you prepare new things by means of a book, when you are not favorable to the form of a book? Because, I say, this concerns decorum; the topic of writing in response to a need. But, today there are some who have blurred vision in so much light of the world, and prefer to feed on acorns after finding a fruit; their dislikes are a threat to those who prepare better things. And once already, the royal favor was called upon to protect Lorenzo Valla [1407–1457] against the fury of the Sophists, for he had corrected the dialectic and moral philosophy, an action which in some sense he himself narrates in the *Apology to the Pontifex Maximus*[8]. The dislikes of all of the peda-gogues in France and Germany tormented Pierre de la Ramée [1515–1572], Regius professor, who preferred to carefully evaluate, rather than follow Aristotle [384 BC–322 BC], until he was immolated to the Parisian *Manes* of Aristotle on the occasion of those nuptials[9]. Who is unaware of the destinies of Galileo Galilei [1564–1642] and Tommaso Campanella [1568

[8] Lorenzo Valla (1518), *Laurentii Vallensis Pro se et contra calumniatores, ad Eugenium IIII Pont. Max. Apologia. De libero arbitrio. Apologia ejus adversum calumniatores, quando super fide sua requisitus fuerat. Item contra Bartoli libellum, cui titulus, de insigniis et armis, epistola.* Basileae: apud Andream Cratandrum.

[9] Pierre de la Ramée (1543), *Animadversionum Aristotelicarum Libri XX*. Lutetiae. De la Ramée, a Protestant convert, was killed during the St. Bartholomew's Day Massacre (on Aug 24, 1572) two days after the nuptials (to which L. refer) between Margaret of Valois and Herry IV of France.

–1639], faced as they were with the hostility of envious minds who threatened the former with exile, and tormented the latter with prolonged incarceration? Philipp Nicodemus Frischlin [1547–1590] suffered the persecution inflicted upon him by his colleagues until the time of his death, and nevertheless discussed only questions of grammar[10]. No less did Caspar Schoppe [1576–1649] draw upon himself the hatred of all the pedagogues of Italy, because of the new rules set out in his *Philosophical Grammar*[11], admirably adapted, neverthless, as a compendium for teaching. I will say nothing on the subject of René Descartes [1596–1650], the reformer of Philosophy; nothing of William Harvey [1578–1657], the reformer of Medicine[12], neither of whom escaped the envy of their peers and the dislike of the populace, until the truth came out and often triumphed over the very intentions of the slanderers. We will say nothing with regard to so many names, if we relate only our own meditations and not even the discoveries of illustrious men, of whom there is none who does not wish a better method of teaching that several also have experienced in esteeming the capacity of their own sons. Indeed you will find many children in this time and above all the sons of the most learned men, who even in their early years displayed prodigious erudition, on account not so much of the greatness of their intelligence, as of the art of their education. For although the faculty of judgment does not arrive before their adult years, it may, however, be exercised in childhood by querying; such is the circumstance por-

---

[10] Philipp Nicodemus Frischlin (1584), *Quaestionum Grammaticarum libri VII ex probatissimis auctoribus collecti*. Venetii.

[11] Caspar Schoppe (1659), *Grammatica Philosophica*. Amstelodami: Pluijmer.

[12] William Harvey (1628), *Exercitatio Anatomica de Motu Cordis et Sanguinis in Animalibus*. Francofurti: sumptibus Guilielmi Fitzeri.

trayed in Plato's [428/427 BC–348/347 BC] reminiscence, and the related pattern exhibited in the *Meno*, where Socrates, directing attention to the first obvious things and to the power of sense, not by teaching but only by questioning, prompts a child to engage in reflections that would require an effort even for anyone who is very perspicacious: namely, the incommensurability of the diagonal and the side of the square. Those who acknowledge these things are by no means lacking, but they espouse odd reasons to the contrary, arguing that the number of learned men was already excessively great and that premature education was driving young people lacking in authority and experience to public offices; that the harvest of the Know-it-all and inexperienced cavillers would have to be straightened; that precipitous counsels would necessarily ensue and that any action undertaken by the young senators was adverse. But these people receive our counsels in another sense: we do not act in order that young people come to the public offices, but in order that they may be worthy of such offices. For life is short and art is long: thus the instruction cannot be too hasty. This will become more evident if we first discuss the whole method of the studies (although our commitment focuses predominantly on the training of jurists) in order to achieve greater clarity in the subsequent topics. In effect, both Hugo Grotius [1583– 1645] in his famous *Letter about the Study in Political to Benjamin Auceruim Royal Ambassador*[13], as well as Christoph Coler [1570–1604] in another on the same topic[14], Gijsbert Voet [1589–1676] and Gerhard Meier of Bremen [1616–1695]

---

[13] Hugo Grotius (1663), *Ad Beniamin Auberium Maurerium, Christianissimi regis ad faederatas inferioris Germaniae provincias legatum ordinarium, epistola:* [*Inest Consilium de studiorum ratione*]. Helmestadii: Mullerus.

[14] Christoph Coler (1621), *De studio politico ordinando epistola ad ... Stanislaum Zelenium Vitellium de Zelanka*. Argentorati: Zetzner.

in the *Theological Libraries* [15], Michael Havemann [1597–1672] in the *Amusium*[16], and Hermann Vulteius [1555–1634] and Hendrik Moreelse [1615–1666] in the *Dissertations on the Study of Law*[17], treated the topic again by reconsidering the method of study, and dwelt on all of the disciplines, traces of which, as we have demonstrated in the *Specimen of Philosophical questions Collected from Right*[18], were found in the *Corpus Juris*[19]. If perchance our reflections fall into error, Good Reader, think how many, and how frequently, useful suggestions have been made, and then, once the opposing considerations have been balanced, the mistakes are set aside. Finally, bear in mind that the arguments we will set forth concerning the things that must be done and learned are by no means a meritorious reflection of things we our-

---

[15] Gijsbert Voet (1644), *Exercitia et bibliotheca studiosi theologiae*. Rheno-Trajecti: Strick; Gerhard Meier (1660), *Bibliotheca Theologica contracta libelli duo*. Bremae.

[16] Michael Havemann (1644), *Amusium sive Cynosura Studiosorum*. Hammipoli: Sump. Autoris.

[17] Hermann Vulteius (1594), *De Studio Juris* (in *Jurispr. Rom.*). Marpurgi; Hendrik Moreelse (1658), *Dissertatio de manuductione studiosi iuris per academiam ad rempublicam*, in Gerardus Johannes Vossius [1577–1649] and others, *Gerardi Jo. Vossii et aliorum Dissertationes de studiis bene instituendis*. Traiecti ad Rhenum [not included in AA VI, 2, sources directory, see note 18].

[18] Gottfried Wilhelm Leibniz [1646–1716] (henceforth Leibniz) (1664), *Specimen questionum philosophicarum ex iure collectarum*, in AA VI, 2.

[19] Adolf Berger [1882–1962] (1953, repr. 1991), *Enciclopedic Dictionary of Roman Law*. Philadelphia, *ad vocem Corpus Juris Civilis*, "A collective designation of the Emperor Justinian's codification, used first in the edition by Dionysius Gothofredus (Godefroy) [1549–1622] in 1583. The denomination encompasses the *Institutiones*, the *Digesta* (or *Pandectae*), the *Codex* (*Codex Justinianus*) and the *Novellae*. No collective title was given to his codification by Justinian himself. He mentions only once (C.5.13.1.pr.) *omne corpus iuris* (= the entire domain of law)."

selves have done or said- let such presumption be far from our minds - , because long ago we had no knowledge of these topics; but also, we pray you to believe us, that we have acted as the whetstone that sharpens the iron, but the same by itself has no power to cut[20]. Thus, I bid you farewell, and if our counsels are to your liking, I beg you to follow them or, if they are displeasing, to improve them.

---

[20] The sentence is drawn from Horace [65 BC–27 BC], *Ars poetica*, 394-395, "ergo fungar vice cotis, acutum reddere quae ferrum valet, exsors ipsa secandi".

PART I

The new method for learning and teaching jurisprudence, general and common to all other intellectual abilities. The plan of studies in general.

§. 1. The method of the study is approximately a way of using reason, that is, a way to reach the condition of perfect actions.

§. 2. This condition is also called habit[21], which I define as: an acquired permanent readiness to act.

---

[21] The term *habitus* is used here (see *infra* §. 3) by L. in the same meaning given to the word by Thomas Hobbes (1655), *Elementa Philosophiae* 1, *De corpore*. Londinium: Crook, XXII, 20, Engl. transl. London 1656, in William Molesworth [1810–1855] (ed.) (1839), *The English Works of Thomas Hobbes of Malmesbury*. I, London: Bohn, 378–379, "To what has been said of motion, I will add what I have to say concerning habit. *Habit*, therefore, is a generation of motion, not of motion simply, but an easy conducting of the moved body in a certain and designed way. And seeing it is attained by the weakening of such endeavours are to be weakened by little and little. But this cannot be done but by the long continuance of action, or by actions often repeated; and therefore custom begets that facility, which is commonly and rightly called *habit*; and it may be defined thus: HABIT *is motion made more easy and ready by custom; that is to say, by perpetual endeavour, or by iterated endeavours in a way differing from that in which the motion proceeded from the beginning, and opposing such endeavours as resist*".

Historically, the term *habitus* acquired its technical meaning in the thought of Aristotle, who first defined virtue as a habit, a condition, a state of mind, a second nature formed for exercise. For the meaning of the term in the history of philosophical thought, see Tom Sparrow and Adam Hutchinson (eds.) (2013), *A History of Habit, from Aristotle to Bordieu*. Plymouth: Lexington Books.

§. 3. A subject of habit is whatever is capable of action. For it is clearly evident that even inanimate things can become accustomed to particular actions. Thus chemists make the alcoholic spirit very volatile by vigorous shaking and they unanimously teach that metals themselves will be able to ascend above the stills within a month after distillation and many cohobations[22]. Thomas Hobbes [1588–1679] taught in *On the Body*[23] that as a result of many flexures even the laths acquire, to a certain extent, the habit of returning to their original position.

§. 4. No one who has read Girolamo Rorario's [1485–1556] booklet *Why Brutes Use Reason Better than Men*[24], or the *Plinian* miracles of the tightrope walker elephant, or the panegyrics of the elephant and dog in the *Letters* of Justus Lipsius [1547–1606][25], can doubt that brutes are

---

[22] Ephraim Chambers [c. 1680–1740] (1741), *Cyclopedia*. I, London, *ad vocem*, "In chemistry, a repeated distillation of the same matter, with the liquor drawn from it; that liquor being again and again returned upon the matter left at the bottom. (…). *Cohobation* is a kind of circulation; only differing from it in this, that the liquor is drawn off in *cohobation*, as in common distillation, and thrown back again; whereas in circulation, it rises and falls in the same vessel, without ever being carried out".

[23] Hobbes, see note 21, 349–350, "Nor are habits to be observed in living creatures only, but also in bodies inanimate. For we find that when the lath of a cross-bow is strongly bent, and would is the impediment were removed return again with great force; if it remain a long time bent, it will get such a habit, that when it is loosed and left to its own freedom, it will not only not restore itself, but will require as much force for the bringing of it back to its first posture, as it did for the bending of it at the first."

[24] Girolamo Rorario (1648), *Quod animalia bruta ratione utantur melius homine*. Parisiis; about Girolamo Rorario, see Aidée Scala (2004), *Girolamo Rorario: un umanista e diplomatico del cinquecento e i suoi Dialoghi*. Firenze: Olschki, 47.

[25] Justus Lipsius (1586), *Epistolarum selectarum centuria prima*. Antverpiae, *Epist. L, Jane Hautene* (Jan van Haut; therein the panegyric of the elephant); Id. (1605), *Epistolarum selectarum*

teachable. All these are things which endow with greater credibility the recent demonstration of the horses leading the dances in Vienna.

§. 5. Since infants, in their early years, differ little from brutes in the visible use of reason, not inconveniently their teachers may by no means inappropriately borrow many techniques from animal trainers: for the tamers of horses, dogs, birds, have their own peculiar abilities in speaking, singing or hunting.

§. 6. The technique of which they generally avail themselves is the supply of food, granted in abundance when the animals respond obediently, but denied when they disobey.

Quis expedivit Psittaco suum χαῖρε
Corvos quis olim concavum salutare,
Picasque docuit nostra verba conari?
Magister artis ingenique largitor
Venter, negatas artifex sequi voces[26]

For instance, it is said that the Balearic population does not give food to children before they have accomplished their assigned goal. And

Pueris dant crustula blandi
Doctores, elementa velint ut discere prima[27].

---

centuria prima Ad Belgas. Antverpiae, *Epist. XLXIV*, *Ad Contubernales Suos* (therein the panegyric of the dog).

[26] Persius [34–62], *Saturae, Prologus,* but the Latin text in George Gilbert Ramsay [1839–1921] (ed. and transl.) (1927), *Juvenal and Persius*. London: W. Heinemann; New York: G.P. Putnam's Sons, 310–311, is, *Quis expedivit Psittaco suum χαῖρε/Picasque docuit nostra verba conari?/Magister artis ingenique largitor/Venter, negatas artifex sequi vocés* ["Who thought the magpie to ape the language of man? It was that master of arts, that dispenser of genius, the Belly, who has rare skill in getting at words which are not his own"].

The punishment of fasting, *das Cariren* [in German in the text, e.n.], applied in many boarding schools, derives from this custom.

§. 7. This tactic may be used with children but not with nobler minds who are already making use of reason, and who should thus be rewarded with nourishment not so much for the body but rather for the soul, *i.e.* honor[28]. Hence, there has arisen a system of classes and places in primary schools and promotions in academies. And in ancient days those who had persevered excellently were led home by other children with words of great praise, as we know from the example of Cicero[29].

§. 8. So far we have described the basic characteristics of habits. The cause or manner of acquiring a habit is either supernatural infusion or natural familiarization. In sentient beings, insofar as they are sentient, the latter is referred to as teaching.

§. 9. Infusion is either divine or diabolical. We have examples of the divine in the apostolic gift of tongues[30], although some do not believe it to have lasted beyond the duration of ecstasy, in the sense that the perception was

---

[27] Horace [65 BC–27 BC], *Saturae.* I, 1, 25, "even teachers sometimes give cookies to children to coax them into learning their A B C.", in Henry Rushton Fairclough [1862–1938] (ed. and transl.) (1955), *Horace, Satires, Epistles and Ars Poetica.* Cambridge MA: Harvard University Press.

[28] The passage from the text recalls the *Ratio atque institutio studiorum,* famous even at the time of Leibniz, (1599). Romae: In Collegio Societatis Jesu; Engl. transl. in Allan P. Farrell, S.J. (1970), *The Jesuit* Ratio Studiorum *of 1599.* Washington D. C.: Conference of Major Superiors of Jesuits, in *www.bc.edu/sites/libraries/ratio /ratio1599*, Common rules of the teacher of the lower classes, n. 39, "[...] Faithful observance will be better secured by the hope of honor and reward and the fear of disgrace than by corporal punishment".

[29] Plutarch [45–120], *Vitae parallelae, Cicero*, 2.

[30] *Acts of the Apostles*, 2, 1–4.

not permanent and thus could not become a habit. In ecclesiastical history we have a similar example with regard to St. Ephraem the Syrian [c. 306–373], who gained immediate familiarity with the Greek language due to the prayers of St. Basil the Great [330–379]. In our time, there are examples of evil infusion in his slaves[31]. Not even today can we believe divine infusion to be absent; for we implore divine blessing for our studies.

§. 10. From infusion, let us proceed to habituation, which occurs as the outcome of the quantity of an impressive action. Moreover, the quantity is either extensive or intensive: the extensive element involves a multitude of actions, while the intensive aspect refers to the magnitude or the strength required in order for the habit to become ingrained. The former requirement is widely known in the form of the common statement that habit is acquired by means of repeated actions; with regard to the latter, popular wisdom is usually silent.

§. 11. The effectiveness of multiple or frequent repetition of acts is confirmed by the common saying:

> *Adde parvum parvo, magnum cumulabis acervum*

And Ovid sings:

> *Gutta excavat lapidem, consumitur anulus usu,*
> *Et teritur pressa vomer aduncus humo*[32]

---

[31] Of the devil, evidently; Leroy Earl Loemker [1900–1985] (ed.) (1989), *G.W.Leibniz, Selected Papers and Lecters*. Dordrecht: Kluwer Academics, 90, reference 3, "Leibniz seems thus to accept witchcraft in 1667; later he commends the work of the Jesuit Friedrich Spee [1591–1635] (*Cautio criminalis*, 1631) and of the Protestant pietist Philip Jacob Spener [1625–1705], with whom he began a correspondence while at Mainz, in opposing the widespread injustice of the witch processes (cf. *Theodicy*, I, Sec. 97)".

[32] Ovid [43 BC–17/18 AD], *Epistulae ex Ponto*. IV, 10, 5, "Drops of water hollow out a stone, a ring is worn thin by use, the hooked plough

Aesop's [c. 620 BC–564 BC] tortoise, faster then the eagle[33], applies here, and likewise the German proverb *wer langsam geht, komt auch nach*[34]. This results in the expedient, widely employed by the human race, of attacking a thing by its individual parts, if it cannot be dealt with as a whole. We split marbles with a file, carry away mountains with baskets, and drain lakes with a bucket. So in arithmetic we calculate large sums by their parts and in geometry we resort to dividing plane surfaces into triangles.

§. 12. From this principle there arises the need for repetition, which mainly depends on the most essential attribute of habit: permanency. Experience shows that as a result of practice some figures and images are quickly received but equally hastily dismissed: such is the case, for instance, of wax tablets; others, instead, as in the case of a bronze tablet, are acquired and lost more slowly. In the same way, some people are quick to fan the flames of anger like straw, but equally quick to dampen them. It is precisely for this reason that the Pythagoreans believed no one fall asleep before

Omnia totius repetiverit acta diei[35].

---

is rubbed away by the soil's pressure." in Arthur Leslie Wheeler [1871–1932] (ed. and transl.) (1988 revised by G. P. Goold), *Ovid, Tristia, Ex Ponto*. Cambridge: Harvard University Press.

[33] Aesop, *Fabulae*. "407. Aquila et Testudo. Testudo aquilam magnopere orabat, ut volare sese doceret. "'Rem petis,'" inquit aquila, "'naturae tuae contrariam, nam quomodo poteris volare, cum alas non habeas?'" Testudo autem nihilominus aquilam obsecrabat ut se volucrem facere vellet. Itaque eam ungulis arreptam aquila sustulit in sublime ibique demisit, ut per aera ferretur sed, cum in rupes decidisset, comminuta interiit.".

[34] Even the slow traveler reaches his destination.

[35] He will have repeated all the things learned in the day.

Indeed it is harmful if repetition is continually delayed as the year unfolds, as is commonly the case in schools; rather, it would be more advisable to recapitulate a day's studies in the evening before the onset of night-time, and then repeat the most important part [of the studies] of the day at the end of the week, the most important part [of the studies] of the week at the end of the month, and the most important part [of the studies] of the months at the end of the year; and to meditate again on the most important arguments one by one, by degrees.

§. 13. From the same principle the distinguished academics Wilhelm Schickard [1592–1635] derived a unique system for teaching the Hebrew language, which he has exhibited in his *Clock*[36], *i.e.* he taught 12 children at the same time, divided the grammar between them so as to assign the rules of nouns to some, the rules of pronominal forms to others etc., this part of the syntax to a given group, another part to others different group. He also distributed among them also his concise *Lexicon*, assigning to one the letter א; to another the letter ב, to yet another letter ג etc. So it happened that while the one was presenting the part he had learned or was responding to the master; the others, being attentive, learned the part of their fellow pupil by playing. For this very same reason it would be advisable that in today's schools the same topic not be assigned to many pupils, but that the lesson be instead distributed among individual students, who together will build up a beautifully harmonious group.

§. 14. The arguments presented so far have concerned the multiplicity of actions; we now proceed to an assessment of the role of intensity, that is to say, magnitude (or strength). A single action, with some extraordinary force of impression is more effective than many repeated

[36] Wilhelm Schickard (1626), *Horologium Hebraeum*. Lipsiae.

actions, *e.g.* we remember more easily some specific fact, such as an unexpected prank, an action that proved to bring us a special stroke of luck, as well as an action which brought us praise or disgrace. From this principle, *infra* in § .23 about Mnemonics, we will demonstrate that the more strongly impressed the marks [for this term, see *infra* §. 23] are on our consciousness, the more they reinforce memory.

§. 15. It is very wise, however, to temper and blend multitude and magnitude. This is particularly important if the action increases gradually towards perfection, starting with infinitesimal efforts. Chemists prescribe the same thing with regard to the use of fire in inducing habitual alterations in inorganic bodies. Milo of Croton [the wrestler, 6th-cent. BC] asserted that he measured his strength through such a trick: Every day he carried a calf for a certain distance: thus while the weight of the calf was increasing, his own strength likewise increased imperceptibly, to the point that he was eventually able to lift a large bull in the Olympic Games, in front of the whole of Greece. The same method could be adopted in teaching the art of drinking if the measure of the glassful imbibed were increased every week. Indeed, a Frenchman at Sulsbach spa, who happened to have the occasion to watch Germans drinking many increasing mugs of water, assumed that in Sulsbach there was a drinking school, a *Sauff=Schule*, where Germans learn by quaffing water what they will be able to do with wine. Even children, starting from alphabetic letters and then proceeding to syllables, gradually become proficient in reading words; and in arithmetic, the more the numbers recede to the left, the more they grow tenfold. As regards the degrees of repetition, readers are referred to our comments in §. 13. The same method is useful, for example, in memorizing a speech to be delivered orally: the technique involves learning a first part by heart, then the first and the second, then the first with the second and the third, etc. This device is used in numerous sissies' games. The result is truly admirable as everything remains easily impressed in the memory. The stern reader will forgive me if I utilize these trifles as examples, for trifles help us to be more skillful in following serious instructions.

§. 16. We have thus examined the question of developing a habit or a routine, or of the development of the habit even among those who lack common sense. We must now turn to teaching. To teach is to form a habit in a sentient being as such, or through his sense. Accordingly, this art as a whole is called *Didactics*. For even those who spontaneously learn are effectively teaching themselves; therefore they are called αυτοδιδάκτων [in Greek in text, self-taught, e.n.].

§. 17. Furthermore, as medicine is to the living being, so doctrine is to the soul: and since the duty of the physician is to heal, 1) safely, 2) quickly, 3) pleasantly; it follows that the same is also required in the care of the soul, namely to teach 1) completely, 2) quickly, 3) pleasantly. Of these approaches, the first is designed to ensure that everything is well in that which is being taught, the others are designed for wellbeing; the first for the habit itself, the others for the most suitable manner of introducing it. The first, moreover, contains two aspects, to teach truths, but also to fix them permanently, so that they do not fall away immediately, just as physicians must likewise avoid recurrence of disease.

§. 18. And this first requirement, to teach good things, concerns the object of the habit, which we will discuss *infra*. A multitude of actions, on the other hand, makes sure that they are fixed steadily, while magnitude ensures rapid absorption and stabilization of the habit; these are the common causes of a habit for inanimate beings, as pointed out in §. 10 and ff.

§. 19. The ultimate objective, that is, to teach in a pleasant way, belongs properly speaking to only to the realm of animate beings. For animals are characterized by a peculiar ability to grow accustomed to routines, so that they become spontaneously more receptive to the instructions they will receive; this is accomplished by giving them pleasure when they learn, pain when they close their ears to any novelty. Such an outcome is achieved in beasts by means of food and blandishments; in men by means of utility (for instance, food) and honor (as in the case of flattery). This was already dealt with in § §. 6. 7.

§. 20. Furthermore, they learn if it is not only the objective which is proposed to them that is pleasant, but the means of learning as well. As far as the objective is concerned, readers are referred to the discussion in §. 19. The means of learning are pleasant if they are taught by playing. Comedies and tales are wonderfully appropriate to this aim. Numerous strategies have been devised for this purpose: playing cards based on geographical, astronomical, historical, cheironomical concepts, etc. and dice containing the alphabet. For instance, (St.) Jerome [347–420] used them in order to devise a memorizing system for *Pauline*[37]. Similarly, witticisms, epigrams, paintings, poems, essays. This is the topic of the excellent *Painted*

[37] St. Jerome in Frederick Adam Wright [1869–1946] (ed.) (1954), *Selected letters of St. Jerome*. London: William Heinemann; Cambridge MA: Harvard University Press, *CVII*, *To Laeta, A Girl's education*, 345, "Have a set of letters made for her, of boxwood or ivory. And tell her their names. Let her play with them, making play a road to learning, and let her not only grasp the right order of the letters and remember their names in a simple song, but also frequently upset their order and mix the last letters with the middle ones, the middle with the first. Thus she will know them all by sight as well as by sound".

Ethics[38], devoted to the Prince of the Youth of Alterburg (which the fates only showed on the earth), the *Emblems* by Andrea Alciato [1492–1550][39], the *Politics* by Diego De Saavedra y Fajardo[40] [1584–1648], the *Theology* in the *Heart School* by Benedictus Van Haeften [1588–1648][41] and also that very ingenious game, which Franz Christian Rosenkreuts remembered in the *Weddings*[42], where, as in the *Latrunculi* game[43], virtues in white, and vices in black dress, fight each other with admirable dexterity.

---

[38] Probably, Johann Christofph Wagenseil [1633–1705] (1693), *Ad J. Fechtium de infundibuli sui occasione, consilio et instituto, epistola.* Altdorfi.

[39] Andrea Alciato (1621), *Emblemata*. Patavii: apud Petrum Paulum Tozzium. This is the latest edition of the work published for the first time in Augsburg in 1531.

[40] Diego de Saavedra y Fajardo [1640–1642], *Idea de un principe politico cristiano rapresentada en cien impresas*. en Monaco en Milan (Engl. transl. by J. Astry, 1700, London). The work illustrates the pacifist approach of the author and his concept of authority, anti-Machiavellian, enemy of fictions and deception, in harmony with the Christian ideas. Strangely, L. mentions only the followers of Machiavelli ("Machiavellisti") to criticize them, s. *infra*, II, §. 99, but not Machiavelli.

[41] Benedictus van Haeften (1629), *Schola cordis*. Antverpiae: typis H. Verdussi.

[42] Pseudonym of Johann Valentin Andreae [1586–1654] (1616), *Chymisce Hochzeit Christiani Rosencreuts, anno 1459*. Strasburg (Engl. transl. by E. Foxcroft, 1982, London: Minerva Books). About the relationships Leibniz, Rosenkreuts and Van Helmont, *s.* Maria Rosa Antognazza (1999), *Trinità e incarnazione. Il rapporto tra filosofia e teologia rivelata nel pensiero di Leibniz*. Milano: Vita e Pensiero, 314–315 (Engl. transl. by Gerald Parks, 2007, *Leibniz on the Trinity and the Incarnation: Reason and Revelation in the Seventeenth Century*. New Haven, CT: Yale University Pres); Allison Coudert (1995), *Leibniz and the Kabbalah*. Dordrecht: Kluwer.

[43] Ulrich Schädler (2001), "Latrunculi–a forgotten Roman game of strategy reconstructed". *Abstract Games*, 7, 10–11.

§. 21. We have spoken, first, about the cause of process involved in becoming accustomed to a certain type of activity, a process that is common to inanimate things, brutes and men, namely habituation, which we addressed from §. 10 up to and including §. 15; we then addressed the cause of acquiring a habit, the latter process being common only to brutes and men, namely teaching. This aspect has been addressed from §. 16 up to here. What remains to be discussed is the cause of the habit peculiar to man: education.

§. 22. Such habits, peculiar to man alone, concern memory, invention, or judgment; hence the approach to the learning of these habits is likewise threefold: mnemonics, topics, analytics. Thus propositions (which are peculiar to man alone) can be memorised, made or judged. On the other hand, topics and analytics are included in the single lemma of logic[44], from which it is clear that logic and memory constitute parts of didactics. To the latter, not without reason, is added methodology.

---

[44] As known, notwithstanding Aristotle [384 BC–322 BC] is considered as the founder of the logic as science which deals the forms in which the thought moves in reasoning, he had not exactly given the name of logic to his doctrines (which include the Topics and Analitics, mentioned by Leibniz in the text), set forth in the works *Categoriae, De interpretatione, Analytica priora, Analytica Posteriora, Topica, De sophisticis elenchis*. The term "logic" was adopted by peripatetic his followers; of them in particular, Andronicus of Rhodes (fl. 1th. BC), grouped together the mentioned Aristotle's works under the name of *Organon*, or "tool" of thought; about the passage of which in the text, after more than sixty years, Gioele Solari's [1872–1952] synthesis does not fade, Id. (1947), "Metafisica e Diritto in Leibniz" *Rivista di filosofia*, 40, "In *Nova Methodus* special emphasis is given to *ars inveniendi* (Aristotelian topics) and *ars judicandi* (Aristotelian analytics): the former aims to discover new truths, to solve problems going through from consequences and known effects to unknown causes and principles; the latter aims to demonstrate discovered truths and to solve disputed and dubious truths." [ed. transl.].

Mnemonics provides the substance, methodology the form, logic the application of substance to the form.

§. 23. The foundation of mnemonics[45] is a sensible thing called a mark[46], linked with the thing to be remembered signalled by a certain relationship, which is either one of comparison—similitude, or dissimilarity—or one of connection, such as that of whole and part, part and part, cause and effect, sign and the thing signified. Thus language was invented in order to overcome the difficulty men faced in remembering things. For words are not only the signs of present thoughts manifested to others but also marks of one's past thoughts to oneself, as Thomas Hobbes demonstrated at the beginning of the first section of *On the body*[47]. Among the range of different marks, those that affect the senses are the most important mnemonics, to the point that I would say of adding §. 14, as in the case of words that are not only heard, but [heard] with delight, for instance poems, or so-called

---

[45] "Tertia ars est *Mnemonica*, seu ars retinendi et in memoriam revocandi quae didicimus, quae ars multis elegantibus utitur compendiis et inventis, quorum aliquando usus esse potest in vita. In primis autem portio ejus, ars reminiscendi, scilicet, excoli debet, cujus ope nobis in memoriam revocamus illis quibus opus habemus, et quae in memoria nostra latent, sed non soccurrunt; aliud enim est retinere, aliud reminisci, nam eorum quae retinemus non semper reminiscimur, nisi aliqua ratione admoneamur" [Leibniz, *Consilium de Encyclopaedia nova conscribenda methodo inventoria* (15–25 June 1679), in Louis Couturat [1868–1914] (ed.) (1903), *Opuscules et fragments inédits de Leibniz*. Paris: Alcan, (repr. 1961) Hildesheim: Olms Verlagsbuchandlung, 37].

[46] See note 47.

[47] Hobbes, see note 21, 14, "From which it follows that, for the acquiring of philosophy, some sensible moniments are necessary, by which our past thoughts may be not only reduced, but also registered everyone in its own order. These moniments I call MARKS, namely, sensible things taken at pleasure, that, by the sense of them, such thoughts may be recalled to our mind as are like those thoughts for which we took them".

clappantes words[48], which are added in many dictionaries to the considerable benefit of pupils. Similar considerations can be put forward for allusions, the expedient that Schickard used in *Hebrew Clock*[49] to imprint the Hebrew roots [of the words, e.n.] in the learners. And one marvels at the extent to which the harmony of languages and the appropriateness of their items serve this purpose so usefully. Moreover, it is not only the auditory perception of the mark that has a relationship with memory, for vision of the mark likewise plays a role. The hieroglyphs of the ancient Egyptians fulfill this aim, and even those of the contemporary Chinese people, which are described extensively in Athanasius Kircher's [1602–1680] *Oedipus*[50]. Similarly, the arrangement of things in children's bedrooms, on the wall of a room opposite the door, and other distributions in specific premises, also play a significant role: readers should consult authors who have written on the subject of mnemonics, first and foremost Johann Heinrich Alsted [1588–1638] in the *Treasure of Mnemonics*[51], and Janus Caecilius Frey [c.

---

[48] Johann Friedrich Nolte [1694–1754] (1744), *Lexicon Linguae Latinae Antibarbarum Quadripartitum*. Lipsiae et Helmstadii: apud Christian Frideric Weygand, 1618, "Rhytmica eumdem in fine sonum habentia, barbare *termini clappantes* dicta sunt ut: *Qualis rex, talis grex. Mors hominum est ita, sicut fuit vita*".

[49] Schickard, see note 36.

[50] Athanasius Kircher [1652–1654], *Oedipus Aegyptianus*. Romae: ex typografia Vitalis Mascardi.

[51] Johann Heinrich Alsted (1621), *Thesaurus artis memorativae*. Francofurti. For relationships Alsted-Leibniz, see Paolo Rossi [1923–2012] (1985), *Clavis Universalis*. Bologna: Il Mulino, 267 (Engl. trans. by S. Clucas (2006), *Logic and the Art of Memory*. London New York: Continuum); Francis Amelia Yates [1899–1981] (1966), *The art of memory*. London: Routledge and Kegan Paul, 369; more recently, Maria Rosa Antognazza, Howard Hotson (1999), *Alsted and Leibniz: on God, the Magistrate and the Millennium*. Wiesbaden: Harrossowitz.

1580–1631], in the *Road to Sciences et Arts*[52]; to which should be added the *Winkelmannian* sketches of stories through images, which should not be underestimated.

§. 24. The foundation of the topics, or the art of invention, are the dialectical arguments, that is, the transcendent relations[53], such as the whole, the cause, the matter, the similar, etc. And, as we have diffusely explained in our *Dissertation about Combinatorial Art*[54], propositions grow out from things connected by any such relations by means of the combinatorial art. Nor are to be despised the contributions that Raimond Lull [c. 1233–1315][55] gave on this matter in several works and Johann Heinrich Bisterfeld [1605–1655] in the *Epitome of Art of Meditation*[56].

---

[52] Janus Caecilius Frey (1628), *Via ad divas scientias artesque, scientiarum notitia, sermones extemporaneos, nova et expeditissima*. Parisii.

[53] "Quarta est *Topica* seu ars inveniendi, id est dirigendi cogitationes ad aliquam veritatem ingnotam vel eruendam, vel media finis cujusdam reperienda" [Leibniz (note 45), 37].

[54] Leibniz (1666), *Dissertatio de Arte Combinatoria*. Lipsiae, in AA, VI, 1.

[55] Raimond Lull (1274), *Ars compendiosa inveniendi veritatem*. Lull's entire *Opera latina* (1978–) is being published by Brepols, Turnhout (Belgium); Ana H. Maróstica (1992),"*Ars combinatoria* and time: Lull, Leibniz and Pierce". *Studia Lulliana* 32, 106, "The *ars combinatoria* of Ramon Lull is a method by mean of which he tries to find and explore (by using certain rules) all possible combinations (or manifestations) of primitive concepts: the so called divine dignities. This method was conceived as a new way of answering, with mathematical infallibility, questions of any type, and, consequently, of obtaining true knowledge".

[56] Johann Heinrich Bisterfeld (1657), *Elementorum Logicorum Libri tres*. Lugduni Batavorum: Verbiest.

§. 25. Analytics or the art of judging[57] seems to me to be almost completely reducible to two rules: 1) no word is to be accepted without being explained, 2) no proposition is to be accepted without being proved. These, in my view, are far more effective than the four *Cartesian rules* in the *prima Philosophia*, the main one of which states that whatever I perceive clearly and distinctly is true[58], whereas such a rule deceives in many ways[59].

---

[57] "Sequitur *Logica*, qua tantum hoc loco comprehendo artem illationum, sive artem iudicandi quae proponuntur, quae sumenda est ex usu hominum loquentium scribentiumque" [Leibniz (note 45), 36]; in late revision note "D" of *NM*, added by L. at the end of the century [G. Grua (1948), *G.W. Leibniz, Textes inedits*, Paris, II, 704], and printed in a footnote to the critical edition of *NM* in AA VI, 1 (note 18), L. notes that, "Logica verisimilium est opus adhuc desideratum, ut saepe monui, ubi probabilitas non tantum petitur ab externis seu ab auctoritate, vel plurium vel sapientium (quo uno eam parum recte definivit Aristoteles, quem in ea re probabilistae morales sunt secuti), sed etiam et maxime quidem ex ipsa rei natura, quia alia aliis facilius contingere possunt, eoque sunt credibiliora. In praxi autem non tantum quid sit verisimilius, sed quid tutius; quamquam in hoc, ut aestimetur quam tutum sit aliquid, cursus consideretur verisimilitudo. Sic ergo capienda est oppositio inter verisimilius et totius; ut verisimilitudo boni aut liciti maior, superetur a minore verisimilutidine mali connexi, cum malum timendum est multis parasangis maius bono sperando. Logica utem verisimilium a nullis magis quam iureconsultis exculta est, qui de probationibus plenis aut minus plenis, praesumptionibus, coniecturis, indiciis, passim et multi egerunt; etsi certis principiis nondum constitutis"; about *logica probabilium*, see of the same Leibniz (1704), *Noveaux esssays sur l'intendiment humain*, in Peter Remnant and Jonathan Bennett (eds. and transl.) (1996), *New essays on human understanding*. Cambridge: Cambridge University Press, IV, 2, § 14, and *retro* introductory essay, all the par. 9].

[58] René Descartes [1596–1650] (1641), *Meditationes de prima philosophia, in qua Dei existentia et animae immortalitatis demonstratur*. Parisiis: Apud Michaelem Soly.

[59] Solari, see note 44, 40, "The Cartesian criterion of evidence since these days is abandoned: to the four rules of Cartesian analytics, considered vague and general, Leibniz opposes two rules: to define everything, to demonstrate everything. These rules, applied to

§. 26. Methodology, or the art of arranging, concerns the method. A method may be either *natural*, in which case it obeys the rule that everything can be known without a second, but the second cannot be known without the first, and thus the first must be placed before the second; or *occasional*, for which no general rule can be formulated, but it [the rule] varies in an infinite number of ways. On this topic Jacopo Aconcio [1492–1567] wrote extensively in the pamphlet *About Method* and in the *Letter on Satan's Stratagem*[60] as an appendix; additional writings

jurisprudence, meant the need to demonstrate the concepts or the first elements of law and then to recompose them synthetically in complex concepts and propositions for the purposes of the foundation of rational jurisprudence "against the Cartesian evidence, points out Mario di Dario, (ed. and Italian transl. of the first part of *NM*) (1965), *Leibniz, Il metodo generale degli studi.* Naples, 42, n. 43, "Vico expresses an identical opinion". Indeed, Giovan Battista Vico [1668–1744] (1710), *De antiquissima Italorum sapientia.* Neapoli: ex Typographia Felicis Mosca, cap. VII, par. V, *De certa facultate sciendi* (in Lucia M. Palmer [1929–2007] (ed. and transl.) (1988), *Vico, On the Most ancient wisdom of Italians.* Ithaca NY: Cornell University Press, 101, from which I quote, "But if someone is confident of having looked all through a thing in clear and distinct idea [of it], he can easily be mistaken and may often think that he knows the thing distinctly when he has still only a confused knowledge of it, because he does not know all [the elements] that are in the thing and which distinguish it from others. But if he will scrutinize all the 'place' distinguished of *Topics* with a critical eye, then he will be certain that he knows the thing clearly and distinctly because he has turned the matter over in his mind and answered all the question can be asked with respect to the subject under discussion. And by completing this process of questioning, topics itself will become criticism".

60 Jacopo Aconcio (1558), *De Methodo, hoc est, de recte investigandarum tradendarumque Scientiarum ratione*. Basileae: per Petrum Pernam; Id., (1565) *Stratagematum Satanae libri octo.* Basileae: apud Petrum Pernam.

on this topic by Johann Neldel [1554–1612][61] and Abraham Calov [1612–1686][62] are also of interest.

§. 27. So far [we have spoken] on the causes of habits, dwelling on their most characteristic features (the multitude and magnitude of actions) and their general aspect (pleasantness); we have also devoted attention to special elements (mnemonic art, topics, analytics, methodology). There follows the object of habit, namely, the action itself with regard to which the habit has developed.

§. 28. Accordingly, the habit is either of the body or of the soul. The habits of the body concern either a permanent action, the ἀποτέλεσμα [in Greek in text, the effect, e.n.], or a temporary fact. The arts that produce a work either improve nature by application, and subsequent cessation of the agent and the patient, and then ceasing, as is the case with agriculture, horticulture, pastoralism (the oldest art), and likewise the art of medicine, chemistry, veterinary treatment; or they accomplish their task without external assistance (single-handedly) and accomplish the entire work, as can be observed with those that link, separate, or transform until a certain desired shape emerges from the arts themselves. Painting, for example, consists in union, sculpture in separation, in transformation of all activities which give a certain form to substances that at first are liquid and subsequently become coagulated. The art of melting, beating and shaping metal or glass fall into this category. For the moment, I will not describe the infinite blend of

---

[61] Johann Neldel (1607), *Pratum logicum, organi Aristotelici septis inclusum ...sive praxis et usu organi Aristotelici genuinus*. Francofurti.

[62] Araham Calov (Calovinius) (1637) *Tractatus de methodo docendi et disputandi*. Rostochii.

arts leading to the variety of objects deriving from these acts, which the illustrious Erhard Weigel [1625–1699] expounded in detail in the *Euclidean Analysis*[63]. However, it is certain that all of them consist either in the application of a natural agent, or in the conjunction, or separation or processing of the substances, or in a composite *mélange* of these activities.

§. 29. The arts involved in a transitory event, that is, those that consign no work to posterity, are commonly said to be exercises; they consist either in advancing the motion of something else, or simply in their own motion. As examples of advance, we may consider the art of sailing, driving a cart, riding, shuffling playing cards with dexterity, throwing the dice in such a manner as to ensure the dice falls in the desired direction; the art of shooting arrows, throwing a small or large ball, the game of the cones, the game of the birch tablet, etc. Motion is either of the whole body or of only a part of it. It is of the whole body in the art of jumping, climbing, running, in acrobatics, to which could conceivably be added the art of flying, which is symmetrical to the art of swimming. The movement of a distinct part is different according to the diversity of the individual parts, such as eyes in the art of crying, the art of speaking or singing in a distinguished and elegant language; likewise the art of distinguishing the flavors of wines and other beverages and foods or drinking in the throat belong to this category, as does the readiness of many (although an art of the internal viscera is not otherwise possible) in regurgitating the ingested food already in their stomach whenever they wish. Similar observations can be made on the subject of moving one's lips in such a manner that another person can understand one by their motion, a

[63] Erhard Weigel (1658), *Analysis Aristotelica ex Euclide restituta.* Jenae: apud Grosium.

topic discussed by Franciscus Mercurius Van Helmont, Jr. [1614–1699] in his recently published dissertation *The Alphabet of Nature*[64]. I will mention nothing about the other arts of many who bend their fingers and joints in singular and unusual ways, or about the conjurer's art, *von der Sauckel=Tasche*[65], which also concerns the swift movements of pickpockets. From the very same source comes the art of instrumental music, which is simultaneously performed by the fingers and the feet, or by means of a pewter. Finally, the harmony among all these parts is achieved by the art of gestures with a singularly effective result, on which Scipione Chiaramonti [1565–1652][66] wrote eloquently. The histrionic art also falls within this topic, which although once despised, today 'not without reason' is highly prized even amongst great men.

§. 30. And these are the habits of the body, even though a notable difference can be observed among them. Furthermore, despite the differentiation, all of them are exercised by means of the body: indeed, the body countenances many habits simultaneously and, I would say, is so greatly attuned to using habit that even if the mind has thoroughly learned all the rules, it cannot practice a technique save with the habituation of the body being added, as for example in ball games, in jumping, or

---

[64] Franciscus Mercurius van Helmont (1657), *Alphabeti vere naturalis Hebraici brevissima delineatio*. Sulzbaci: Typis Abrahami Lichtenthaleri (in Allison Coudert and Taylor Corse (eds. and transls.) (2007), *Van Helmont, The alphabet of nature*, Leiden Boston: Brill. Van Helmont built a monadology system, which, in many respects, is a singular anticipation of that of L. (the latter seems to have taken from Van Helmont the word "monad").

[65] Hand tricks, play with glasses and balls; see Simon Witgeest (1745), *Natürliches Zauber-Buch oder Neu-eröffneter Spiel-Platz*, Nuerberg.

[66] Scipione Chiaramonti (1625), *De coniectandis cuiusque moribus et latitantibus animi affectibus*. Venetiis.

in the art of music, whether vocal or instrumental, etc. And these properly are the habits of the body. The other habits, in truth, are properly in the mind, and the body obeys only the mind which orders. In no way does the body add anything to art; the same is true in the majority of arts that produce permanent αποτέλεσμα [in Greek in the text, results, e.n.], and in the game of *Latrunculi*[67] or [otherwise stated, e.n.] *Aggerario*[68] and in the others that rely both on skill and on the strength of the player.

§. 31. Let us turn now to the habits of the mind. Every action of the mind is thought, for the act of exercising one's will is none other than thinking of the goodness of a thing. Every thought, in turn, is a proposition concerning something, for mere simple terms are found only among brutes: man's imagination is never without some reflection.

§. 32. Every proposition is either singular, hence history (for example a magnet holds up the iron coffin of Muhammad [c. 570 AD–632 AD] in Mecca of Arabia, assuming for the sake of example that this is true); or a universal contingent depending on induction from singular events, hence observation (for example, a magnet lifts iron); or *necessary universal, provable* from the terms themselves, hence *science*: for example, whatever moves is moved by some other thing, or, if a magnet lifts iron, there must be corporeal effluvia passing from the magnet to the iron.

§. 32. [a.] History, therefore, is the mother of observations. On its nature, constitution, classification Francis Bacon, Baron of Verulam [1561–1626], excellently [wrote] in the incomparable treatise *The*

[67] See note 65.
[68] So in *Sachverzeichnis* AA VI, 1, 358.

Advancement of Learning[69], and no less brightly in his *New Instrument of Sciences*[70]. For verily, the same matters also involve history, observation and theorems (by which science is spurred into activity); let us consider an example concerning History: the wife of Paulus Fabius Maximus [d. 14 AD], who lived under Caesar Augustus [63 BC–14 AD], was garrulous; Observation or *Chria*[71]: women are garrulous; Theorem or Maxim: no secret is to be entrusted to a garrulous person; therefore, we classify propositions in general, not on the basis of the copula and signs, as in §. 31, but on the basis of the terms.

§. 33. Terms, furthermore, can be either simple or compound. Simple terms are those which cannot be made clear by more familiar terms, because they are communicated immediately to sense, that is, they are themselves sensible qualities. That which has sensible qualities, or is perceptible, is called a being. And this is the best definition of a being: for whenever we wish to prove that something is, we do so by the fact that we or others sense it, either in itself, by immediate sensation; or mediated by the sensation of something else with which it forms an inextricable whole. Qualities taken together at the same time (or imaginability, *imaginabilitas*) constitute

---

[69] Francis Bacon (1605), *The Two Books of Francis Bacon: Of the Proficiencie and Advancement of Learning, Divine and Humane. To the King*. At London: Printed for Henrie Tomes.

[70] Francis Bacon (1620), *Novum organum*. Londinii.

[71] "In rhetoric, a sentence proposed as a theme for rhetorical exercise, with its logical development", *A Latin dictionary* (repr. 1879), Founded on Andrews' edition of Freund's Latin dictionary, revised, enlarged, and in great part rewritten by Charlton Thomas Lewis [1834–1904], Ph. D. and Charles Short LL.D. Oxford: At Clarendon Press, *ad vocem Chria*). *Adde* Leibniz (note 45) late revision note "D", Z-11-12, 284 (note 57). The example related by L. is narrated by Tacitus [56–after 117], *Annales*, I, 5, 1–2: the "garrulous" woman was the wife of Paulus Fabius Maximus, a friend of Octavianus Augustus.

essence, existence is constituted by sensibility. From the thought of many beings taken together there arise relations or the affections of being. Thus from co-imaginability or co-essence there arises comparison: the same, different, similar, dissimilar, contrary, genus, species, universal, singular. From consensibility or coexistence, on the other hand, there arise the connections: whole, part, order, one, many, necessary, contingent, togetherness, cause, etc. Universal metaphysics derives from this.

§. 34. Sensible qualities in particular, moreover, are perceived by some only in mind; others in fantasy, or by means of mediating bodily organs. Only two sensible qualities are perceived in the mind: 1) thought, 2) causality. Thought is a sensible quality of the human intellect or of some "I do not know what" within us, which we observe to be thinking. But, how this thinking actually comes about is something we cannot explain any more than what white is, or what extension is. It can be deduced, by a demonstration that this quality is also in God and angels. Logic, therefore, the most notable of sciences after metaphysics, which Aristotle structured in the form of mathematical demonstration, deals with [literally, moves about near, e.n.] that sensible quality called thought.

§. 35. The other quality perceptible only by the mind is causality, when one can deduce from an effect, by demonstration, that the effect in question does indeed have some cause, even though latent. And this quality, abstracted from other qualities, for example, motion, figure etc., is in the cause of the world, that is to say, God, and moreover in the causes of certain miracles in the world, namely, the angels, and finally in our mind as the cause of the motion of the body. This notwithstanding, we cannot explain the rule of causality, this concerns the doctrine of *pneumatics,* which deals with the external actions of an incorporeal entity;

while logic deals with their internal action, that is to say, thought (which also concerns practical philosophy, or the doctrine of the pleasant, of the useful and the righteous, or of what is a shared value in a community). The demonstration of the existence of God and of his attributes likewise belongs to this subject, as does that of angels and of the incorporeal mind within us, or of the immortality of the soul. With regard to these topics, with appropriate meditations we have attained mathematical certainty through a surprising mode of reasoning, which I believe to be greatly superior, for our peace of mind and for faith in eternity, than if we had discovered perpetual motion or the quadrature of the circle.

§. 36. Qualities developed through corporeal organs are either sensible or common to many organs, namely: number (which is perceived by all the external senses), and is the ground of arithmetic, and extension with its various modes (which is perceived only by sight and touch), and is the ground of geometry. Furthermore, whatever has another sensible quality besides extension and number is called body. Anything that is devoid of this added quality is called a vacuum. Here there arises the field of physics. The simplest sense is touch, through which we perceive motion. It is the task of general physics to explain these things because, as we will show next, there is nothing in the other qualities but a subtle motion, by which they can all be explained, if we assume extension. There are also special qualities of touch: solidity, fluidity, tenacity, extension, smoothness etc. Information should be gathered most diligently about these and about light and colors or about sounds, smells, tastes, so that their causes in matter and motion may be better known.

§. 37. After the abstract philosophy of qualities there follows the concrete philosophy pertaining to things into which the latter coalesce. Here it is important to note that the qualities of things are considered historically and nothing is demonstrated anew, but only subsumed, according to what was previously demonstrated in the abstract philosophy. Thus we are concerned with God, angels, our mind; fire, vapors, meteors, water and various species of spirits; soil, and various kinds of soil or minerals; plants; and finally animals. Here, therefore, we do not consider the interconnection of qualities and their relation to the subjects, but the connection of the subjects with the qualities. This part of philosophy can be called ἐιδογραφία[72]; the preceding part: ποιογραφία[73].

§. 38. Finally, we conclude with Cosmography[74], in which the connection of subjects to each other is set out, showing how they are distributed in the world: the

---

[72] "*Tertia decima* est scientia corporum organicorum, quas vocare solent, species, hanc possis appellare *Idographiam*. Species autem accurate distinguendae, non communi more per dichotomias, seu per qualitatum quibus dignosci possunt per combinationes", [Leibniz (note 45), 39– 40; in late revision note "D" of *NM* (note 57), 288, "Eidografia igitur duplex est Pnenumatica et Somatologia. Pneumatica in Theologiam, Angelographiam, Noologiam et Psycologiam dipesci potest. Somatologia similarium, mixtorum, foret (…)"].

[73] "*Decima* est scientia qualitatum sensibilium, quam vocare soleo *Poeographiam*. Qualitates hae quoad licet definiendae sunt, distinguendae per varietates et gradus, enumerandaque, subjecta in quibus existunt et a quibus fiunt, denique quae ex ipsis consequuntur", [Leibniz (note 45), 38; in late revision note "D" of *NM* (note 57), 288, "ποιογραφία. Huc pertinet comprobatio veritatis rerum extra nos, ex quibus maxime demonstrativa est Existentiae divinae notitia; quae fluit ex ipsa notitia nostri cum nostra existentiae et variarum in nobis perceptionum intime conscii simus. Ex iisdem et immortalitas animae demonstratur. Et utramque demonstrationem meditationibus nostris nonnihil adiutam esse intelligentes iudicarunt"].

[74] *Duodecima* est *Cosmographica* seu scientia majorum mundi corporum [Leibniz (note 45), 39; in late revision note "D" of *NM* (note 57), 288: Cosmographia, quae est mundi tamquam alicuius individui Historia et simul tamquam speciei scientia, in qua].

mechanical and theoretical history of celestial motions, astrognosy[75] and the more recent observations, briefly the history of the universe and of memorabilia since its creation. This field of argument includes chronology, universal history and that of certain regions, nations, states, ways of life etc. I believe that with thorough partition of the disciplines as set forth heretofore, I have exhausted the pertinent range of topics; and have outlined the elements of the sciences briefly but soundly.

§. 39. In the paragraphs extending from §. 27 up to this point, we have spoken of things on which we can acquire knowledge. We will select from these the elements which are intended to promote knowledge, and outline briefly how the study of these aspects should proceed. The first thing an infant has to learn is language. Specifically, one should make sure that the child absorbs Latin through practice with the same speed with which he learns his own language; but it is not appropriate to burden the child with an excess of Latin names, for example of plants, animals, etc., as such names rarely occur. This twofold language learning will be achieved if, during a certain part of the day, for example in the morning, Latin is spoken in conversational exchanges between the teacher and the pupils, while from noon onward the children are exposed to the language between the maids and the mother of the home. Alberico Gentili [1552–1608][76]

---

[75] In late revision note "D" of *NM* (note 45), 288, "quomodo scilicet revera in mundo hoc disposita sunt: observationes motuum coelestium, Agnostrosia et ex his estructa Astronomia recentiorum, speciatim etiam res nostri globi rerumque inde usque ab origine memorabilium, Geographia physica et civilis, Chronologia, historia rerum humanarum universalis et certarum regionum, nationum, personarum, statuum, generum vitae, rerum et qualitatum particularis"].

[76] Alberico Gentili was an Italian jurist. He left Italy due to his Protestant faith. Regius Professor of Civil Law at the University of

adopted this method in simultaneously teaching three languages to his infant son. He spoke Latin with his son, French with his wife, and addressed the servants in English, which they spoke as their home language. Another study that is appropriate for our time concerns gestures; in this regard, children should spend their time every day among men of good morals and endowed with cultural achievements, so that their progress is promoted by watching those around them. Finally, let the third study be of history, both in reference to the general development of previous times in a historical perspective, and also, more specifically, to the history of sacred institutions and the state of the contemporary world.

§. 40. When a boy is six years old, he should be sent to a public school, where he can become accustomed to engaging in public relations and may even form friendships lasting for life. He should live only for limited periods with his parents, so that he may learn to seek refuge in his own prudence; he should acquire familiarity with gymnastics, the art of music and dance, gladiatorial arts and javelin throwing, as well as painting and other skills necessary in life or for elegance; moreover, first and foremost he primarily [should acquaint himself] with the elegance of words. A deeper knowledge of ancient history and the most diligent attention to mathematics, namely arithmetic, geometry, optics, statics and astronomy should be added. As far as the natural sciences are concerned, only the names of herbs, minerals, trees, animals, mechanics tools should be included, focusing on subjects that belong to *The visible world in pictures*[77] by John Amos Comenius [1592–1670], but this book should

---

Oxford as from 1580, his work (1598) *De iure belli libri III*. Hanoviae, had a great influence on Hugo Grotius's thought.

[77] John Amos Comenius (1658), *Orbis sensualium pictus*. Noribergae: sumtibus Michaelis et Joannis Friderici Endteri.

be painted more diligently and illustrated with appropriate colours. The exercise of style should be performed not only through the composition of written material, but also in discussion and certainly in extemporaneous speech, instructing the young boy in the foundations of discourse, establishing relations among topics, and developing an argument by means of combinatorial art.

§. 41. From the age of twelve to eighteen years, he should be treated with greater liberality, allowing him to be close not to his tutors but to his friends. He should be shown the greatest secrets of nature and art, the basics of mechanics, so that he can learn by means of these at least the material, tools, basic rules and prices; likewise he should become acquainted with the system of trade between nations, so that he may discern among goods, and have knowledge of prices and the places from where such goods derive. He should already learn the rudiments of medicine, anatomy, the properties of simple elements, essences for the preparation of medicines and chemical compounds. It is preferable that every man be a doctor and jurist and theologian to a certain extent; that is, he should know at least the fundamentals of theology and positive jurisprudence. He should learn the statutes of his nation and the laws of the kingdom, but also to a certain extent [those] of the other [nations] so that he can travel abroad more confidently. He should learn French and Italian; and so that may interpret the Scripture itself, he should learn even Hebrew and Greek to an appropriate degree, in order to be able to understand the Old and New Testament. He should publicly declaim and appear in comedies. Indeed, as rightly [noted by] Hugo Grotius, Rhetoric as the completion of all other arts should be learned only when the majority of disciplines have been assimilated. This exercise should be conducted not only in Latin but also in the young man's own language.

Above all, however, he should become competent in that profession in which he will be able to display his talents one day. Furthermore, he should have knowledge of books, for it is extraordinary how greatly such an understanding is not only regarded as a sign of distinction, but is also of notable usefulness. During this time he should live not in a school, but in a university or at a court or in another important place where he will have the benefit of the potential to increase his knowledge and acquire familiarity with illustrious men, an opportunity that is the foundation of a promotion today. For no longer is it a foregone conclusion that a graduate from a university will be called to public office. Once it was customary [for political leaders and those holding office] to write to a guild in order to request the name of some excellent young aspirant; nowadays it is necessary to make oneself known in a range different sciences. Accordingly, it is not desirable that universities be situated in small localities devoid of any significant reputation.

§. 42. As from his eighteenth year, or—if his natural ability is slower—from his twentieth year, until his promotion, his time and energy should be dedicated to travelling. During his travels he should devote attention to his health, as described in the fine treatise *On Travelers' Medicine* by a physician of Augsburg[78], whose name I do not remember; he should observe and write down the advantages in food, drinking, buildings, clothes, agriculture, mechanics that he discovers in certain peoples. He should comply with local laws and customs, and should endeavor to glean knowledge from important men, firstly from secretaries and ministers of state, such knowledge being more accessible to foreigners than to

[78] Probably, Christoph Schorer [1618–1671] (1663), *Medicina peregrinantium*. Ulm [not included in AA VI, 2, sources directory].

natives. If he listens to memorable stories, or particular accounts concerning nature or technics, he should write them down diligently. The purpose of the journey will thereby be obtained, as it seeks to report not only on the merchandise, but also on the techniques adopted. In particular, if a certain region excels in some form of manufacturing, he should endeavour to investigate associated techniques. No further details are called for here, as illustrious men have dwelt on this matter before. Indeed these are issues concerning the plan of studies, in general, which derive from our old and recent reflections during stops at inns, jotted down without books, which we hastened to write down. Thus there was no opportunity to fill the margins with a heavy apparatus of quotations. If we have not already published or reported useless things, we have at least avoided the crime either of those who copy or of those who are mere innovators only in the matter of style.

PART II

Special, solely restricted to the Jurisprudence

§. 1. Jurisprudence is the science of the Law connected to a case or fact. Since we plan to expound the corresponding method, two aspects must be addressed: 1) delineating the Idea of the perfect jurist and all that is connected to his completion, as outlined by Cicero [106 BC–43 BC] in *De Oratore*[79]; 2) tracing the path to perfection or, if you prefer, stopping at a lower level[80]. Similarly Plato expounded the Idea in the books *de Republica*[81]; moreover, in *de Legibus*[82] he touched on the aspects each person may be allowed to attain.

---

[79] Cicero, *De Oratore*, in Edward William Sutton, Harris Rackham (eds.) (1942), *Cicero, De Oratore* (*On the Orator*). Cambridge, MA, London.

[80] The Latin text is "vias designemus ad perfectionem grassandi, aut sicubi placeret, in secundis tertiisque consistendi"; here L. is quoting from another work of Cicero, *Orator, Ad M. Brutum*, I, 4, "(...) prima enim sequentem honestum est in secundis tertiisque consistere", "For it is no disgrace for one who is striving for the first place to stop at second or third.", in George Lincoln Hendrickson, Harry Mortimer Hubbel (eds.) (1971), *Cicero Brutus (Orator)*. Cambridge MA, London. From these passages, it undoubtedly emerges that the ideal jurist in L. thought is one who can manage rhetoric according to the model of Cicero and Quintilian [35–100] (see *infra* §. 66, 67).

[81] Plato, *De Republica* (Πολιτεία) in G. R. F. Ferrari (ed.), Tom Griffith (transl.) (2000), *Plato, The Republic*. Cambridge: Cambridge University Press.

[82] Plato, *De Legibus* (Νόμοι), in R. G. Bury (ed. and transl.) (1967–1968), *Plato, The Laws*. Cambridge, MA.

§. 2. What pertains to the instruction of the perfect jurist can be divided, as in theology, in the following manner: a Didactic or Positive part, which includes those rules that are explicitly contained in the *Libri Authentici*[83], and they are of a certain right; a Historical part, which describes the origin, authors, changes and the repeal of laws; an Exegetical part, which interprets the same *Libri Authentici*; and finally, above all others, a Polemical or Controversial part, which defines cases not covered by the laws, adopting reason and similarity.

§. 3. Of these, the Didactic and Polemical parts from the proper subject-matter of jurisprudence, whereas the Historical and Exegetical sections are to be considered merely as aids[84]. The latter two subjects are theoretical; the former two are practical. Effectively, a jurisconsult of such kind is sufficiently trained in the first two, if he knows what is lawful in a given case: even a person skilled in commerce and trade, although lacking any knowledge of Latin, possesses the appropriate understanding, albeit on a different basis, or indeed with no knowledge of Latin at all; for instance if someone dares to deny [the arguments], he who is only experienced will be unable to build a demonstration on the basis of history[85] and laws: accordingly, his approach will more

---

[83] *I. e.* the source book, "I define *Libri Authentici*, as at least in general I would recommend, not only the ancient books, but also the recent, such as the rescripts of the Diet, the Saxon body of laws, and the statutes or the reforms of each republic" (so the same L., *infra*, §. 93).

[84] The first version in text is "(...) sunt requisita tantum", "are only needs"; I prefer to follow the revised text by L. "sunt adiumenta tantum" [see revision note "D" 19–20, (note 45)].

[85] On this point L. disagrees with Quintilian, although the latter seems to be an indispensable reference of judicial rhetoric (see *infra* §. 66, 67): according to Quintilian, history helps to narrate, not to demonstrate something, see *Institutio Oratoria* in Donald Andrew

suitably deserve the name of empirical, rather than a designation that communicates an understanding of the real philosophy of law.

§. 4. Moreover, in moving from theology to jurisprudence we have rightly transposed the example of our division into sections, because the similarity among the two disciplines is surprising. Both have a twofold principle: on the one hand, reason, hence natural theology and natural jurisprudence, (of which Ramón Sibiuda [c.1385–1436][86] and Theophilus Raynaud [1587–1663][87] developed the former, Grotius, Hobbes and others the latter; of these will be done mention *infra* in §. 70., [but 71, e. n.]), on the other, scripture, that is to say any of the *Libri Authentici*[88] containing positive laws, then divine, here human. It should be noted, however, that some have inappropriately extended this comparison even to medicine, philosophy and mathematics[89]. Hippocrates [460 BC–379 BC], Galen [129–c. 201] and Aristotle [384 BC–322 BC] were often

---

Russel (ed.) (2001), *Quintilian, The Orator's Education.* Cambridge MA, London: Harvard University Press, 10, 1, 31.

[86] Ramon Sibiuda *Liber naturae sive creaturarum* (aliter *Theologia Naturalis*), circa annum 1435 ab eo compositus, Latine impressus anno 1484. (1966, Stuttgart, Bad Cannstatt: Frommann) [not included in AA VI, 2, sources directory]; see also Johann H. Alsted, (1615), *Theologia naturalis*. S.l.: prostat apud Antonium Hummium, 1, "Theologia naturalis, est sapientia rerum divinarum, quatenus illae faciunt ad manifestationem creatoris lumine naturae cognoscibilis.".

[87] Teofilo Raynaud (1629), *Moralis disciplina, ad praestruendam Theologiae practicae*. Lugduni: Jacob Cardon.

[88] See note n. 83.

[89] See Carl Schmitt [1888–1985] (1922, revised edition 1934 by Dunker & Humblot), *Politische Theologie: Vier Kapitel zur Lehre von der Souveränität*, Berlin (Engl. transl., by G. Schwab (1985), *Political Theology*. Cambridge MA, London, chap. 3, 37, "The clearest philosophical expression of that analogy is found in Leibniz. Emphasizing the systematic relationship between jurisprudence and theology, he rejected a comparison of jurisprudence with medicine and mathematics".

guilty of error; Euclid [fl. 300 BC] is not believed because he makes statements, but because he proves that which is otherwise in divine and human laws, where the will stands in the place of reason[90].

§. 5. No wonder then, that what happens in jurisprudence equally happens in theology, because theology is a particular category of jurisprudence taken universally; that is to say, it deals with right and laws which are respected in the state, or rather in the reign of God over humans; morals falls into the category of private law, the rest into that of public law. Accordingly, rewriting, to a certain extent, our own treatise *On Combinatorial Art*[91], p. 29, infidels are, as it were, like rebels, the church is like good subjects; ecclesiastics persons and indeed political magistrates are like ministers and subordinate magistrates; excommunication like banishment; the doctrine of holy Scripture and the word of God is like the laws and their interpretation; the canon of sacred books is like the *Authentia* of laws [92]; fundamental errors like capital crimes, the final judgment, the last day and the prevailing compensation of Christ are like the judiciary process; the termination and compensation for others; the forgiveness of sins corresponds to the right of pardons, eternal damnation to capital punishment, or life imprisonment, which

---

[90] It is a quote from Juvenal [c. 50–after 127], *Saturae*. 6, 223, in George Gilbert Ramsay, see note 26, 100-101, *Hoc volo, sic iubeo, sit pro ratione voluntas* ["Be it so; but this is my will and my command: let my will be the voucher for the deed"; or "This I will, thus I command, let my will be in place of a reason", ed. transl.].

[91] Leibniz, see note 54.

[92] *I. e.*, of Justinian Laws in their Latin version (the so-called *Authenticae*), whose authenticity was doubted at first: see Álvaro d'Ors [1915–2004] (1997), *Auctoritas–Authentia–Authenticum*, Pamplona, 143–151; and for preliminary information, see Berger, note 19, *ad vocem Authenticum*.

is equivalent to the death sentence. In brief, almost the whole of theology depends for the greater part on jurisprudence. How often is there mention of a testament, inheritance, servitude and adoption in St. Paul [c. 5–c. 67] With regard to the explanation of the concept of testament, a substantial part of the controversy about the Lord's Supper[93] has been consumed between theologians of the Augsburg confession and the Reformers. A word on Fausto Sozzini [1539–1604][94] is relevant here: precisely because he came from jurisprudence to theology, it is surprising how intensely he was to embarrass all others. Hence, he could not be better refuted than by that man who had dealt equally with jurisprudence and theology, namely the incomparable Hugo Grotius in his book *de Satisfactione Christi*[95]. The illustrious Matthias Zimmermann [1625–1689] wrote a specific dissertation[96] in which he carefully examined the loopholes that Sozzini's disciples seek to find within the juridical concepts of *acceptilatio*[97]. Whether and how far a rule prevails in

[93] This controversy concerns the real presence of Christ in Holy Comunion; see Thomas R. Schreiner, Matthew R. Crawford (2010), *The Lord's Supper*. Nashville, TN, 211.

[94] Fausto Sozzini (1578), *De Jesu Christo Servatore*, in Elisabetta Scribano (ed.) (2004), *Fausti Socini, Opera Omnia*. Siena: Ciaccheri.

[95] Hugo Grotius [1583–1645] (1617), *Defensio fidei catholicae de satisfactione Christi adversus Faustum Socinum Senensem*. Leiden, in (1732) *Hugone Grotii Operum Theologicorum, T. quartus, Opuscola Diversa*. Basileae, (Engl. transl. (1889) of *Defensio Fidei* by Frank H. Foster, Andover: Draper).

[96] Matthias Zimmermann (1666), *Acceptilatio Sociniana*. Lipsiae: typis viduae Henningi Coleri.

[97] For the concept of *acceptilatio* in Roman law, see Gai, 3, 169, "Item per acceptilationem tollitur obligation. Acceptilatio autem est veluti imaginaria solutio. Nam quod ex verborum obligatione tibi debeam, id si velis mihi remittere, poteris sic fieri, ut patiaris haec verba me dicere: QUOD TIBI EGO PROMISI, HABESNE ACCEPTUM? et tu respondeas: HABEO". The word later took on

matters of faith has recently been discussed by the noble couple referred to as the *Walenburch Brothers*[98]; in contrast Johann Hülsemann [1602–1661], the illustrious theologian of the Augsburg Confession, has proceeded in the opposite direction, likewise composing a specific treatise, *de praescriptione*[99]. Briefly: in theology so great is the multitude of juridical controversies that among the ἀνέκδοτα [in Greek in the text, unpublished, e. n.] of the distinguished Johann Georg Dorsche [1597–1659] a posthumous work will remain with the title of *Jurisprudentia Theologica*[100].

§. 6. Didactic jurisprudence will not ineptly be named in imitation of Euclid's *Elements*, which were followed in the titles of their books: Thomas Hobbes, in *On the Citizen* and *On the Body*[101], Johann von Felden [d. c. 1668][102] and Samuel Pufendorf [1632–1694] in *Elements of Jurisprudence*[103]. Elements are composed of two teaching modes: by explanation of terms or definitions, as is made clear in the title *on the meaning of the words,* and by propositions or precepts, as indicated in the title *the rules of the law*.

---

the meaning of debt remission. For the theological transposition see Sozzini, note 94, 216; Grotius, note 95, 320.

[98] Adrianus [1609–1699] et Petrus [1610–1675] de Walenburch (Bishops) (1666), *De praescriptionibus catholicis.* Antwerpiae: apud Lucam de Potter.

[99] Johann Hülsemann, *Tractatus de praescriptione* in, by the same, (1640) *Breviarium theologiae*. Wittembergae.

[100] Johann Georg Dorsche was a Lutheran Theologian known for his large production of theological *Disputationes*.

[101] Thomas Hobbes (1642), *Elementa philisophiae, sectio tertia: De Cive*. Parisiis; Id. (1655), *Elementa philisophiae, sectio prima: De Corpore*. Londinii.

[102] Johann von Felden (1664), *Elementa Juris Universi, et in specie Publici Justinianei*. Francofurti et Lipsiae.

[103] Samuel Pufendorf (1660), *Elementorum jurisprudentiae universalis libri duo*. Hagae Comitis.

§. 7. Definitions, that is, the explanations of juridical terms, should be taught in a small separate book, in order to ensure the absence of any confusion with the precepts or rules. This can be titled: Partitions of law. Its method should not be alphabetical, but precise and complete. It is striking how in a complete, natural method, a thing explains a second thing through another, and memory is helped. Additionally, in this case tables are very useful; firstly we may, at a glance, view the whole map of a science in a general table, like a geographical map, and then proceed to examine the particular details, as if they were the individual provinces. These tables, unknown to the ancient authors, were often used first by Pierre de la Ramée and his disciples: subsequently, in those concerning ethics and politics Theodor Zwinger [1533–1588][104] exercised the utmost care, as did Johann Thomas Freige [1543–1583][105] with regard to those concerning law. An innumerable multitude of others followed them, but they did not fully attain the goal we desire, the method that I call natural. In fact, as the incomparable Bacon of Verulam rightly objected to Pierre de la Ramée and his followers (Ramists), the latter group of scholars devoted such scrupulous care in formulating the subdivisions that they ultimately achieved the result of delimiting rather

---

[104] Theodor Zwinger (1566), *Aristotelis Stagiritae De moribus ad Nicomachum libri decem: tabulis perpetuis, quae commentariorum loco esse queant, explicati & illustrati.* Basileae: Per Ioan. Oporinum & Eusebium Episcopium; Id. (1589), *Icones sive imagines vivae, literis cl. virorum, Italiae, Graeciae, Germaniae, Galliae, Angliae, Ungariae.* Basileae: Apud Conr. Valdkirch; Id. (1565), *Theatrum vitæ humanæ: omnium fere eorum, quæ in hominem cadere possunt, bonorum atq[ue] malorum exempla historica, ethicæ philosophiæ præceptis accommodata.* Basileæ: Per Ioan. Oporinum, Abrosium et Aurelium Frobenios fratres [all books by Zwinger are not included in AA VI, 2, sources directory].

[105] Johann Thomas Freige (1571), *Partitiones Juris Utriusque.* Basileae.

than understanding the subject, which, meanwhile, escaped like an eel, or otherwise stated, left useless straws of subdivisions in place of the grain of the peculiarities.

§. 8. Since, however, the method of teaching jurisprudence also includes the method of orderly arrangement of the topics, we will now examine the directions the various authors followed[106]. Care in the art of collecting all details pertaining to law dates back to very ancient times, and was practised also by *Cicero*, according to the testimony of Aulus Gellius [130–180][107]. At a later stage, the ancient jurists likewise threw themselves on the same work and composed not only disorderly books of questions and responses, but also *Digesta*[108], that is, orderly arrangements as the name itself indicates, and *Institutiones*[109]. Nevertheless, because their writings have come down to us in mutilated or torn form, we can but seek to

---

[106] The Latin text of this passage is "videamus quas varii vias inverint"; L. is probably remembering a passage from Cicero, *Pro Murena*, 26, "Praesto aderat sapiens ille qui inire viam doceret" ("and here was that same wise man to teach us in which direction we should go", e. transl.)

[107] Aulus Gellius, *Noctes Atticae*. I, 22, 7.

[108] See Berger note 19 *ad vocem Digesta*, "(from *digerere.*) In juristic literature. Some Jurists (Alfenus Varus, Celsus, Julian, Scaevola, Marcellus) wrote a comprensive work under this title. Neither the system nor the kind of presentation is uniform, but the general feature is that both *ius civile* and praetorian law are taken into consideration. Often excerpts from earlier work of the same author (*Responsa*, *Quaestiones*) are collected and put into somewhat systematic order (*digerere*)".

[109] See Berger note 19 *ad vocem Institutiones*, "Elementary law textbooks primarily for students. Institutions were written by Gaius, Florentinus, Callistratus, Paul, Ulpian, and Marcian. Some of the works may have originated in the lectures of their authors. One part of Justinian's codification is also entitled *Institutiones* [see note 109]".

divine something from the inscriptions of Justinian[110] laws[111]. In *Institutiones*[112], Tribonianus [c. 485?–542][113] maintained a different method from that presented in the *Digesta*[114] and the *Codex*[115]. In *Institutiones* he set out

---

[110] Justinian I, [c. 482–565], was a Byzantine (East Roman) emperor from 527 to 565. One of the main aspects of his kingdom was the uniform rewriting of Roman law, known by the collective designation *Corpus Juris Civilis* [see note 19], which is still the basis of civil law in many modern states.

[111] See Berger note 19 *ad vocem Corpus Juris Civilis.*

[112] See Berger note 19 *ad voces Corpus Juris Civilis* and *Institutiones Iustiniani*, "A part of Justinian's codification compliled in 533 after the final draft of the Digest [see note 108] had been finished, and published on November 21, 533. It entered into force simultaneously with the Digest, published a few weeks later.[…] The work was intended as an elementary manual—hence its title *Institutiones sive Elementa*—for law sudents in their first year. It was edited by the law professors, Theophilus and Dorotheus, under the supervision of Tribonian".

[113] See Berger note 19 *ad vocem Tribonianus*, "Justinian's principal collaborator and adviser in his legislative works. […]".

[114] See Berger note 19 *ad voces Corpus Juris Civilis* and *Digesta Iustiniani*, " The main part of Justinian's legislative work Announced ib December 15, 530 by the constitution '*Deo Auctore*', it was published on December 16, 535 by the constitution '*Tanta*' (in Latin) and '*Dedoken*' (in Greex'), and it entered in force two weeks later. The grandiose work is a compilation of excerpts from the juristic literature of the classical epoch. More than 9,000 texts are distribuited into fifthy books, each of which—except for books 30–32 on legacies and *fideicommissa*—are didived into titles of various extent containing the texts pertinent to the topic indicated in the superscriptions (*rubrica*) of the title. […] By a special instruction of the emperor the compilers were authorized to omit all superfluous, imperfect, and obsolete material and to make alterations in the excerpted fragments taking into consideration the changes introduced by later imperial legislative activity and Justinian's own enactments. The commission composed of law professors in Costantinople and Beirut, high officials, and prominent practitioners, under the chairmanship of Tribonianus made use of that authorization in a very large measure, not only in order to introduce into the collected texts later legislative changes but also to insert some reforms of the older

three objects of right, persons (*personae*), things (*res*) and actions (*actiones*)[116]: thus in the chapter of persons he set forth paternal authority (*patria potestas*)[117], the power of the master over a slave (*potestas dominica*)[118], marriage (*nuptiae*), guardianship (*tutela*)[119], supervision (*cura*)[120]. In other words, he dealt with every power that is immediately enforceable over persons without the involvement of things. Another chapter deals with all cases in which things are the principal element involved, that is to say, cases where the obligation does not hold for a given person but rather for a certain thing. Consequently these are aspects concerning *jus in re*, either *inter vivos*, hence ownership, usufruct[121], use, habitation; or by succession, thus

law where the classical doctrines or ideas seemed to them less appropriate for their time. [...]".

[115] It is a collection of imperial constitutions published in the middle of December 534 which is part of Justinian's legislative work *Corpus Juris Civilis*, see Berger note 19 *ad voces Codex Iustinianus*, *Corpus Juris Civilis*.

[116] Ernest Metzger (1998), "Actions", in Id. (ed.), *A Companion to Justinians's Institutes*. Ithaca NY: Cornell University Press, 208, "The law of actions is the last of the three in the institutional scheme, and is quite different from the subject that precede it. While the earlier subjects are concerned with substantive rules and principles, the law of actions is concerned with redress. It is not quite the same as 'the law of procedure', however; it often includes matters that might easily have been treated under law of persons or of things. This is because actions evolved as a subject over time when procedure was not distinct from substantive law.".

[117] Patrick MacChombaich de Colquhoun [1815–1891] (1849), *A Summary of the Roman Civil Law*, London, 446.

[118] MacChombaich de Colquhoun, see note 117, 446.

[119] MacChombaich de Colquhoun, see note 117, 579.

[120] Metzger, see note 116, 258.

[121] David Carey Miller (1998), "Property", in Metzger, see note 116, 66, 67, "This is the most important form of personal servitude and the other forms are derivatives of it. The personal servitudes [such as use, habitation, e. n.] were so designated because they featured a vesting of all or part of the beneficial interest of the right of ownership in a person other than the owner, the right being personal to that

inheritance with or without testament, legacy, *fideicommissum*[122] etc. On the other hand, there are other types of cases where the things are involved less than principally so that a certain person, not a certain thing, is obliged; this is called *jus ad rem*[123]. *Jus ad rem* arises either from con-

---

person and so inalienable. Justinian (J. 2.4. pr) definition identifies the nature of usufructs as to the removal to someone other than the owner of the rights to the use and the fruits, subject to the substance of the property remaining unimpaired. (…) The owner retained the bare property (G. 2.30) and the right of disposal (*abusus*) of it. (…) As Nicholas shows, there is only a superficial similarity between the usufruct in Roman law and the separation of beneficial interest and title on the basis of equitable and legal ownership as developed in English law. One might go further and note the difference between usufruct and trust device derived from English law and used in various systems to separate beneficial interest and title. The difference follows from the fundamentally distinct starting points applying to the forms. The Roman usufruct is a natural by-product of a unitary right to ownership made up of separable components (the right to use, to fruits, and of disposal). The English trust, on the other hand, developed on the basis of the distinct forms of legal and equitable ownership.".

122 "(…) a trust created by will" (Andrew M. Riggsby (2010), *Roman Law and Legal World of the Romans*. Cambridge: Cambridge University Press, 119); "It may be noted that a Roman form of trust is the *fideicommissum*, but this was a device of law of succession which made possible the settlement of property within the prevailing notion of ownership" (Carey Miller, see note 121, 67).

123 Harold J. Berman (2003), *Law and Revolution II. The impact of the Protestant Reformations on the Western Legal Tradition*. Cambridge, MA: Harvard University Press, 116 (and n. 49), "The concept of *jus ad rem*, not to be found in the Institutes, had been invented by the scholastic jurists of the twelfth century and had become an integral fundamental concept of European law". According to Berman, it is due to the German jurist Johann Apel [1486–1536] [(1535) *Methodica dialectices ratio ad Jurisprudentiam adcommodata Authore Johanne Apello*.Noribergae; Id. (1540), *Isagoge per dialogum in quattuor libros Institutionum D. Iustiniani Imperatoris Authore Johanne Apello*. Wratislaviae, e. n.], the criticism and reworking of the subdivision of right such as, "declared in Justinian's Institutes, into 'persons', 'actions', and 'things'. The author of the Institutes did not define these terms in a satisfactory way and did not in fact organ-

tract[124] or quasi-contract[125]; or from delict[126] or quasi-

---

ize his exposition around them. Apel contended, first, that the category 'persons' is incidental to 'things'. He then went on to divide 'things' (*res*) into 'right in a thing' (*jus in re*), to which he applied the term 'ownership' (*dominium*), and 'right to a thing' (*jus ad rem*), to which he applied the term 'obligation' (*obligatio*), under which he also subsumed 'actions'".

[124] "A 'Contract' can be defined roughly as an agreement that can be enforced by the courts or other governmental mechanism" (Riggsby, see note 122, 121); "It is an important difference between Roman Law and the common law that, though both compromises, Roman law puts the emphasis on specific contracts and common laws on general modes of contracting. The Roman law of contract was dominated by eight specific contracts: sale, hire, partnership, commission (*mandatum*), loan for consumption (*mutuum*), deposit and pledge. This list covers the whole range of commercial and social life. But it is in the nature of any such list to be less than completely comprehensive. (...)" (Peter Birks [1941–2004] (2014), *The Roman Law of Obligations*. Oxford: Oxford University Press, 30).

[125] "This category comprised a number of situations that were not strictly contractual (but were largely analogous to contract), in which liability *in personam* arose. It is difficult to find any common principle or link among them." (Paul J. du Plessis (2010), *Borkowski's Textbook on Roman Law*. Oxford: Oxford University Press, 253); for example, "1. If a person manage the affairs of an absent person without the knowledge of the absentee, both parties are under obligations to one another, '*quasi ex contractu*'. 2. Tutors and pupils are under obligations *quasi ex contractu* to one another, as are also. 3. Persons who are joint owners of the same things. 4. The heir and the legatees. 5. The person who has received money by mistake. If money has been paid merely to escape a penalty it cannot be recovered, although was not due." (Gordon Campbell (2008 reprint), *Compendium of Roman Law Founded on the Institutes of Justinian*. Clark NJ, 126); "The difference from contract is the absence of agreement. These obligations are not incurred voluntarily, by being undertaken. They are imposed willy-nilly when the event happens. In that point they resemble delictual obligations. But they differ from delictual obligations in that the events which trigger them are allowed or even encouraged, not forbidden. So the quasi-contractual events are those but bring into being involuntary obligations." (Birks, see note 124, 124).

[126] "Roman and Common Law have similar ideas of a 'wrongful act which does not involve a breach of contract and for which the injured party can recover damages in civil action'; we call this a 'tort', and in

delict[127]. To the third chapter there belong actions: both exceptions, replications and the whole due process and finally the duties of the judge. In the *Digesta*[128] and indeed the *Codex*[129], Tribon-ianus[130] thoroughly examined only the actions according to the order of Perpetual Edict, while in the other two related titles, he succinctly treated issues concerning persons and things.

Roman law the parallel category of act is called 'delict'. (...) The main difference between tort and delict is that included under the heading of delict are several offenses (theft, most assaults) that we routinely treat as crimes today." (Riggsby, see note 122, 187).

[127] "That leaves quasi-delict. Nobody has ever come up with a view which commanded universal acceptance. There is a difference from quasi-contract. All the quasi-delict are events which the law forbids: no *litem suam facere*, no pouring or throwing from houses, no placing or hanging above public ways, no stealing in ships, inns and stables. But, if this suffices to make line between the quasi categories, the next question is, Why are these figures not delicts? What is 'quasi' about them? The judge tends to spoil almost every attempt to answer this question. The other three all show a number of features which could provide the distinction. They are all cases in which the liability is vicarious, the occupier, innkeeper and so on being made to answer even for the acts of the others. They are all cases of liability without personal misfeasance, liability which ca extend to pure omissions. They are probably all cases of liability without proof of any fault in the defendant himself. (...) One feature which is common to the quasi-delict is that they all involve defendants in special positions. You have to become *iudex* before you can *litem suam facere*, and so on. They all involve breaches of duties imposed not just on people generally but specifically on judges, occupiers, innkeepers. At first sight, this seems to have no jurisprudential weight. In short, so what? However, I think the answer does lie in this direction. The business of elegant classification is delicate. (...) But in fact they seem to have been divided between forbidden events which anyone could commit (delicts) and forbidden events which could be only within the context of a special relationship (quasi-delicts)." (Birks, see note 124, 126–127).

[128] See note 114.

[129] See note 115.

[130] See note 113.

§. 9. The medieval juriconsults likewise developed no clear doctrine of the art of right, inasmuch as they were already content if they overwhelmed Laws with Glosses[131] and Judges with Counsels. Just as the theologians of those times constantly relied on Thomas when forming their opinions, on the philosopher Aristotle when drawing up their summaries, similarly jurists smear their annotations over the *Corpus Juris*[132]. Indeed, they seem convinced it is their bounden duty to utilize the method of Laws, as if they exercised authority in logic as well. Such a method has proved pleasing to quite a few notable persons even in this highly cultured age. Aegidius Mommer [1520–1570] in his dissertation *de Studio Juris*[133] denies that one should consider common places different from Laws, a different method in comparison to that of Laws, for it is only the Laws that you must have at hand: all the rest is to be set aside. Even Justus Meier [1566–1622], the director of the *Collegium Argentoratense*[134], covertly expresses anger, in the *Praefatio,* towards those jurists who dare to prefer their own method to that of *Imperatoriae*. In addition, Anthon Matthaeus [1564–1637] in the *Collegium Fundamentorum Juris*[135], argued openly that a new method of right would be pointless and possibly even harmful in the contemporary circumstances. He admitted that the Justinian method

---

[131] In the medieval legal tradition, the glosses are exegetic remarks to texts, phrases or single words of Justinian's Corpus, written as marginal or interlinary notes; see Berger note 19, *ad voces Glossae and Glossatores*.

[132] See Berger note 19.

[133] Aegidius Mommer (1600), *Epistola ... de ratione legendi discendique Jura.* Herbornae Nass.

[134] Justus Meier (1657), *Collegium Iuridicum Argentoratense totius jurisprudentiae absolutum systema exibens*. Argentorati.

[135] Anton Matthaeus (1638), *Collegia iuris sex unum fundamentorum juris, alterum institutionum, tertium & quartum earundem, quintum pandectarum, sextum codicis, quibus adjectæ sunt disputationes quædam extraordinariæ*. Groningæ: typis Johannis Sas.

was not ideal, but he believed that such a defect was of trifling importance given that methods set forth by others are equally imperfect. Furthermore, he admits that it would be desirable for another body of laws to be in force, drawn up by the public authorities. However, the work involved in the discovery of a new method appears to be twofold, inasmuch as one must have recourse to both approaches, because in addition to the Justinian, the new method must likewise be impressed upon memory.

§. 10. However, against the flaws of the Justinian method, we will explain the usefulness of the new approach. First, the work is effectively twofold in the Justinian method, since the method of the *Institutiones*, that of the *Digesta* and that of the *Codices* differ from one another. The method contained in the *Institutiones*, for persons, things and actions is superfluous; actions derive either from the right of persons, or from the right of things, persons themselves, for example, slaves and the sons of the family, being considered as things: thus the action of *vindicatio* is given no less for a slave than for a horse. And even for a family's son the concept of ownership comes into play, although it is restricted by the state within certain limits. In addition, briefly stated, this method has not been derived from the profound and underlying concepts of right, but from fact. Persons and things are terms of fact, authority (*potestas*) etc. are terms of right. Moreover, if [Tribonianus] sometimes wished to choose the method of fact, why did he not continue, why did he not subdivide persons and things according to physical and ethical facts, *e. g.* persons into deaf, mute, blind, hermaphrodites, male, female, prepubescent, minors, adults, rich, poor nobles, magistrates, rustic labourers, foreigners, heretics, schismatics, etc., and things into divisible, indivisible, valuable, vile, cheap, movable, immovable, self-moving, treasures, money, fungible things, quadrupeds, horses, wild beasts, etc.?

Why, I ask, did he not set out titles of right in this manner and, for each one, why did he not explain and illustrate the proper right? Evidently, he recognized that endless repetitions would not follow from this method, nor could an argument be attributed to a general concept. It is as if a land surveyor were to divide his science not according to the form, but according to the matter, and to carry on with the measurement of fields, pastures, sandy, clay, stony plains. Who would not laugh at a new Euclid of such a nature? Consequently the division of jurisprudence derived from considerations of the concrete [case] is the source of all the confusion, and it concerns rather than those who write either treatises or indexes, i.e., works that can collect from the various titles the rights of women, the mute, the deaf, etc. It cannot be denied that nowadays even the method of the specific sections of laws is not entirely satisfactory: nowhere is ecclesiastical law conveniently inserted, nowhere feudal law, nowhere bankruptcy law. Certainly, in *Digesta* and *Codex* the perpetual cause of order is the old system of right, which is as valid for today's system as a pig for Minerva.

§. 11. The new method surely will bring incredible advantages, if it is drawn up accurately. The first benefit deriving therefrom will be a wonderful compendium of things to be learned, while by means of the general rules the infinite special rules will be learned at the same time, and from premised genres they will gradually descend to the species, where only those that are not obvious by mere subsumption under general rules will need to be mentioned. Indeed, as rightly warned by Von Felden in the preface of the *Elementa*[136], what need is there to inculcate in particular that the minor needs a curator, while in another passage it is those who are furious who have

---

[136] See note 102.

such a need, and in another it is those who are absent, if the rule is made evident by the same general principles of policy: all those who can not attend to their own business need a curator. And then, memory itself will be helped exercising the greatest care in the most natural connection of things which gently descend, if they are considered according to the limits set by the definition of genre, or difference of genre will give rise to the differences among species. Finally, since an accurate method is not possible without accurate definitions of terms (the definition of genre can be regarded as the key to differences which constitute species), a solid knowledge of right will be imbued with the same method; allowing definition of the doubtful cases of right through general reasoning. And thus memory as well as judgment clearly depends on the perfection of the method.

§. 12. The desperate cases will not be medicated by the pomade of Anthon Matthaeus[137]. He admits Tribonianean errors of method, therefore he will admit that a better method has to be adopted: in short, a new Body of Law. What, then, is averse to methods, if nothing else, at least, than the σκιαγραφίας [in Greek in the text, the project, the draft, e. n.] of the new body [of law]? The idle talk about the doubling of labor amounts to nothing, because it takes no labour to learn a natural method; indeed, by perceiving the precise definitions of the concepts one obtains a perfect method to deal with a different topic. Such a method will, in truth, be an index of the Body of Justinian law, and it will be helpful to place the corresponding passages of the laws in the margin.

§. 13. Various (authors) have treated the method of law in different ways. I will not follow all of them, not Jean de

---

[137] See note 135.

De Coras [1515–1572][138] or Matthias Stephani's [1570–1646] dissertation *de arte Juris*[139], not the method of Hugues Doneau [1527–1591] in *Com.*[*mentariis*] [140], not Franz Julius Chopius' *de vera Philosophia Juris*[141]; not Joachim Hopper's [1523–1576] *Seduardus* [142], not the *Principia*[143] by Martin Delrio [1551–1608], not that of Sulszbach, edited by Van Helmont Jr., Ottavio Pisani's [fl. 1660/1666] excellent *Lycurgum*[144] recently reprinted in Latin and German, nor that which Von Felden[145], or Pufendorf[146] or Richard Zouchaeus [1590–1661 [147] commendably attempted, not the order of Grotius, which, while it may not be the best according to the opinion of the illustrious Jakob Thomasius[148], it is certainly not the

---

[138] Jean de Coras (1560), *De iuris arte libellus*. Lugduni: Apud Antonium Vincentium.

[139] Matthias Stephani (1630), *De arte iuris, et eius principiis.* Gryphiswaldae: Koep [not included in AA VI, 2, sources directory].

[140] Hugues Doneau (1595–1597), *Commentariorum de iure civili libri viginti octo.*–5 v., 4o, Francofurti: apud Andreae Wecheli heredes, Claudium Marnium et Ioan. Aubrium.

[141] Franz Julius Chopius (1650), *Philosophia juris vera.* Lipsiae: Ritzsch.

[142] Joachim Hoppers (1590), *Seduardus.* Antuerpiae: In Officina Plantiniana, apud viduam et Ioannem Moretum.

[143] Martin Antonio Delrio (1589), *De principiis iuris libri duo.* Lugduni: Apud Franciscum Le Feure.

[144] Ottavio Pisani (1666), *Lycurgus Italicus.* Sulzbaci: Typis Abrahami Lichtenthaleri; Id. (1666), *Der Italienische Lycurgus: Gesetze und Ordnungen.* Sulzbaci: Typis Abrahami Lichtenthaleri.

[145] See note 102.

[146] See note 103.

[147] Richard Zouchaeus (1636), *Elementa Jurisprudentiae Definitionibus, Regulis, & Sententiis selectioribus Juris Civilis illustrata.* Oxoniae: Leon. Lichfield.

[148] Jakob Thomasius [1622–1684], was a German academic philosopher and jurist. In the spring of 1661, at the age of fourteen, Leibniz began his studies at the university in Leipzig where he came under the influence of Thomasius, who became the young man's mentor and adviser. See Christia Mercer (2004). Leibniz and His

worst; it is easier to defame than to emend. Let us recall once and for all Johann Althusius [1563–1638] and Hermann Vulteius [1555–1634], the former in *Diceologia*[149], the latter in the *Jurisprudentia Romana*[150]: they sought to render right as a science not only in words but also in execution. In truth, each confused fact and right. Indeed, this first immediate division belongs to Althusius: jurisprudence is twofold, the one dealing with fact, the other with right. But where lies the truth: does jurisprudence deal precisely with fact and with fact alone, or does there genuinely exist a species of jurisprudence which does not deal with right? Vulteius, among other things, disagrees with this, since he leads obligation back to right applied to persons, as if it were opposed to right applied to things. We will discuss this issue later, with regard to right as applied to things for which the obligation of the owner intervenes purely as a bare fact, as if it were, for example, a *quasi-contractu*, thus treating it as a case in which possession arises and he [the owner] is obliged to undertake restitution. We will now cover other topics in more detail.

§ 14. Nevertheless, because we have attributed to ourselves faculty to pass judgment on others, we will allow the same with regard to the publication of our reflections. We will make sure, therefore, that we obtain a solid method from the definitions of things. Jurisprudence is

---

Master: The Correspondence with Jakob Thomasius. In: Paul Lodge (ed.) *Leibniz and his Correspondents*. pp. 10–46. [Online]. Cambridge: Cambridge University Press. Available from: Cambridge Books Online [http://dx.doi.org/10.1017/CBO9780511498237.002 [Accessed 12 May 2016].

[149] Johann Althusius (1618), *Dicaeologicae libri tres*. Prostant Frankfurti: Apud Christophorum Corvinum.

[150] Hermann Vulteius (1602), *Jurisprudentiae Romanae a Justiniano compositae libri duo*. Marpurgi: Typis Pauli Egenolphi Typography Acad.

the science of the actions, insofar they are called just or injust. Just and unjust is defined as whatever is publicly useful or harmful. Publicly, that is, firstly for the world, or for God who is its rector, and secondly for mankind, and finally for the state: with this subordination, in case of conflict the will or the utility of God, if it be permitted to speak thus, is to be preferred to the utility of humankind and this to the utility of the state, and this to one's own utility. Hence, one may speak of divine, human, and civil jurisprudence. To talk about one's own utility, however, is a topic of politics not of jurisprudence.

§. 14 [a]. Morality, that is, the justice or injustice of an act, derives however from the quality of the acting person in relation to the action springing from previous actions, which is described as moral quality[151]. But just as the real quality is twofold in relation to action: the power of acting, and the necessity of acting; so also the moral power is called right, the moral necessity is called obligation[152].

---

[151] As pointed out by Christopher Johns in his dissertation (2007), "The science of Right in Leibniz's Practical Philosophy", 12, and subsequently in Id. (2013), *The science of Right in Leibniz's Moral and Political Philosophy*. London: Bloomsbury, 7, L. is certainly influenced by Grotius definition of right, Hugo Grotius [1583–1645] (1625), *De Jure Belli ac Pacis*. Parisiis, I, 1, IV, "Jus est qualitas moralis personae competens ad aliquid juste habendum vel agendum"; for a recent English translation Stepfhen C. Neff (ed. and transl.) (2012), *Hugo Grotius, On the Law of War and Peace*, Cambridge.

[152] In a late revision note "D", see note 45, 301, "potentia est necessitas, id est posse et non posse non".

§. 15. The *subject*[153] of moral quality is person and thing. Person is rational substance, and is either a natural or civil person. Natural persons are God, angel, and man. God is the subject of supreme right, without any obligation. A civil person is a corporation guild, which, because it has a single recognizable will through some sign, for example through obtaining a majority of the vote, through drawing lots, etc., [the civil person] is, therefore, able to oblige and to be obliged. A thing is likewise a subject of rights and obligations[154], for example if some-

---

[153] Riccardo Orestano [1909–1988] (1960), "Diritti soggettivi e diritti senza soggetto". *Jus*, 150–151, stresses that L. was one of authors who first used the term *subjectum juris* in the modern sense of holder of rights and obligations, rather than subject *to* the law. Concerning the reversal of this meaning in the XVII cent., Orestano refers to John Dewey [1859–1952] (1938), *Logic–The Theory of Inquiry*. New York (Ital. transl. 1949 Turin, 131) and informs us that in the language of some jurists of XVI cent. (for example Matteo Gribaldi Mofa [1504–1564] (1544), *De Methodo ac ratione studendi in jure*. Lugduni) the term *subjectum juris* was used to indicate the legal concepts (contract, will, judgement etc.).

[154] L.'s enunciation *res* as *subjectum juris* has no confirmation in Justinian Institutes, nor, to the best of my knowledge, in legal literature before L. Furthermore, in the late revision note "D" (see note 45, 301), "Est persona, nam cum rei videtur inesse ius aut obligatio, intellegitur persona indefinite qua rem habebit, ita ut res transeat cum iure et obligatione. Persona est subsistens rationale idque vel naturale vel civile. Naturale veluti Deus aut homo"; and therefore, "Res quoque sed modo iam dicto, *per reductionem ad personam* [italics added] censetur subiectum iuris et obligationis". Giovan Battista Agostino Bono [1731–1799] (see about L. Bulferetti (1947), "Agostino Bono giurisdizionalista piemontese editore e critico degli scritti giuridici del Leibniz". *Rivista di filosofia*, 137), one of the earliest commentators of L.'s juridical works, in his "Ad Partem Jurisprudentiae G.G. Leibnitii Praefatio", in Louis Dutens [1730–1812] (ed.) (1767), *Gothofredi Guillelmi Leibnitii, Opera omnia nunc primun collecta, in classes distributa, praefationibus et indicis exornata*. Genevae: apud Fratres de Tournes, t. 4, pars tertia, 18, so paraphrases the thought of the Philosopher, "Jura et obligationes acquiruntur rebus et personis, personam autem intelligimus non solum

thing is bequeathed for a service, the right [to that service] will remain in all of successors; if anyone holding office, albeit important, causes damage to someone else, the office in question will be obliged [for compensation, e. n.], and the obligation shall pass to the successors. Likewise, if something is bequeathed to a horse, for example trappings, it cannot be doubted that since the horse has been alienated, the thing passes to the [new] owner of the horse; the same right is applied to the slave, who is not to be considered as a person, but as a thing. In truth, in every real right the thing is the subject of obligation. Moreover, the whole matter of succession pertains to the subject, because succession is the movement of a right or of an obligation from one subject to another. Here too, topics that are common to many are to be discussed.

---

naturale uti homo, sed etiam civile uti collegium". In *Ars Combinatoria* (see note 54), 189, 42, we find the following affirmation: "Res sunt mobiles, immobiles, dividuae (homogeneae), individuae, corporales, incorporales; et speciatim: homo, animal cicur, ferum, rabiosum, noxium; equus, aqua, fundus, mare etc. *Et omnes omnino res de quibus peculiare est jus* [italics added]". Having, thus, every *res* its *ius peculiare*, it seems that this is the meaning we should give to the *reductio ad personam* of *res* as *subiectum iuris*, made by L. This passage of *Ars Combinatoria* and the definition of *res* in text do indeed appear consistent with Roman Law principles, if we consider that *res*, according to Romans, were entities, that is, terms of reference in law, different from *personae* (Umberto Vincenti (2007), *Categorie del diritto romano*. Napoli, 46); and if it is true that for Romans, the personal right is not the right of the person as such, but rather the *status*, *i.e.* a particular, not general, condition of the person, (Michele Barillari [1875–1965] (1913), *La dottrina del diritto di G. G. Leibniz*. Napoli, subsequently in (1915) *Società Reale di Napoli. Atti della Reale Accademia di Scienze Morali e Politiche*. vol. XLIII, Napoli, 74), then we could say the same about *res*, which also have their particular *status* in Roman law, for example *bona paraphernalia*, or dowry.

§. 16. The object of rights and obligation is the body of subject, a thing, a third person. The right over my body, as subject, is called freedom; the right in things is called faculty, and has the following species: *dominium directum* in the substance of the things; *utile*, that is, the right of use and enjoyment in the form[155]; the right of servitude

---

[155] *I.e.*, as in *dominium directum*, absolute ownership over the thing, that involves the right also to modify the substance (*materia*) of the same thing; *dominium utile* is the right only of use or enjoyment of a thing, respecting its conformation (*forma*). It is worth adding Berman, see note 723, 170, "The absence of full rights of property among feudal tenants as well as among the Franciscans gave impetus to the creation in the thirtheen century of the legal concept of *dominium utile* or 'beneficial ownership', which gave a right of possession and use but not disposal, as contrasted with 'direct ownership', *dominium directum*, which included a right of disposal. The holder of a *dominium utile* had the rights of a beneficiary of the holder of the *dominium directum* (...). Sixteenth-century German Romanists also gave new emphasis to the distinction between *dominium directum* and *dominium utile*" (Berman, see note 723, 168). Among these Romanists, according to Berman (see note 723, 170), the German jurist Johann Apel is worthy of note, "Ownership rights *in* a thing (*jus in re*) included, for Apel, not only full ownership (*dominium directum*) but also beneficial ownership (*dominium utile*), including the right to possess and enjoy the fruits of the land or goods of another. Such beneficial ownership had previously been classified as a right to a thing (*jus ad rem*), based on a contractual or other obligation, rather developed by Conrad Lagus [1500–1546], *dominium directum* lost its connotation *Herrshaft*, 'lordship', and became synonymous with *proprietas*, in German *Eigentum*, 'one's own'. At the same time, proprietary rights less than full ownership, such as the rights of lessee or pledgee, come to be classified as property rights in land or goods of another (*jus in re aliena*), rather than as part of the law of obligations. Apel's division of civil law into the law ownership and the law of obligations, controversial at the time came to prevail in Germany and other countries.(...) Everywhere in the West today [but not in Italy!, see art. 1376 of Italian civil code, 'In contracts whose object is the transfer of ownership of a given thing, the creation or transfer of a real property right or the transfer of rights, property, or the right are transmitted and can be purchased as a result of the consent of the parties legitimately

in parts of the form, that is, in qualities; the right of retaining and acquiring by *usucapio*[156] a condition, and other real rights. The right over a person is defined as authority, and varies in many ways, sometimes of life and death, sometimes of punishment, sometimes of reproach, etc. Obligation means not obstructing the freedom, faculty, and authority of another, the obstruction of which is called injury. And the obligation not to impede another's authority over me is positive, by virtue of which I must do or bear something. This is likewise called obligation κατ'ἐξοχήν [in Greek in the text, for excellence, absolute, e. n.]; the remaining obligations, *i.e.* not to impede the freedom of another and thus not to obstruct the freedom of another, or to seize his things, are mostly negative [not to do, e. n.]. Moreover, whatever interests me and indeed is either the thing itself, or something of equal worth or estimation, is also object of my right. Such matters that pertain to the price of things.

---

expressed.', e. n.], as in Apel's scheme, a simple contractual obligations to sell land, for example, does not in itself, without some form conveyance, normally give rise to a transfer of property rights in the land, valid against the whole world, but gives ride only to the right to remedy against the seller for breach of contract".

Berman's view of reducing the Western system of transfer of property rights exclusively to the Apel scheme, cannot be shared on this point. It should not be forgotten that Romans already held the view that the mere contract was unable in itself to transfer the *dominia rerum* (*traditionibus et usucapionibus, non nudis pactis dominia rerum transferuntur*, CI, 12, 3, 20).

[156] Du Plessis, see note 125, 184, "*Usucapio* was prescriptive acquisition—a person became owner of property by holding it for the prescribed period of time. It was of great importance in practice since it allowed persons who possessed property to convert their interest into full *dominium*. The consequence was to reduce the problems caused by uncertainty over ownership"; more in deep, see William A. Hunter (1903), *A Systematic and Historical Exposition of Roman Law in the Order of a Code*. London, 288.

§. 17. The cause of moral quality is nature and action. Nature is the cause of freedom and faculty and of the corresponding obligation in another not to impede. Action is the cause of authority over an acting person, to do or undergo something by acting on himself, or on his assets; and this is possession, or injury, or agreement (*conventio*)[157]. Possession grants a real right in the first place over my body, because firstly I possess the body, hence freedom, secondly over other things which belong to nobody, hence the faculty. Whence arises for me the right of claiming a thing as mine where I find it: and the obligation to the other of not impeding such a claim. Only in the state of nature does injury give the damaged entity the right to freedom, power and all authority, that is, the law of war against the offender who violates human society. But in the states, on the contrary, this permission was limited by the prince for equity, so that the damaged person must be content with estimation by value, punishment being reserved to the state if injury was intentionally inflicted. Injury, then, is a source of delict and quasi-delict[158].

The agreement contains within itself all the promises and acceptances to which there pertains the doctrine of interpretation of words, terms, etc. The quasi-contracts[159] pertain to a real right. Many rights and obligations, however, are not seen to descend from these sources of natural law, but from Law, for this reason, these rights and obligations derive from only one of these sources, namely from an agreement, because people have agreed to submit such matters to a legislator.

---

[157] George Mousourakis (2012), *Foundamentals of Roman Private Law*. Heidelberg: Springer, 187.

[158] See notes 126 and 127.

[159] See note 125.

§. 18. For this reason, all the obligations of public judgments, whether they tend to corporal punishment, or to a pecuniary punishment, pertain to the source of pacts: every subject of the state has promised that he would deem valid its decrees, either universal, such as laws, or singular, such as judgments. The law, however, rules that he who has promised must keep his promise: he is, therefore, obliged under the basis of the very pact of promised fidelity. Therefore, it is clear that to this topic constitutes a source of *Die Policey-Ordnungen*, namely the police regulations, through which are regulated life, way of life, cost of clothes, of banquets, briefly all the actions of subjects: by the same token, such regulations are designed to prevent criminal acts, those concerning crucial goods, namely public peace, the security of citizens and the respect of God and magistrates. The public law comes from the identical source of pacts, and likewise, finally, both civil and criminal trials, whose purpose is the enforcement of judgment, which is the actualization of moral qualities, so that whoever has authority or moral necessity also has natural authority or moral necessity.

§. 19. Thus, we have deduced the main chapters of the entire body of law. The modes of acquiring a right are as follows: 1) the law of nature, precisely the freedom and faculty to act over the things belonging to no one, § 17. 2) Succession §. 15, which does not produce any new right, but transfers the old right. Only descendants who were born as true scions of a family succeed without a testament, on the grounds of pure right, but this concerns only those goods belonging to the parent, because their soul was born in the manner of a vine-shoot from the soul of the parent; the intestate succession of others concerns the source of pacts, because it derives from law. Testaments, on the other hand, would be of no effect under pure right, if the soul were not immortal. But because the deceased still live [beyond earthly life, e. n.], they remain therefore masters of things, and the heirs they leave behind are to be regarded as representatives in their own affairs (*procuratores in rem suam*[160]). 3) The third way of acquiring a right is possession of a thing belonging to no one, with the intention to possess it in the future. From this arises the right to possess and manage for the future, which is a real right. 4) An agreement, such as an incorporeal delivery, through equivalent symbols to the thing, or words, that concern everything, descend from the body of civil right or law, as in the case of criminal actions and processes. An agreement, however, can be traced back not only to possession, but also to injury, because to deceive is to damage with intent. 5) Injury, as rupture of human society in its pure natural state, cancels out every right, or rather gives to one the absolute right over another and his things. This right is, however, restricted by the laws of the state.

§. 20. On the other hand, the causes of right in one person are a kind of loss of right in another and it concerns the process of acquiring obligation. Conversely, the ways of losing an obligation are causes of recovering a right, and can be defined as liberation. Examples include 1) death without heirs, 2) payment, to which there corresponds compensation, and 3) the agreement, to which forms part of law. I thus consider that I have sufficiently ordered the main chapters of right, on the basis of the most evident principles of pure right. There is no other cause of right and obligation, whether contrary and destructive, that is not contained in these principles. It requires a special effort to render the matter more specifically. The things we have said regarding the method of arranging right were

---

[160] Birks, see note 124, 127, "Formally a representative of me, in substance about your own business, you would be called a representative *in rem suam*, a representative in your own affair".

appropriately presented as the premise in this passage, because not only didactic, but polemical jurisprudence as well must be arranged according to this method.

§. 21. Neither should we omit, here, the counsels of illustrious men on the inclusion of polemic jurisprudence within the confines of the didactic form of this discipline. If the more frequent controversies are to be resolved by public authority, then a new accurately set out body of right is to be drawn up. In this respect, due attention should be paid to the splendid meditations of the illustrious Bacon, whose outstanding work is contained both in the *Essays*[161], and in the *Advancement of the Sciences*[162]. In short, it seems to me that three characteristics are necessary in the new body of law, which must be fully written out, without rambling digressions and set forth in an orderly manner. This will ensure the absence of repetition, obscurity, contradiction.

§. 22. It is time to return to our elements of law. In §. 7 above, these were divided into definitions and precepts. The definitions can be included in a book which, on the basis of its character, can be called Partitions of Law (a title that even the most illustrious man, Johann Otto Tabor [1604–1674][163], gave to one of his own works) in which the most common terms are clarified and explained, their definitions and subdivisions being described by the method of which I spoke. Certainly philological curiosities, synonyms are to be left aside. However, while obvious terms need no attention, the

---

[161] Francis Bacon (1638), *Sermones fideles, sive interiore rerum.* Lugduni Batavorum.

[162] See note 19.

[163] Johann Otto Tabor (1641), *Iurisprudentiae methodicae partitiones elementariae.* Strassburg: sumptibus Friderici Spoor.

meaning of any equivocal word, especially if it is conspicuous and is likely to become a source of confusion, should be made clear, choosing the best known signification. Meanwhile, considerable benefit will be gained by reading *Signpost of Right*[164], by the illustrious Johann Rebhan [1604–1689], who devoted this work first and foremost to the explanation of terms. On the other hand, causes, contraries, effects, objects and subjects do not belong to the definitions or explanations of terms, but to the rules or precepts.

§. 23. Let us now examine the Matter and Form of Jurisprudence Precepts. As far as Matter is concerned, only those that are expressly embodied in laws, are certain in terms of law and right and are minimally controversial should be included; similarly, only those that are still in use are to be given careful consideration, less attention being devoted to those that were repealed, for, it is necessary for the beginner to start from the current law, as we will show below. Additionally, it is advisable to exclude all precepts which are well-known from natural law itself and from sound principles of reason, or that even a peasant would be able to understand after having grasped the basic learned terms (which therefore we have premised in the definitions). In effect, almost the whole doctrine of agreements derives from natural law, while inheritance, due process and crimes arise from positive law[165]. Like-

---

[164] Johann Rebhan (Rebhannus) (1606), *Hodegeta juris*. Argentorati.

[165] The term *ius positivum* does not belong to Roman Law, which knows only the distinction between *ius scriptum* and *ius non scriptum*, Berger, see note 19, *ad vocem Ius scriptum*; the expression was used for the first time by Abelard [1079–1142] as opposed to *jus natural*, see Karl Olivecrona [1897–1980] (repr. 1971), *Law as fact*, London: the latter is made of eternal and immutable rules; the former is "posited" by man, therefore, according to Aquinas [1225–1274], it is conventional, see Annabel S. Brett (repr. 2003), *Liberty, Right and*

wise to be omitted, finally, are not so much juridical questions, but rather, issues that are of a historical nature, for example, why Justinian is called *Alamannicus* (victor of Alamanni), *Francicus* (victor of Franks)[166]; or philological, for example, whether the testament correctly derives from *testatio mentis,* that is, action of testifying to the will of the mind; or philosophical, for example, whether Justinian has rightly defined the right of passage (*iter*), drive (*actus*), way (*via*)[167]; whether *mutuum*[168] is a transference of ownership. Only those precepts which decide what is the right in some given case are to be proposed. Therefore, once all the following issues have been omitted, namely precepts that are 1) uncertain; 2) repealed; 3) well-known;

Nature. Cambridge, 93. In the English language the term *Positive law*, in the sense above, was used for the forst time by Thomas Hobbes [1588–1679] (1651), *Leviathan*. London, in R. Tuck (ed.) (1996), *Hobbes, Leviathan*. Cambridge, 197, "Another division of Laws, is into natural and Positive. Natural are those which have Laws from all Eternity; and are called not only Natural but also Moral Laws (…). Positive are those which have not been from Eternity; but have been made Laws by the will of those that have had the Sovereign power over others; and are either written, or made know to men, by some other argument of the will of their legislator.".

[166] So in Justinian Digest *Preamble*, "In Name of Our Lord Jesus Christ. The Emperor Caesar, Flavius, Justinianus, Alamannicus, Gothicus, Francicus, Germanicus, Anricus, Alanicus, Vandalicus, Africanus, Pious, Happy, Renowed, Victor and Triunpher, ever Augustus, To The Youth Desiderous of Learning The Laws"; see A.D. Lee (2007), *War in Late Antiquity: A social History*. Oxford: Blackwell Publishing, 39–40.

[167] Carey Miller, see note 121, 68.

[168] Birks, see note 124, 119, "This is (…) type of loan. We translate it as 'loan-for-consumption'. Not very elegant and not quite accurate, in the sense that money is not naturally 'consumed?', and if I borrow eggs I do not necessarily mean 'to consume' them. Perhaps I want to give them away or sell them or throw them at a politician. It makes no difference. So 'for consumption' is an approximation. (…) It is more to exact to say 'loan where repayment is to be made by way of exchange in kind'. But that is cumbersome. 'Exchange-loan' might be acceptable, but is not self-explanatory".

3) mot recounted in known sources, then this booklet of elements will be highly appreciated by virtue of its brevity and supreme readability.

§. 24. The form of the precepts consists in the orderly arrangement of titles and subtitles. The nature of titles should be that of definitions, so that it will be not disadvantageous if the precepts are inserted between the definitions even with other typefaces. Hence, firstly, care should be taken, as far as possible, to abstract general precepts. There are indeed some most general precepts, called *Brocardica*, and these are abstracted from various matters even of a completely different kind, for example, *every sort of loss of right is voluntary*, or *no one may be deprived of his right against his will*. This rule is so universal that it does not suffer any significant exception. Why therefore, is there a widespread tendency to add the condition: *unless as a penalty from a superior*? But the reason why they oppose this argument is that they fail to penetrate the principles of moral issues, for what is removed from a superior is removed from one who is consenting. More specifically, we have agreed, as argued above, that the acts of a superior are to be considered valid. However, a possible counterargument may consist in the existence of a superior with whom there was no agreement, for example, God, by right of creation. He, therefore, deprived the Egyptians, fully without their consent, of all their rights. But in order for the comparison to be correct, it is necessary to know that no right is given to God, and thus not even the removal of a right. Death is not properly the loss of right, because only the person in itself is lost. Nor does payment (which can even be paid to an unwilling recipient) cease to be valid, any more than the usufruct by consolidation[169]. The nudity of right[170] vanishes, not right itself, which, instead, is completed. I could show by means of countless examples how many times such *Brocardica* are built by a proliferation of captious statements that have no basis in necessity. But at times—it has to be admitted—we come across some *Brocardica* which of necessity have many exceptions, but I judge these to be of a somewhat inept kind. How often, in fact, is a rule made defective through a trivial fault that impairs its entire function. For the function of a rule is to calm the mind, which draws confidence from the certainty that the predicate mantains its validity for all subjects. But, if the rules have exceptions, or are misleading, then they cannot be trusted. What, therefore, is usually repeated, namely the assertion: *there is no rule without exception*, seems to me the same as the statement: *I am lying now*; or that of the Skeptics: *nothing is known, not even this, the affirmation that nothing is known.* We dealt with such statements in our *Specimen of Philosophical Questions Collected from Right, Question 12.* Now this rule at once asserts and denies itself. Because, in fact, no rule is without exception, and this very axiom is itself a rule, therefore it will not be without exception. Consequently, some rule is without exception. Then, because no rule is without exception; it is therefore false that no

---

[169] *I. e.* the merging of usufruct in property, that is the reversion of the right of *usus* and *fructus* to the owner, "A usufruct was terminated by the death of the usufructuary or by deprivation of civil law bearing-status (J. 2.4.3). The usual form of usufruct was for the lifetime of the usufructuary, but usufruct for a fixed term ended upon the death of usufructuary before the expiry of the period. *Upon termination, the rights of* usus *and* fructus *automatically reverted to the owner* (J. 2.4.4) [italics added]." (Carey Miller, see note121, 67).

[170] *I. e.*, for example, mere ownership (*nuda proprietas*) without any content (when the owner has no right to use the object or to take the fruits); by termination of the usufruct (see note 110) mere ownership ceases and the property right becomes complete and actual.

rule is without exception. But let us pass over this paradox, for what must meanwhile be regarded as certain is that this little saying conceals sloth and ignorance. For even among Grammarians (from whom this motto was taken) Franciscus Sanchez de las Brozas [1523–1601][171], and later Schoppe[172], have shown some rules that admit of no exception; in this regard, apparent counter-examples that are commonly considered by the uneducated to be instances of an exception are more properly to be analysed as either an ellipse, or a pleonasm of another word. The same vice reigns in philosophical rules, from which it has spread to juridical subjects. Indeed, as that most illustrious scholar Johann Adams Scherzer [1628–1683][173] has warned in the preface to his *Philosophical Manual*, among the rules one also finds certain maxims which have more delimitations than meanings: for example, *from such cause, results such an effect.* [Numerous] endeavours have been made, by resorting to hedges and subtle nuances, to defend such a distinction, but in the end [they] come back to this: *in univocal causes* [*i.e.* in specific causes, so that specific causes result in related effects, e. n.]. What is, on the other hand, a univocal cause? It can be defined as a circumstance in which precisely from such a cause there arises such an effect. The rule must therefore be conceived in the following manner: where such a cause results in such an effect; then from such a cause arises such an effect. If you were invited to a viewing of a show based on this inanity, could you stifle your laughter, my friends[174]? This may help to

---

[171] Franciscus Sánchez de las Brozas (1556), *De arte dicendi liber unus*. Salmantica: excudebat Andreas a Portonarijs; Id. (1970), *1: Opera grammatica- 2: Opera philologica:* T. 1-2. Hildesheim: Olms.
[172] Schoppe, see note 11.
[173] Johann Adam Scherzer (1658), *Vademecum sive manuale philosophicum quadripartitutm*. Lipsiae: Kirchenerus.
[174] Leibniz is quoting here from Horace [65 BC–27 BC.], *Ars Poetica*. 5.

explain why the most illustrious Thomasius[175] is at great pains to provide an accurate explanation of the philosophical rules and will, I sincerely hope, present it to the public before long. Likewise, as soon as possible, if God grants us strength, we will undertake to draw up a reformed version of the *Brocardica*, leading all of them to perfect universality, and rejecting as unfit those that cannot tolerate the latter condition. In the meantime, it is not necessary to paste onto a rule those limitations which, through combinations, can be deduced from the other rules that are expounded or have to be expounded in the same book. For example, whoever makes a promise must fulfill it; unless he has already done so, or unless he has been freed from the obligation, or can compensate in a different manner, etc. Why is there a need to add all this? By themselves, they are obvious from the rules that have to be set out, although useless repetitions and thick books are piled up in the attempt to present them yet again. So far, no true remedy has been found for these evils, thus I cannot determine which author of juridical rules should be recommended first and foremost; however, Augustinus Barbosa [1589–1649][176] and Juan Bernardo Diaz de Luco [1495–1556][177] are certainly to be commended, not to mention those who have sought to summarize the rules of right in large lexica *in folio*.

---

175 See note 148.

176 Augustinus Barbosa (1660), *Tractatus varii: quorum I. De axiomatibus iuris usu frequentioribus. II. De apellativa verborum-uutriusque iuris significatione. III. De locis communibus argumentorum iuris. Etc.* Lugduni: sumptibus Philippi Borde, Laurentii Arnaud, & Claudii Rigaud, in via Mercatoria, sub signo Temporis.

177 Juan Bernardo Diaz de Luco (1564), *Regulae iuris cum suis ampliationibus & restrictionibus, ex variis codicibus excerptae.* Lugduni: Apud Guliel. Rouillium.

§. 25. And these [are the problems, e. n.] concerning the most general precepts or *Brocardica*. Intermediate precepts, restricted to certain matters, although not so specific, follow now. For example, *no one to whom respect is owed is to be summoned before the judge*, not even such figures as a parent, an advocate, or a magistrate having the right of punishment, etc. And this is demonstrated by the nature of the summons before the Court. If this occurs by force; those who refuse are brought to court by compulsion. Instead, any person to whom reverence is owed should not be mistreated. Such a consideration is a principle of pure natural right, which is evident even to peasants. We must therefore make sure that, wherever possible, general rules are conceived in order to abbreviate the burden of learning. Thus the aim should be to determine whether it is possible to conceive a rule having a certain degree of necessity, which Aristotle termed καθόλου πρῶτον [in Greek in the text, universal principle, e. n.] by, that is, a reciprocal rule, such that the subject is equal to the predicate, so that the subject of this predicate cannot be found from the general considerations. There are matters that concern all those we studied in our *Combinatorial Art*[178]; for example: all and only those persons who hold another's things in their power are required to maintain an inventory or a sworn description of items. And reciprocally, he who is bound to such a specification has another's things in his power. In fact, even an heir who intends to renounce an insolvent inheritance[179] is bound to this sort of specification, because *a posteriori* it is evident that he has retained

[178] See note 54.

[179] The Latin text is "hereditatem, quae solvendo non est"; see the same sentence in *D.*35.2.3 and 42.6.1.2; Alan Watson (ed. 1985, reprint 2011), *The Digest of Justinian.* 4 vols., Philadelphia PA: Philadelphia University Press, vol. 3, translates these passages as "estate which is insolvent".

another's things. Similarly, on the matter of torture I conceive this general rule: *only a person who would be condemned,* rebus sic stantibus[180], *if the proceedings were civil, should be tortured in a criminal trial*. For in a criminal trial nobody is to be sentenced, unless he has confessed. Therefore, a person who has been demonstrated guilty of a crime should be compelled to confess. It follows that torture cannot be waived even for one who cannot prove his exception, *sondern muss er sie auf der Tortur erhalten.* For in civil proceedings, a person who cannot prove an exception[181] has to be condemned. This is the only rule equivalent to many types of sufficient evidence for torture, which commonly are applied. In this way in most matters the concept can be reduced to the reciprocal proposition. On this the most illustrious Johann Von Felden [d. c. 1668] gave many warnings, in his *Annotations to Hugo Grotius's Elements of Jurisprudence*[182], and in his *Elements of Jurisprudence*[183]. So much for the intermediate precepts. The most specific precepts, in truth, belong for the most part to positive right and they consist of formalities, and once you remove the general precepts, they are really rather few. Often, one rule or another may represent a whole title. As a model of this work will provide some excerpts, with

---

[180] This Latin sentence, is for "things thus standing"; largely used also in modern law (in public international law, for example, it means that a treaty is valid until a fundamental change in the circumstances which led the parties to enter into the treaty itself) in the text seems to mean "according the circumstances or facts of the proceedings".

[181] The term comes from Roman Legal System where an *exception* was a specific defence opposed to the plaintiff's claim to render it ineffective and exclude the defendant's condemnation; Berger, see note 19, *ad vocem Exceptio*.

[182] Johann von Felden (1653), *Iohannis a Felden I.V.D. Annotata in Hug. Grotium De jure belli et pacis.* Amstelodami: Apud Iodocum Ianssonium.

[183] Von Felden, see note 102.

God's help, from the books *On presumptions* by Giacomo Menochio [1532–1607] and *On Proofs* by Giovanni Mascardi [1540/45–1585] [184]. These books, however great, could be summarized in little more than 100 most natural rules. In this way it could be possible to derive all the remaining obvious consequences. We will therefore entitle our work: *Compendium for the Proof and Presumptions of Menochio and Mascardi.*

§. 26. From the titles and their arrangement, we come to subtitles. Subtitles include the following: form or definition, subject, cause, effect, contrary to or destructive of a given argument. I do not disregard the observation that different authors have distributed these topics differently, but when more accurately considered, all topics are reduced to these. In their partition, Matthaeus Wesenbeck [1531–1586][185] is especially diligent, and even those who have composed the classes of actions[186]: Johann Oldendorp [1488–1567][187] and Arnold van Haersolte [c. 1546–late 16th][188]. But it pertains to the doctrine of topics to talk more diffusely about the subtitles. Therefore, these subtitles are to be considered in any title or matter.

§. 27. And these topics concerning the Didactic Jurisprudence, or Elements of Right are to be learned not only by jurisconsults, but also by theologians and physicians. For

---

[184] Giacomo Menochio (Menochius) (1636), *De praesumptionibus, conjecturis, signis et indiciis commentaria.* Coloniae Allobrogum: Sumptibus Iacobi Crispini; Giovanni Mascardi (Mascardus) (1593), *De Probationibus.* Venetiis.

[185] Matthaeus Wesenbeck (1565), *Paratitla in Pandectarum Libros.* Basileae.

[186] See note 116.

[187] Johann Oldendorp (1543), *Actionum Forensium Progymnasmata in VII Classes Distincta.* Coloniae.

[188] Arnold van Haersolte (1583), *De Actionibus.* Antwerpiae.

it is fitting for each and every theologian, jurisconsult, and doctor to be familiar with the didactic part of theology, jurisprudence, and medicine. However, it is not necessary for the one to interfere in controversies and subtleties of the other, which are dealt with in the polemical part of each discipline. And I know that great men repented of having scorned jurisprudence in their youth, spurning much that could be useful for theologian, as we have demonstrated above in §. 5.

§. 28. We have thus dealt with Didactic Jurisprudence. Now we must turn to the Historical aspects. Historical Jurisprudence is both internal and external[189]: the former penetrates the very substance of the Jurisprudence; the latter is only a support, and necessary. The internal history of Right is that which examines the various rights of the republics: these once were in force according to the works of Aristotle and Theophrastus [c. 371 BC–287 BC], but they have not persisted until our time. We have the Mosaic laws in the Holy Scripture, of which, a little after Justinian, a certain Graeculus[190] undertook the comparison with the Romans, while today, in truth, Philipp Zepper [1592–1655][191] has brought to fulfillment a more

---

[189] Paolo Cappellini (1984), *Systema Iuris*. I, Milano, 244, points out that the originality of Leibniz—in his tension toward an humanitarian ideal of a systematic unification of the sources of the learning—has consisted in more than a discovery, because it applies to historiography the *locus* 'external-internal: a distinction widely used in humanitarian jurisprudence, which came from dialectical schemes.

[190] Unknown author (IV cent.) of the book *Collatio Legum Mosaicarum et Romanarum*, edited by Pierre Pithou [1539–1596] (1573) in Paris: Loiselius, and wrogly attributed to Licinius Rufinus [c. 185–c. 238]; see Moses Hyamson [1862–1954] (1913), *Mosaicarum Et Romanarum Legum Collatio with Introduction, Facsimile and Transcription of the Berlin Codex*. Oxford: I; 229.

[191] Philipp Zepper (1604), *Legum Mosaicarum forensium explanation*. Herbonae Nassorum: Corvinus.

accurate work on that matter. Traces of the the laws of the Egyptians, Persians, Scythians are found in Herodotus, in the fragments of Ctesias [440 BC?–after 397 BC?][192] and Diodorus [c. 90 BC–c. 27 BC][193]. Pausanias [110–180][194], in a very diligent way, enumerated the institutions of the Greeks, and those of our era such as another Pausanias: Johannes Meursius [1579–1639][195]. The laws of the Romans may be known adequately from their historians, on which *infra*. First Friedrich Lindenbrog [1573–1648][196] collected and published in a single volume the laws of people before the Barbarians became civilised, that is the laws of the Longobards, Goths, Franks, the Salic Laws, and other documents of similar antiquity. I will say nothing about the Bullarium of the Popes[197], nor of the Gallic code[198], and the *Landrecht*[199]

---

[192] Ctesias (1557), *Ex Ctesia Agatarchide et Mnenone excerptae historiae*. [S. l.]
[193] Diodorus Siculus (1611), *Bibliotheca, sive rerum gestarum libri XVII*. Hannoniae.
[194] Pausanias (geogropher), *Ἑλλάδος περιήγησις*, in William Henry Samuel Jones [1876–1963] (1918–1935), *Pausanias, description of Greece*. V voll., Cambridge MA.
[195] Johannes Meursius (1617), *Atticarum lectionum libri IV*. Lugduni Batavorum; Id. (1624), *Athenae Atticae sive de Praecipuis Athenarum antiquitatibus*. Lugduni Batavorum.
[196] Friedrich Lindenbrog (1613), *Codex legum antiquarum, in quo continentur Leges Wisigothorum, Edictum Theodorici Regis, Lex Burgundionum, Lex Salica, Lex Alamannorum, Lex Baivvariorum, Decretum Tassilonis Ducis, Lex Ripuariorum, Lex Saxonum, Angliorum et Werinorum, Frisionum, Longobardorum, Constitu-tiones Siculae sive Neapolitanae, Capitulare Karoli M. et Hludowici Impp. &c.* Francofurti: Apud Johannem & Andream Marnios & consortes.
[197] Laerzio Cherubini [d. c. 1626] (ed.) (1638), *Bullarium Romanum novissimum: ab Leone Magno usque ad S.D.N. Urbanum VIII*, 4 vols. Romae.
[198] (1600), *Le corps du droit François avec amples annotations et observations*. Coloniae Allobrogum.

and Saxon *Weichbild*[200], the statutes of the Poles[201], the Body of Prussian Right[202], the customs of the Italians extensively collected by Cardinal Domenico Toschi [1535–1620][203], nothing of the Saxon-Hungarian Rights, the customs of the Marks, and the other almost endless costoms of different peoples. From all these others collected in various places, if God is willing, we will one day write a Legal Theater, and compose παραλλήλως [in Greek in the text, in parallels, e. n.] of all of the peoples, places, times on all of the [juridical] matters. The history of Roman law, in particular, was also drafted by Valentin Forster [1530–1608] in the *History of the Law*[204] and Jacques Godefroy [1587–1652] in his *Handbook*[205]; I miss, however, a more particular survey, which would focus on what has been changed afterwards either by some Tribune through *Plebiscita*[206], or by some Consul or other through *Senatusconsulta*[207], or by the Praetor

---

[199] (1566), *Kayserlich und Königlish Land–und Lehenrecht satzungen, sitten unf gebreuch wie die unsere Teutsche Vorfaheren lang wol hergebracht und erhalten (Speculum suevicum)*. Francofurti.

[200] (1482), *Sächsiches Weichbild, Lehenerecht und Remissorium mit Glosse*. Augusta Vindelicorum.

[201] Johann Herburt de Fulstein [1508–1576] (ed.) (1563), *Statuta regni Poloniae in ordine alphabetici digesta*. Craccoviae.

[202] (1584), *Corpus juris Prutenicum:–Jus Culmense*. Thorunii; (1620) *Landrecht des Herzogtums Preussen*. [S.l.]

[203] Domenico Toschi (1620), *Selecta de jure statuum in Imperio sive de Regum, Principum tam ecclesiasticorum quam secularium nec non Comitum et Civitatum privilegiis, iuribus et consuetudunibus*. Francofurti.

[204] Valentin Forster (1565), *De historia iuris civilis romani, libri tres*. Basileae.

[205] Jacques Godefroy (1654), *Manuale Juris Seu Parva Juris Mysteria*. Genevae: Antonius.

[206] Berger, see note 19, *ad vocem Plebiscitum*, "Legislative measure passed by the assembly of the plebeians".

[207] Berger, see note 19, *ad vocem Senatusconsultum*, "Decisions, decrees of the senate issued in response to request for advice from

through *Edicta*[208], or by the Emperor through *Constitutiones*[209], until Roman law finally developed in this form. Therefore, we, who gladly attempt things neglected by others, will treat this matter at some time with a booklet: *The Authors of the Roman Law*.

§. 29. The External History, necessary for jurisprudence, is the Roman History which helps to understand Civil Law, the Ecclesiastical History to penetrate Canon law; the History of the middle ages to decipher Feudal Law, and of our time to comprehend the Public Law.

§. 30. Roman history is fourfold: of the Free Republic, the Augustan history, the history of the Greek emperors before Justinian, and then, after Justinian. The history of the free republic has been handed down both in the Lucius Annaeus Florus [d. 130] *Compendium of the Roman History*, adorned by Johann Freinsheim [1608–1660][210], and in the other Florus[211], the commentator of Livy, on which Martial [c. 41–c. 102]:

Pellibus exiguis arctatur Livius ingens,

---

one of the high magistrates who after presenting the matter asked the senators for their inidividuals opinions".

208 Berger, see note 19, *ad vocem Edictum*, "Either the whole edict published by the magistrate on the album whe he assumed his office or a single clause thereof".

209 Berger, see note 19, *ad vocem Consitutio*, "It is a general term wchich embraces all types of imperial enactment.".

210 Johann Freinsheim [1608–1660] (ed.) (1632), *Lucii Annaei Flori Rerum romanarum editio nova, accurante Joanne Freinshemio*. Argentorati.

211 Lucius Annaeus Florus [d. 130], *Epitome de Tito Livio*. It seems to be the same Florus (see note 210). The misunderstanding concerning two different writers may have occurred because of the vexed question relative to the biography of the historian; see about Jolanda Giaccone de Angeli (ed.) (1977), *Patercolo e Floro*. Torino, 303–305.

Quem mea vix totum bibliotheca capit[212];

then in Marcus Junianius Justinus [c. 2th cent, abridger of Pompeus Trogus [fl. 1th-cent. BC][213], which Matthias Bernegger [1582–1640[214] accuralety refined. In undoubtedly more detailed terms of a description of Roman history before Augustus Livy of Padua [59 BC–17 AD][215] has been provided by Dionysius of Halicarnassus [c. 60 BC–after 7 BC][216], and Plutarch [45–120] in the *Parallels*[217]. Cassius Dio [155–235][218], in truth, has consecrated to memory the transition of Rome from democracy to the monarchy. It will not be fruitless to add more recent authors: Johann Graf Zamoyski [c.1540–c.1605][219], Carlo Sigonio [1520–1584[220], Francesco Robortello [1516–1567][221], Paolo Manuzio [1512

---

[212] Martial, *Epigrammata libri*, XIV, 190, "In vellum small huge now Livy is dressed;/My bookshelves could not him uncompressed", thus translated by John Wight Duff (1963), *A Literary History of Rome*. London, 467.

[213] Marcus Junianius Justinus [c. 2th cent.] (1630), *Justinus Trogi Pompeii Historiarum Epitomator*. Francofurti; of Trogus [fl. 1th cent. BC] *Historiae Philippicae* abridged by Justinus in the book just mentioned, we have only *Fragments*, see Otto Seel [1907–1975] (ed.) (1956) *Pompei Trogi Fragmenta*. Lipsiae.

[214] Matthias Bernegger (1631), *Ivstini In historias Trogi Pompeii epitomarum editio nova*. Argentorati.

[215] Livy, *Ab Urbe condita*.

[216] Dionysius of Halicarnassus, *Antiquitatum Romanarum libri XI*.

[217] Plutarch, *Vitae parallelae*.

[218] Dio Cassius (1606), *Historiae Romanae libri XLVI*. Hanae.

[219] Johann Graf Zamoyski (1563), *De Senatu Romano libri duo*. Venetiis. Apud Iordanum Ziletum.

[220] Carlo Sigonio (1579), *Historiarum de occidentali imperio libri 2*. Basileae.

[221] Francesco Robortello (1559), *De vita et victu populi Romani sub imperatoribus Caes. Augustis*. Bononiae.

–1574][222], Adrien Turnèbe [1512–1565[223], Justus Lipsius [1547–1606][224], Joseph Scaliger [1540–1609][225], Thomas Dempster from Muresk [1579–1625][226], Ottavio Ferrari [1607–1682][227], Fortunio Liceti [1577–1657][228], Jan Gruter [1560–1627], in first place his *Critical Torch* (that is, the Treaty of Philological Treaties) and the *Inscriptions*[229], on the supplements of which the most illustrious Thomas Reinesius [1587–

---

[222] Paolo Manuzio (1557), *Antiquitatum romanarum liber de legibus: index rerum memorabilium*. Parisiis: Apud Bernardum Turrisanum, via Iacobęa, in Aldina bibliotheca.

[223] Adrien Turnèbe (1597), *Lucubrationes Variæ. C. Plinii Historiæ naturalis Præfatio emendata & annotationibus illustrata. In M. T. Ciceronis I. Academicas Quæstiones, II. De Fato, III. De Legibus libros tres, una cum Apologia, IV. In Orationem pro C. Rabirio perduellionis reo, Commentarii eruditiss.* Heidelbergae: apud Hieronymum Commelinum.

[224] Justus Lipsius (1600), *Della grandezza di Roma e del svo imperio.* Roma: Appresso Stefano Paolini.

[225] Probably, Joseph Justum Scaliger and others (1603), *Inscriptiones Antiquae totius orbis Romani: in corpus absolutiß. redactae ; Cum Indicib. XXV.* Heidelbergae: Commelinus Cadorinum [not included in AA VI, 2, sources directory].

[226] Thomas Dempster (1613), *Antiquitatum Romanarum corpus absolutissimum*. Lutetiae Parisiorum.

[227] Ottavio Ferrari (1642), *De re vestiaria.*Patavii.

[228] The works of Fortunio Liceti, physician and philosopher, are almost all on medicine and on widely varying topics, for example, Id. (1634), *De monstrorum caussis, natura, et differentiis libri duo* (...). *Multis illustrium autorum locis difficillimis explanatis de masculo parturiente, de feminis in viros mutatis, de hermaphroditorum natura* (...). Patavii: Apud Paulum Frambottum; the books that seem to be related to the Roman customs could be, Id. (1645), *De anulis antiquis liber singularis*. Utini; Id. (1662), *De lucernis antiquorum reconditis libb.*. Patavii: apud Matthaeum Cadorinum [not included in AA VI, 2, sources directory].

[229] Jan Gruter (1602–1634), *Lampas, sive fax artium liberalium*. 7 vols., Francofurti: prodit sumtibus Ionæ Rhodii e Collegio Palthenianiano; Id. (1602), *Inscriptiones antiquae totius orbis Romani in corpus absolutissimum redactae*. [S.l.]: Of. Commeliniana.

1667][230] wore himself out. I will not say anything about the *Pallium*[231] by Claude Saumasie [1588–1653] and the *Roman Army*[232], or the *As*[233] by Guillaume Budé [1467–1540], or the *Sesterces*[234] by Johannes Friedrich Gronovius [1611–1671], or the *Paenula*[235] by Bartolus Bartholinus [d. 1690], or the *Adversaries*[236] by Caspar von Barth [1587–1658], or on the various works by others writers of Roman history. We could extend this list by adding those who in the notes to the authors have compiled their own books of Collects for the occasion. This history has made it possible to outline the Laws of the Twelve Tables, the Laws of the Praetors[237], the origin of the Jurisconsults and many other rules, which Romans respected in the age of Cicero or before. At that time, the Roman Jurisprudence never deviated from natural law, because the laws were not bent to the whims of the despots.

---

230 Thomas Reinesius (1682), *Syntagma inscriptionum antiquarum: cum primis Romæ veteris, quarum omissa est recensio in vasto Jani Gruteri opere cujus hoc dici possit Supplementum; opus posthumum*. Lipsiæ: Sumptibus Jo. Fritschii hæred. & Jo. Fr. Gleditsch, typis Johann Erici Hahnii.

231 Claude Saumaise (1622), *Notae in Q. Sept. Florentis Tertulliani librum De pallio*. Lutetiae Parisiorum: Sumptibus Hieronymi Drouart.

232 Claude. Saumaise (1657), *De re militari romanorum liber*. Lugduni Batavorum.

233 Guillaume Budé (1516), *De asse et partibus ejus libri quinque*. Parisiis: Badius.

234 Johannes Friedrich Gronovius (1643), *De sestertiis commentarius*. Daventriæ.

235 Bartolus Bartholinus (1655), *Commentarius de paenula*. Hafniae: sumptibus G. Holstii, Typis viduae M. Martzani.

236 Caspar von Barth (1624), *Adversariorum commentariorum libri LX*. Francofurti: Aubry & Schleich.

237 Berger, see note 19, *ad vocem Jus Praetorium*, "'The law which the praetors introduced in order to support, to supplement or to amend the jus civile (*D.* 1.1.7.1)'".

§. 31. Augustan history extends from Augustus [63 BC–14 AD] to Constantine the Great [after 280?–337]. This account of history also includes various books of the historians edited by Friedrich Sylburg [1536–1596][238], and several times rearranged in Belgium. Dio Cassius [155–235][239], Suetonius [70–130][240], Tacitus [56–after 117][241], Velleius [c. 19 BC–c. 31 AD][242], the Greek writer Herodian [170–249][243], Aelius Lampridius [4th-cent][244], and others of lesser value should also be mentioned, for example, the illustration of the *Panegyrics* of various [writers] who are now for the most part added to the *Epistles* of Pliny the Younger [61–c. 115][245]. To these should be added those who flourished under the Emperors: Philo [c. 25 BC–c. 50 AD][246], Josephus [37–c. 100][247], Martial [c. 41–c. 102][248], Statius [c. 45–c. 96][249]; and even Ecclesiastical writers: Tertullian [160–220][250],

---

[238] Friedrich Sylburg (1588), *Historiae Romanae Scriptores*. Francofurti: apud Andreæ Wecheli heredes, Claudium Marnium, & Ioann. Aubrium.

[239] See note 248.

[240] Suetonius *De XII Caesaribus libri VIII.*

[241] Tacitus, *Annales*.

[242] Velleius Paterculus, *Historiae Romanae ad Vinicium libri II.*

[243] Herodian of Alexandria (1535), *Historiarum libri IX.* Basileae

[244] Aelius Lampridius, one of the six Scriptores in Isaac Casaubon (ed.) (1606), *Historiae Augustae. Scriptores sex*. Parisiis.

[245] Pliny the Younger (1606), *Epistolae et Panegyricus*. Coloniae Allobrogum.

[246] Philo of Alexandria, *De legatione ad Gaium*. For news about the kingdom of the emperor Caligula (12–41) [not included in AA VI, 2, sources directory].

[247] Josephus Titus Flavius, *De bello Judaico libri VII.* For news about about the kingdom of the emperor Vespasian (9–79).

[248] Martial, see note 212. For news about emperor Domitian (51–96).

[249] Statius, *Silvae.* For news about Emperor Domitian (51–96). [not included in AA VI, 2, sources directory].

[250] Tertullian, *Liber de Pallio* in Claude Saumasie see note 231. Tertullian explains the reason to wear the mantle of philosophers,

Cyprian [200–258][251], Eusebius [263–339][252]. On the other hand, under the Emperors, Roman law deviated substantially from its ancient simplicity. First Augustus introduced the *Fideicommissa*[253] and codicils (*codicilli*[254]), under Hadrian the *Edictum Perpetuum* was prepared[255]; partly the Code, partly the jurisconsult fragments indicate what Marcus Aurelius [121–180], Lucius Verus [130–169], Marcus Aurelius Commodus [161–192], Septimius Severus [145–211] and Antoninus Pius [86–161], Diocletian [244–311] and finally Maximian [c. 250–c. 311] would later gather.

§. 32. Greek history before Justinian, from Constantine the Great [after 280?–337] onward, can be drawn from the writers of ecclesiastical and profane history: Ammianus Marcellinus [c. 332–after 391][256], John Zonaras [fl. 12th-cent.][257], Paulus Orosius [c. 375–c. 420][258], Jor-

---

according to the Greek style, instead of Roman *toga*, and gives news about the society of his era.

[251] Cyprian, *Ad Donatum*. In this work, Cyprian describes the decadence of Roman society, gladiatorial shows, theater, unjust courts, the emptiness of political success etc. [not included in AA VI, 2, sources directory].

[252] Eusebius of Caesarea (1544), *Ecclesiasticae historiae Eusebii Pamphili libri X. Ejusdem de Vita Constantini libri V.* Lutetiae Parisiorum.

[253] See note 122.

[254] Berger, see note 19, *ad vocem Codicilli*, "A written document containing dispositions of a testator to be valid after his death (*mortis causa*), but not an institution of an heir which was permissible only in a testament. The recognition of *codicilli* is somehow connected with the insitition of *fideicommissa* (under Augustus). (…)".

[255] Berger, see note 19, *ad vocem Edictum perpetui Hadriani*. "A revision and codification of the praetorian and aedilian edicts, made by the jurist Salvius Julianus at initiative of the emperor Hadrian toward the end of his reign (after AD. 132) (…)".

[256] Ammianus Marcellinus (1636), *Rerum gestarum qui de XXI supersunt libri XVIII*. Parisiis.

[257] John Zonaras (1557), *Compendium Historiarum, in tres tomos distinctum*. Basileae [not included in AA VI, 2, sources directory].

nandes [fl. 660][259]; Procopius [500–565], both in the formerly well-known *History*, and especially in the *Secret History*, where he revealed the vices of Justinian, which was published for the first time by Niccolò Alemanni [1583–1626], and was revised by the illustrious Johann Eichel of Helmstedt [1621–1688][260]. The Englishman Thomas Ryves [1583–1652] wrote an *Apology of Justinian against Procopius*[261] and Paganino Gaudenzi [1595–1649] an elegant treaty *On the customs of the Justinian century*[262]. Also to be read here are Sidonius Apollinaris [c. 430–c. 486][263], Ausonius [310–395][264], Claudius Claudianus [c. 370–c. 404][265], the *Epistles* of Quintus Aurelius Symmachus [340–402][266]. One may also add the *Knowledge of the Eastern and Western Empire*[267] edited

---

[258] Paulus Orosius (1583), *Adversus paganos historiarum libri septem*. Coloniae.

[259] Jornandes (1597), *De Getarum sive Gothorum Origine et rebus gestis*. Lugduni Batavorum.

[260] Procopius of Caesarea in Niccolò Alemanni Johann Eichel von Rautenkron (eds.) (1654), *Anekdota Seu Historia Arcana Procopii Caesariensis*. Helmestadii: Mullerus.

[261] Thomas Ryves (1626), *Imperatoris Iustiniani Defensio Adversus Alemannum*. Londini.

[262] Paganino Gaudenzi (1654), *Liber de Justinianaei seculi moribus nonnullis: cum ejusdem dissertatione de successione foeminarum*. Argentorati: typis et sumptibus Friderici Spoor.

[263] Sidonius Apollinaris, *Epistulae* in Jean Savaron (ed.) (1609), *Caii Sollii Apollinaris Sidonis, Opera*. Parisiis.

[264] Ausonius in Josef Justus Scaliger [1540–1609] (ed.) (1575), *D. Magni Ausonii, Opera*. Lugduni.

[265] Claudius Claudianus in Michael Dewar (ed. and transl.) (1966), *Claudian Panegyricus de Sexto Consulatu Honorii Augusti*. Oxford: Clarendon Press; see also by the same Claudius Claudianus, *De bello gotico*, in Giovanni Garuti (ed) (1991), *Cl. Claudiani, De Bello Gothico*. L'Aquila [not included in AA VI, 2, sources directory].

[266] Quintus Aurelius Symmachus (1606), *Epistularum libri X*. Parisiis.

[267] Guido Panciroli (1593), *Notitia utraque dignitatum cum orientis tum occidentis ultra Arcadii Honoriique tempora: et in eam Guidi*

with notes by Guido Panciroli [1523–1599], helpful for understanding book 1.10 [That no heretic, pagan or Jew shall have, possess or circumcise a Christian slave], 11 [Concerning pagan sacrifices and temples], 12 [Concerning those who flee to the churches or raise a disturbance there] of the *Codex*[268]. It is also useful to read the *Anti-Tribonian*[269] by François Hotman [1524–1590].

§. 33. The subsequent Greek history is to be drawn from Georgius Cedrenus [fl. 11th-cent.][270], the dignities of the court from the *Book of the Duties*[271] by the Kouropalates [*i.e.* Georgius Codinus also called Kouropalates, beg. 15th-cent.–c. 1453]. To this should be added the two Greek authors, of whom the one wrote the *History of Mauritius*, the other the *History of the Capture of Constantinople*, both edited with notes by the Jesuit Pontanus Jakob Spanmüller [1542–1626]. I do not remember the names because I do not have the appropriate books[272].

Panciroli commentarium. Venetiis: apud Franciscum de Franciscis Senensem.

[268] The translation of these titles of the *Codex* is by Fred H. Blume [1875–1971, *Annotated Justinian Code*, http://www.uwyo.edu/lawlib/ /blume-justinian/ajc-edition-1/, of which I will also avail *infra* in §§. 57. 58 [accessed on 4 may 2015].

[269] François Hotman (1645), *Antitribonianus sive dissertatio de studio legum, scripta Ao. 1567 ex sententia Mich. Hospitalii et post obitum auctoris edita Ao. 1603*. Hamburgi.

[270] Georgius Cedrenus (1566), *Annales, sive historiae ab exordio mundi ad Isacium Comnenum usque compendium.* Basileae: Oporinus et Episcopius.

[271] Georgius Codinus (1596), *Georgii Codini (sive, ut volgo Curopalatae) de Officialibus Palatii Constantinopolitani, & officiis magnae ecclesiae.* [S.l.].

[272] The authors whose names L. does not remember are: Theophylact Simocatta [7th-cent.], George Sphrantzes [1401–c. 1478, Georgius Trapezuntius, alias George of Trebizond [1395–1472 or 1473] (1604), *Theophylacti Simocattae Ex-Praefecti, Et Observatoris Coactorum, Historiae Mauricii Tiberii Imp. Lib. VIII.. Item Georgii Phranzae Protovestiarii Chronicorum De Ultimis Orientalis Imperii*

Finally, the Greek Laonikos Chalkokondyles [c. 1423–1490] described in detail the origin and deeds of the Turks[273]. The history of the Saracens was written by Georgius Elmacinus [1205–1273] [274]. The expeditions in Palestine, or the holy war, are related in the great book entitled *The Deeds of God through the Franks*[275]. The subsequent Laws of the Greece are in the *Basilica*[276], in the *Epitome*[277] of Harmenopoulos and in other fragments diligently collected by Jacques Godefroy, in the *Handbook*[278], which I will not copy out here. Jacques Cujas [1522–1590][279] illustrated this Greek law in a precise way. In our time, Charles Annibal Fabrot [1580–1659][280] de-

---

Temporibus, De Sultanorum Osmanidarum origine ...post captam Costantinopolim libri III. Epistola Georgii Trapezuntii, Qva Ioannem Palaeologum Imp. Hortatur, Vt Ad Synodum In Italia celebrandam proficiscatur. Omnia Ex Bibliotheca Sereniss. Maximiliani Utriusque Bavariae Principis deprompta, in latinum conversa, et Notis illustrata A Iacobo Pontano Societatis Iesu. Ingolstadii: Sartorius.

[273] Laonikos Chalcocondyles (1615), *Atheniensis Historia de origine ac rebus gestis imperatorum Turcicorum*, Coloniae Allobrogum.

[274] Georgius Elmacinus (1625), *Historia Saracenica, qua res gestae Muslimorum inde a Muhammede Arabe, usque ad initium imperii Atabacaei ... explicantur.* Lugduni Batavorum: tyrogr. Erpeniana, prostant apud Johannem Maire, & Elzevirios.

[275] Guibert de Nogent [1053–1124] (1611), *Gesta Dei per Francos siue Orientalium expeditionum et Regni Francorum Hierosolimitani Historia.* Hanoviae: Typis Wechelianis, apud heredes Ioan. Aubrii.

[276] Berger, see note 19, *ad vocem Basilica*, "A Byzantine codification (termed by Byzantine writers *Basilikos* [sc. *nomos*], i.e. imperial [law]) in sixsty books. (…)".

[277] Constantine Harmenopoulos [1320–c.1385] (1566), *Epitome iuris civilis ex libris pandectarum, codicis, institutionum, et Iustiniani aliorum que principum novellis constitutionibus.* Coloniae Agrippinae: Fabritius & Gymnich.

[278] See note 205.

[279] Jacques Cujas (1566), *Basilicon liber 60*. Lugdunum.

[280] Charles Anibal Fabrot (1647), *Basilicon libri LX... Carolus Annibal Fabrotus,... latine vertit et graece edidit, ex bibliotheca regis christianissimi.* S.l.: s.n.

voted much care to this task. The *Knowledge of Basilica*[281] by Joseph Marie Suarès [1599–1677] has been added to the French edition of the *Basilica*. Up to now many historical narratives lie hidden not only in the East but also in the libraries of Europe. However, there is considerable hope that the *Chronicon Budense*[282], recently translated in Vienna, has collected all of the histories of this kind. Time will gradually make all of these works known.

§. 34. After Roman history, which is useful for understanding Civil Law, there follows the Ecclesiastical history for penetrating Canon Law, which is either total or partial. The total itself is, in turn, either compendious or in detail. It is in detail in the *Centuries of Magdeburg*[283], in the *Annals*[284] by Cesare Baronio [1538–1607], in the *Annals*[285] by Abraham Bzowski [1567–1637], which continue those by Baronio. To these should be added Agostino Tornielli [1543–1622][286] and Jacques Salian [1558–1640][287]. Compendious is [the work] by Johann Pappus [1549–1610][288], by Johann Heinrich Hot-

---

[281] Joseph Marie Suarès (1647), *Notitia Basilicorum*. Parisii.

[282] János Horváth [1878–1961] (ed.) (1973), *Chronica Hungarorum Finita Bude Anno Domini 1473 in Vigilia Penthecostes Per Andream Hess*. Budapesten: Zrínyi.

[283] Matthias Flacius Illyricus [1520–1575] and others (1554–1574), *Ecclesiastica Historia secundum XIII centurias, per aliquot studiosos et pios viros vulgo Centuriatores in urbe Magdeburgica*. Basileae: Per Ioannem Oporinum.

[284] Cesare Baronio (1591), *Annales ecclesiastici*. Romae.

[285] Abraham Bzowski (1621–1630), *Annales ecclesiastici post Card. Baronium*. (voll. 13-19), Coloniae Agrippinae.

[286] Agostino Tornielli (1616), *Annales sacri et profani, ab orbe condito ad eundem Christi passione redemtum: opus Card. Baronii annalibus prævium et connexum*. Francofurti.

[287] Jacques Salian (1620), *Annales ecclesiastici Veteris Testamenti... Tomi IV. Volumine III*. Coloniae Agrippinae: Sumpt. Antonii Hierati.

[288] Johann Pappus (1584), *Historia ecclesiastica*. Argentorati.

tinger [1620–1667][289], who died tragically and undeservedly not long ago; mention should also be made of the *Gothana*[290], which appeared not long afterwards; the *Universal History*[291] by Johannes de Laet [1581–1649], in which, always with great care, the first half was devoted to Ecclesiastical deeds; the *Baronian Epitome*[292] by Henri de Sponde [1568–1643], and the Epitome of the *Centuries of Magdeburg*[293] by Lucas Osiander the Elder, [1534–1604].

§. 35. The Ecclesiastical Partial History concerns the Rites, Martyrs, Churc Fathers, Dogmas, Councils, Heresies, Regimes, Popes, and Ecclesiastical Orders. On the Rites we have Giovan Battista Casali [1578–1648][294]. To this should be added, in the first place, the material which the illustrious Matthias Zimmermann [1625–1689] collected in alphabetical order in the *Commentary to the Tertullian's saying: Christians are made, not born, Part.*

---

[289] Johann Heinrich Hottinger (1655), *Historia Ecclesiastica Novi Testamenti.* Hanoviae: M. Schufelberger. Hottinger drowned with his three children in the river Limmat, as the boat on which he was was sailing capsized.

[290] Veit Ludwig von Seckendorf [1626–1692] (1660), *Compendium Historiae Ecclesiasticae in usum Gymnasii Gothani.* Gothae.

[291] Johannes de Laet (1643), *Compendium historiae universalis civilis & ecclesiaticae: tam Romanae quam Protestantium selectissimis rebus refertissimum ab Augusto ad annum usq[ue] Christi Iesu M DC XL. Deductum*, Lugduni Batavorum: Apud Franciscum Hegerum.

[292] Henri de Sponde (1613), *Annales ecclesiastici ex XII tomis Caesaris Baronii ... in epitomen redacti.* Parisiis.

[293] Lucas Osiander the Elder (1592–1612), *Epitomes historiae ecclesiasticae centuriae XVI.* Tubingae: apud Georgium Gruppenbachium. The work is considered to be a summary and continuation of the *Centuries of Magdeburg* (see note 283).

[294] Giovan Batista Casali (1645), *De veteribus christianorum ritibus.* Romae: Phaeus.

I[295]. Here can be read *The Observations to Baronio* by Isaac Casaubon [1559–1614][296], the Writings by Richard Montagu [1577–1641] [297] which are contrary both to Baronio, and to Casaubon, *The Apparatus*[298] by Claude Saumasie [1588–1653], the various treaties by Jean Daillé [1594–1670][299]. On the Martyrs there are Martyrologies [300] of diverse authors, such as Bede [the Venerable, 672–735], Usuard [Benedictine monk of the Abbey of Saint-Germain-des-Prés, Paris, d. 875], Jan Vermeulen [1533–1585], Baronio, and the *Treaty on the Tortures of the Ancient Christians*[301] by Nicola Gallonio [1556–1605], which also belongs to this subject. Likewise the Lives of the Saints gathered in large tomes by

---

[295] Matthias Zimmermann (1662), *Dissertatio historico-theologica ad illus. Tertull. Apolog. cap. XVIII: fiunt non nascuntur Christiani.* Lipsiae: impensis Christiani Kirchneri.

[296] Isaac Casaubon (1614), *De rebus sacris et ecclesiasticis exercitationes XVI, ad Cardinalis Baronii prolegomena in Annales, & primam eorum partem, de Domini Nostri Iesu Christi nativitate, vita, passione, assumtione*. Londinii: Ex officina Nortoniana apud Ioan. Billium.

[297] Richard Montagu (1636), *Analecta ecclesiasticorum commentationum.* Londini: Impress. per M. Flesher & R. Young.

[298] Claude Saumaise (1649), *De primatu papae. Pars prima cum Apparatu etc.*, Lugduni Batavorum: Ex Officina Elzeviriorum.

[299] For example: Jean Daillé (1661), *De sacramentali sive auriculari Latinorum confessione disputatio*. Genevæ: sumpt. Ioannis Antonii & Samuelis De Tournes.

[300] Martyrologies: Bede (1564), *Martyrologium Venerabilis Bedae presbiteri.* Antuerpiae: ex. off. Christophori Plantini; Usuardus (1538), *Martyrologium.* Strassburg: Jakob Cammerlander; Jan Vermeulen (Molanus (1573), *Usuardi martyrologium, quo romana ecclesia, ac permultae aliae utuntur; iussu Caroli Magni conscriptum.* Lovanii: H. Wellaeum; Cesare Baronio (1631), *Martyrologium Romanum.* Moguntiae: Schönwetter.

[301] But is Antonio, not Nicola, Gallonio (1591), *Trattato de gli instrumenti di martirio, e delle varie maniere di martoriare usate da' gentili contro cristiani, descritte et intagliate in rame.* Roma: A. e G. Donangeli.

Laurentius Surius [1522–1578][302]. On the Fathers who left us writings, many have exercised their diligence: once Jerome [347–420] wrote *The Ecclesiastical Writers*[303], today Roberto Bellarmino [1542–1621][304] among the Roman-Catholics; Johann Gerhard [1582–1637], Lutheran, has left a *Patrology*[305], André Rivet [1572–1651], Reformed, the *Sacred Critical*[306]. The same topic is addressed in the *Censure*[307] by Robert Cooke [1550–1615]; and *The Apocrypha*[308] by John Rainolds [1549–1607] and the book against John Hart [Jesuit, d. 1586][309]. Further on this subject, we have *The Orthodox Writings of the Fathers*, published at the same time, and the work which was actually the prelude to these, namely the *Library of the Fathers*[310], reprinted several times, and now finally edited in Paris after extensive work.

§. 36. The History of Ecclesiastical Dogmas, or anything that has at some time or place ever been examined regarding whatever specific point [of faith], has been carefully collected by Denis Petau [1583–1652][311] ac-

---

302 Laurentius Surius (1617–1618), *Vitae sanctorum ex probatis authoribus a MMS. Codicibus*. Coloniae Agrippinae: sumptibus Ioannis Kreps.
303 St. Jerome (15th-16th cent.), *S. Hieronymi, presbiteri, Liber de Scriptoribus ecclesiasticis, sive de illustribus viris, capita 133: cum praefatione Eusebii*. [S.l.].
304 Roberto Bellarmino (1613), *De scriptoribus esclesiasticis: cum brevi chronologia, ad a. 1612*. Lugduni
305 Johann Gerhard (1653), *Patrologia*. Jenae: Ge. Sengenwaldus.
306 André Rivet (1619), *Critici Sacri Specimen*. Dordrecht: Berewout.
307 Robert Cooke (1641), *Censura quorundam scriptorum*. Helmaestadii: Müller.
308 John Rainolds (1611), *Censura librorum Apocryphorum Veteris Testamenti*. In nobili Oppenheimio.
309 John Rainolds [1549–1607] (1584), *The Summe Of The Conference Between Iohn Rainolds And John Hart*. Londini: impensis Geor. Bishop.
310 (1639), *Nova bibliotheca veterum patrum*. Parisii.
311 Denis Petau (1644), *Theologica dogmata*. Lutetiae Parisiorum.

cording to the opinion of the Roman-Catholics in that great work *On Dogmas* embracing the whole of Theology; by Johann Gerhard [1582–1637] in his very challenging *Catholic Confession*[312] in favor of the Lutherans, which his son Johann Ernest Gerhard [1621–1668][313] gathered in a compendium; similar matters are also dealt with in the *Catalog of the Witnesses of Truth*[314] collected under the direction of Matthias Flacius Illyricus [1520–1575]. Writing, in truth, in favor of the Reformed, Johann Forbesius [c.1568–1634] worked on the Concord of the Fathers, to be incorporated in the remarkable book of *The Historical and Theological Instructions*[315]. The dogmas were, for the most part, established in the Councils: therefore, we should mention here the History of the Councils, which Francesco Longo Coriolano [1562–1625] gathered together in the *Essential Part of the Councils*[316] and Bartholomaeus Carranza [1503–1576] in the *Essential Part of the Councils and Pontiffes*[317]. In this context, the *Tomes of the Councils* were in fact published for the first time in Cologne. Subsequently, several times in France, and last of all with a very costly work, carefully prepared at the expense of the Crown. The French, from what I hear, are preparing another edition, less lavish, with more closely spaced print characters, so that it is

---

[312] Johann Gerhard (1634), *Confessionis Catholicae libri II.* 4 vols., Jenae.
[313] Johann Ernest Gerhard (1661), *Generalis Epitome Confessionis Catholicae.* Jenae.
[314] Matthias Flacius Illyricus (1597), *Catalogus testium veritatis.* Lugduni: Ex typographia Antonij Candidi.
[315] Johann Forbesius (1645), *Instructiones historico-theologicae de doctrina Christiana.* Amstelodami.
[316] Francesco Longo Coriolano (1639), *Summa conciliorum onmium, quae a Sancto Petro usqve ad Gregorium XV papam celebrata sunt, etc.* Parisiis: sumptibus viduae Petri Chevalier.
[317] Barthomolaeus de Carranza (1623), *Summa Conciliorum a Sancto Petro usque ad Julium III. Pontificem Maximum.* Antverpiae.

not completely deprived of that very useful function which smaller things have. Centuries ago, St. Augustine [354–430] wrote for St. Quodvultdeus [bishop of Carthage, d. c. 450] on dogmas rejected in these councils, or *The Catalog of Heresies*, to which Lambert Danaeu [c. 1535–c. 1590][318], a Reformed thinker, added notes; a work *On the Heresies*[319] was also composed by Alfonso de Castro [1495–1558], Roman-Catholic, and Conrad Schlüsselburg [1543–1619], Lutheran, in the *Catalog of the Heretics*[320].

§. 37. Marco Antonio de Dominis's [1560–1624] *Ecclesiastical Republic* comprehensively described [321] the history of the ecclesiastical regimes, or the hierarchy. To this should be added the writings *On the Power of the Pope*[322] by Roberto Bellarmino [1542–1621], and against Bellarmino those by William Barclay [1546–1608][323] and

---

[318] Lambert Danaeu (1578), *Paratitla in D. Aurelii Augustini tomos duos praecipuos, nimirum sextum, et septimum, in quibus illius contra Manichaeos, Priscillianistas, Arrianos, Iovinianistas, ... certamina continentur.* Genevae: Stoer. Saint Quodvultdeus [d. c. 450 AD] is the bishop of Carthage, to whom the Doctor of the Church devoted the work quoted in the text, written on demand of the same Saint Quodvultdeus, "Quod petis saepissime et instantissime, Sancte fili Quodvuldeus, ut de Haeresibus aliquod scribam, etc.", Augustine, *De Haeresibus*, *Praefatio*.

[319] Alfonso de Castro (1543), *Adversus omnes haereses: libri 14.* Coloniae: Novesianus.

[320] Conrad Schlüsselburg (1597-99), *Hæreticorum Catalogus.* 13 vols., Francofurti.

[321] Marco Antonio de Dominis (1620, repr. 2008), *De Republica ecclesiastica libri X.* Spalati: Lamaro.

[322] Roberto Bellarmino (1611), *Tractatus de potestate summi pontificis in rebus temporalibus, adversus Gulielmum Barclaium.* Coloniae Agrippinae: Sumptibus Bernardi Gualtheri.

[323] William Barclay (1609), *De potestate papae, an & quatenus in reges & principes seculares ius & imperium habeat liber posthumus.* Mussiponti.

the king of Great Britain, James [I of England, 1566–1625][324], to which objections were raised by Matthias Torto, the pseudonym of Bellarmino[325], which he revealed when *The Torto's Torture* was published in favor of the King[326]. Additionally, we should mention various Roman-Catholic writers on the ecclesiastical hierarchy, likewise those who wrote on the freedom and privileges of the Gallican Church, of which a long catalog can be drawn up. Such a list should also include even those who wrote in favor of the Emperor Ludwig the Bavarian [1282–1347] against the authority of the Pope: Marsilius of Padua [1275–1342][327], William of Ockham [1285–1347][328], and

---

[324] James I of England (1607), *Triplici nodo, triplex cuneus. Sive Apologia pro iuramento fidelitatis adversus duo brevia P. Pauli Quinti, & epistolam Cardinalis Bellarmini, ad G. Blackuellum Archipresbyterum nuper scriptam.* Londini: Excudebat Robertus Barkerus, illustrissimæ Regiæ Maiestatis typographus.

[325] Roberto Bellarmino (1608), *Matthaei Torti presbyteri, & theologi papiensis Responsio ad librum inscriptum, Triplici nodo, triplex cuneus, siue Apologia pro iuramento fidelitatis: adversis duo brevia Papae Pauli V. & recentes litteras Cardinalis Bellarmini ad Georgium Blacuellum Angliae Archipresbyterum.* St. Omer: English College Press.

[326] Andrewes Lancelot [1555–1626] (1609), *Tortura Torti: sive, Ad Matthaei Torti librum responsio, qui nuper editus contra Apologiam serenissimi potentissimique principis, Iacobi, Dei gratia, Magnae Britanniae, Franciae, & Hiberniae Regis, pro Iuramento fidelitatis.* Londini: Excudebat Robertus Barkerus, serenissæ Regiæ Maiestatis typographus [not included in AA VI, 2, sources directory]; Roberto Bellarmino (1609), *Apologia pro responsione sua ad librum Jacobi Magnae Britanniae Regis, cuius titulus est: Triplici nodo triplex cuneus ... Accessit eadem ipsa responsio iterum recusa, quae sub nomine Matthae Torti anno superiore prodierat.* Romae: Zannettus.

[327] Marsilius of Padua (1599), *Vulgo dictus defensor pacis, sive apologia pro Ludovico IIII. imp. bavaro: tractatus de translatione imperii, ante CCC prope annos scripta.* [S.l.]: Comelin.

[328] William of Ockham (1494), *Dialogus De Imperio Et Pontificia Potestate.* Lugduni: Johann Trechsel.

others whose fragments Melchior Goldast [c.1578–1635][329] collected in a single volume. There is *The History of the Pontiffs* by Platina alias Bartolomeo Sacchi, [1421–1481][330], Onofrio Panvinio [1529–1568][331], Johannes Stella [fl. 1505][332], Johannes Conrad Dieterich [1612–1556][333], etc. To this matter belongs the *History of the Cardinals* and a commentary *On the Cardinals* which appeared recently[334], and there is also a treaty by Johann Freinsheim [1608–1660], which raises the question of the precedence between the Electors of the Holy Roman Empire and the Cardinals[335]. The history of the Episcopacies, monasteries, churches and other institutions of the church affirmed in later times has been collected by Rudolf Hospinian [1547–1626], a Reformed thinker, in his books *On the Origin of Churches and Monasteries*[336], to which can be added Johann Himmel [1581–1642] *On Canon-*

---

[329] Melchior Goldast (1614), *Monarchia S. Romani Imperii*. Francofurti.

[330] Platina (alias Bartolomeo Sacchi) (1479), *Liber de vita Christi ac pontificum omnium*. Venetiis.

[331] Onofrio Panvinio (1557), *Romani pontifices et cardinales*. Venetiis.

[332] Johannes Stella (1570), *De vita ac moribus pontificum romanorum a Petro Apostolo ad Julium II*. Impressum Basileae.

[333] Johannes Conrad Dieterich (1663), *Breviarium Pontificum Romanorum: Breviter Succincteque Exhibens, Ex Testimoniis Avitis Et Domesticis, Vitam Omnium Pontificum A Lino Usque Ad Alexandrum VII*. Giessae Hassorum: Kargerus.

[334] Could be: Alfonso Chacón [1540–1599], Andrea Vittorelli [d. 1653], Ferdinando Ughelli [1596–1670] (1630), *Vitae et res gestae pontificum romanorum et S.R.E. cardinalium ab initio nascentis Ecclesiae*. Romae: typis Vaticanis.

[335] Johann Freinsheim (1660), *De S. Rom. Imperii Electorum et S. Rom. Eccles. Cardinalium praecedentia diatribae quinque*. [S.l.].

[336] Rudolf Hospinian (1578), *De origine, progressu, usu et abusu Templorum et rerum ad templa pertinentium, libri V*. Turici; Id. (1588), *De origine et progressu monachatus*. Turici.

ries[337], and the history of the Universities by Johannes [Jakob] Middendorp [1539–1611][338], Thomas Lansius [1577–1657][339], Johann Limnaeus [1592–1665][340]. The History of Scholastic Theology, which Lambert Daneau [1530–1595] summed up in the *Prolegomena to Peter Lombard,* also belongs to this subject-matter[341]. Here, I could compose a long catalogue of those who wrote in particular the Annals of the different orders, for example of Minors, Dominicans, Cistercians, Carmelites, Augustinians, Carthusians, Minims, Society of Jesus, etc.., if special knowledge of these is necessary for the jurisconsult. Overall, firstly, it is is worthwhile to read the History of the Society of Jesus, especially the version that has been published *in folio* in Rome, which is always updated, whenever some General [of the Society, e. n.] dies. Likewise the *Library of the Society of Jesus*, which has been edited by Philipp Alegambe [1592–1652][342]. We have thus summarized ecclesiastical history, which must be known accurately by the jurist and the contemporary political figures, so that they will not be seized by the ignorant, and, or, according to the custom of the people, but so that, with the principles of all of the opinions having been learned, they can judge without passion and with a purified mind, as the practice of religion is strongly

---

[337] Johann Himmel (1632), *Tractatus de Canonicatu, Iure Canonico, & Theologia Scholastica.* Ienae: Impensis Bircknerianis.

[338] Jakob Middendorp (1602), *De celebrioribus universi terrarum orbis Academiis libri VIII.* Coloniae.

[339] Thomas Lansius (1619), *Commentatio Historico-Politica-Juridica de academiis.* Tubingae: Typis J.A. Cellii.

[340] Johann Limnaeus (1621), *Dissertationum nomico-politicarum prima de academiis*. Altorphi.

[341] Lambert Daneau (1580), *In Petri Lombardi...librum primum sententiarum,....commentarius. Accesserunt prolegomena etc.* Genevae.

[342] Philipp Alegambe (1643), *Bibliotheca scriptorum Societatis Iesu.* Antverpiae.

linked to civil affairs. For the most part, on the other hand, in the individual chapters of the Ecclesiastical History we have quoted authors from all the religions approved in the Empire, so that no one need have fear of being deceived by a man of the adversary party.

§. 38. The History of Germany, or of the Middle Ages, necessary to decipher the Feudal Law, follows the Ecclesiastical History that is necessary to gain insight into Canon law. Numerous minor writers pertain to this matter, such as Otto of Freisig [c. 1114–1158][343], Abbas Urspergensis [c. 1117–1230/31][344], Adam of Bremen [before 1050 and died on 12 October of an unknown year possibly 1081, at the latest 1085][345], Albert of Stade [1190–1261][346], Gubelinus Persona [1358–1421][347], Liutprand [920–972][348], Gunther [c. 1150–c. 1220][349] in Ligurinus, Sigebert of Gembloux [1030–1112][350], Saxo Grammaticus [c. 1150–c. 1220][351] and others here and

---

343 Otto of Freisig (1569), *Chronicon, sive rerum ab orbe condito ad sua usque tempora gestarum libri VIII*. Basileae.

344 Burchard of Ursberg (Abbas Urspergensis) (1569), *Chronicon a Nyno Abysiorum rege, usque ad Friderici II imp. tempora cum paralipomenis rerum memorabilium a Frederico II usque ad Carolum V*. Basileae.

345 Adam of Bremen (1595), *Historia ecclesiastica*. Lugduni Batavorum.

346 Albert of Stade (1587), *Chronicon a condito orbe usque ad 1256 deductum*. Helmstadii.

347 Gubelinus Persona (1599), *Cosmodromium*. Francofurti.

348 Liutprand of Cremona (1514), *Rerum per Europam gestarum libri VI*. Parisiis.

349 Gunther of Pairis, *Ligurinus*, in Erwin Assmann (ed.) (1987), *Ligurinus = Guntheri Poetae Ligurinus*. Hannover: Hahnsche Buchhandlung.

350 Sigebert of Gembloux, *Chronicon*, in Simon Schardius, see note 352.

351 Saxo Grammaticus (1644–1645), *Historiae Danicae libri XVI*. Sorae.

there published in the *Tomes of German History*[352] by Simon Schardius [c. 1535–1573] and others. I will say nothing about those whom John Selden [1584–1654][353] has unearthed in England, and whom Szymon Starowolski [1588–1656] in Poland has reviewed in *A Hundred Polish Writers*[354]. Nor without benefit will readers approach the *Chronicle* of Speyer by Christoph Lehmann [1568–1638][355], of Trier by Wilhelm Kyriander [16th-cent.][356], of Mainz by Nicolaus Serarius [1555–1609][357]. Likewise the *Danish Annals*[358] by Johann Isacius Pontanus [1571–1639], and entirely the *History of the Northern Peoples*[359] by Olaus Magnus [1490–1557, the Icelandic people described by Jónsson Arngrímur the Learned [1569–1649][360], the British by William Cambden [1551–1623][361], the Scottish by George Buchanan [1506–1582][362], the Irish

---

352 Simon Schardius (anonymous) (1566), *Germanicarum Rerum Quatuor celebriores vetustioresque Chronographi*. Francofurti.

353 John Selden (1625), *Analecton Anglobritannicon libri II*. Francofurti.

354 Szymon Starowolski (1625), *Scriptorum Polonicorum Hekatontas: Seu Centum Illustrium Poloniæ Scriptorum Elogia Et Vitae*. Francofurti.

355 Christoph Lehmann (1612), *Chronicon Spirense*. Francofurti.

356 Wilhelm Kyriander (1625), *Augustae Treverorum Annales*. Biponti: Wittelius.

357 Nicolaus Serarius (1604), *Moguntiacae res Moguntiacarum rerum ... libri quinque*. Moguntiae: Lipp.

358 Johann Isacius Pontanus (1631), *Rerum Danicarum historia: libris X unoque tomo ad domum usque Oldenburgicamdeducta*. Amstelodami: Sumpt. Ioannis Ianssonii.

359 Olaus Magnus (1567), *Historia gentium septentrionalium*. Basileae.

360 Jónsson Arngrim or Arngrímur (1610), *Crymogaea; sive, Rerum Islandicarum libri III, per Arngrimum Jonam Islandum*. Hamburgi.

361 William Cambden (1616), *Annales Rerum Anglicarum, Et Hibernicarum regnante Elizabetha, Ad Annum Salutis M.D.LXXXIX*. Francofurti ad Moenum: Rulandi.

362 George Buchanan (1624), *Rerum Scoticarum historia, libris XX descripta*. Francofurti.

in an edition published not so long ago by the *Irish Lyra*[363], the French by Paolo Emili [c.1469–1529][364], Jean du Tillet [d. 1570?][365], Jean de Serres [1540–1598] in the *Inventory*[366], the Spanish by Juan de Mariana [1536–1624][367], the Portuguese by Jerónimo Osorio da Fonseca [1506–1580][368]; the Bohemian by Jan Dubravius [1486–1553][369], the Polish by Martin Cromer [1512–1589][370], of Meissen by Georg Fabricius of Chemnitz [1516–1571][371], the Frisian by Ubbo Emmius [1547–1625][372]; the Westphalian recently by Johann Justum Winkelmann [1620–1699][373], the Belgian by Anton Thysius [the Younger, 1603–1665][374], the Silesian by Joachim Cureus [1532–

---

363 Thomas Carve [1590–1672?] (1651), *Lyra seu anacephalaeosis hibernica.* Viennae: typis Matthaei Cosmerouii.
364 Paolo Emili (1539), *De rebus gestis Francorum ... libri X; additum est de regibus, item* [J.Tilii] *Francorum Chronicon*, Parisiis.
365 See note 364.
366 Jean de Serres (1653), *Inventaire General de l'Histoire de France.* Lyon: chez Claude la Riviere.
367 Juan de Mariana (1605), *Historiae De Rebus Hispaniae Libri XXX.* Moguntiae.
368 Jerónimo Osório (1574), *De Rebus Emmanuelis Lusitaniae Regis ... gestis, libri duodecim.* Coloniae Agrippinae.
369 Jan Dubravius (1552), *Historia regni Boiemiae.* Prostanae: Impressum et finitum in officina I. Guntheri.
370 Martin Cromer (1558), *De Origine Et Rebus Gestis Polonorum Libri XXX.* Basileae: Oporinus.
371 Georg Fabricius (1569), *Georgii Fabricii Chemnicensis rerum Misnicarum Libri VII.* Curante Ernesto Voegelino, Lipsiae.
372 Ubbo Emmius (1596), *Rerum Frisicarum historiae libri X.* Franekerae: apud Aegidium Radaeum ordinum Frisiae typographum.
373 Johann Justus Winckelmann (1667), *Notitia historico-politica veteris Saxo-Westphaliae, finitimarumque regionum, quatuor libri absoluta.* Oldenburgi: imprimebat Joh. Ericus Zimmer.
374 Anton Thysius, (1645), *Compendium historiae Batavicae: a Iulio Caesare usque ad haec tempora.* Lugduni Batavorum: Ex officina Ioannis Maire.

1573][375], the Carinthian by Hieronymus Megiser [1553–1618][376], the Austrian by Johannes Cuspinian [1473–1529][377] and Gherhard de Rous[378], the Swiss by Johann Stumpf [d. 1576?][379], the Slavic by Helmold [c. 1120–after 1177][380], the Venetian by Pietro Bembo [1470–1547][381], the Sicilian by Tommaso Fazello [1498–1570][382], the Swedish by Martin Crusius [1526–1607][383], the Bavarian by Johannes Turmair [1477–1534][384], the Hungarian by Hieronymus Oertl [1543–1614][385] and the *Hungarian Flower* by János Nadanyi [1643–1707][386]. It is not necessary to mention all of them. Here we should add, inasmuch as they pertain to German History, the *Writings* by Marquard Fre-

---

[375] Joachim Cureus (1571), *Gentis Silesiae annales*. Witebergae: Iohannes Crato.

[376] Hieronymus Megiser (1612), *Annales Carinthiae, das ist: Chronica des Ertzhertzogthumbs Khärndten*. Leipzig: Lamberg.

[377] Johannes Cuspinian (1601), *Austria*. Francofurti: typis Wechelianis apud Claudium Marnium, & heredes Ioannis Aubrij.

[378] Gerhard de (van) Rous (Roo, Rhoo) (1592), *Annales rerum belli domique ab Austriacis Habsburgicae gentis principibus, a Rudolpho primo usque ad Carolum V gestarum*. Oeniponti: excudebat Ioannes Agricola.

[379] Johann Stumpf (1548), *Gemeiner loblicher Eydgenossenchafft Stetten, Landen vnd Völkeren Chronick wirdiger Thaaten Beschreybung*. Zürych.

[380] Helmold of Bosau (1581), *Chronica Slavorum*, Francofurti.

[381] Pietro Bembo (1551), *Historiae Venetae libri XII*. Venetiis.

[382] Tommaso Fazello (1558), *De rebus Siculis*. Panormi: J.M. Maida et Fr. Carrara.

[383] Martin Crusius (1595), *Annales Suevici*. Francofurti: Ex officina typographica Nicolai Bassaei.

[384] Johannes Turmair, called Aventinus, (1580), *Annalium Boiorum libri VII*. Basileae.

[385] Hieronymus Oertl (1619), *De Chronycke van Hungarie[n]*. Amsterdam: Cloppenburch.

[386] János Nadanyi (1663), *Florus Hungaricus*. Amstelodami: ex officina J. a Waesberge.

her [1565–1614][387], Melchior Goldast [c.1578–1635][388], Heinrich Meybom [1555–1625][389], Er-pold Lindenbrog [1547–1606][390], Hermann Conring [1606–1681][391] and Christoph Besold [1577–1638][392]. In addition, let us also add those who wrote about the origins of the feudal system, firstly Cujas [1522–1590][393] and Hotman [1524–1590][394]. Likewise, the *Franco-Gallia*[395] by Hotman, and many other men of undying glory: as well as the German Lexicons, of which *infra* on the Exegetical Jurisprudence.

§. 39. Contemporary history, necessary to comprehend Public Law, follows the history of the middle ages, which is necessary to understand Feudal law. I define as Contemporary the period that embraces the last and the present century: the sixteenth and seventeenth centuries. The history of the previous century was highly influenced by religion. Johann Sleidan [1506–1556][396] has described it, as likewise done by his diligent imitators as well: Jasper von Gennep [c. 1500–1564][397] and Lorenz Surius

---

[387] Marquard Freher (1600), *Rerum Germanicarum Scriptores fere hactenus incogniti*. 3 vols., Francofurti.

[388] Melchior Goldast (1606), *Alamannicarum Rerum Scriptores*. 3 t., Francofurti: Porssius.

[389] Heinrich Meibom (1660), *Opuscola historica res germanicas concernentia*. Helmstedt: Mullerus.

[390] Erpold Lindenbrog (1609), *Scriptores rerum Germanicarum septentrionalium vicinorumque populorum diversi*. Francofurti.

[391] Hermann Conring (1643), *De ducibus et comitibus imperii Germanici*. Helmestadii: Mullerus.

[392] Christoph Besold (1620), *De civitatibus Germaniae liberis et mixtis*. Tubingae.

[393] Jacques Cujas (1593), *De feudis libri 5*. Coloniae Agrippinae.

[394] François Hotman (1574), *Commentarius de feudis*. Coloniae.

[395] François Hotman (1665), *Franco-Gallia*. Francofurti.

[396] Johann Sleidan (1555), *De Statu religionis et rei publicae, Carolo V, Caesare, Commentarii*. Argentorati.

[397] Jasper von Gennep (1559), *Rerum Memorabilium, iam inde ab anno Domini M.D. ad annum fere LX in Rep. Christiana gestarum:*

[1522–1578][398]. Pertinent to this period is the *History of Luther*[399] by Johann Cocaleus [1479–1552], among the Roman-Catholics, and by Johann Mathesius [1504–1565][400], among the followers of the Augsburg Confession; moreover, it is not fruitless to read the *Epistles*[401] by Erasmus [1466–1536], likewise by Philip Melanchthon, [1497–1560] as the former was very peace-loving; the *History of the Augsburg Confession*[402] by David Chytraeus [1539–1600], the *Concordia discors*[403] by Rudolf Hospinian [1547–1626], and against the *Concordia concors*[404] by Leonhard Hutter [1563–1616]; the *History of the Council of Trent*[405] by Petrus Suavis Polanus, *i. e.* Paolo Sarpi Veneto [1552–1623], on which a judgment

---

ex plerisque nostrorum temporum historiographis, praecipue autem D. Fontano Theologo Parisiensi, et Ioanne Sleidano collecti; Libri quinque. Coloniae [not included in AA VI, 2, sources directory].

398 Lorenz Surius (1567), *Commentarius brevis rerum in orbe gestarum.* Coloniae: apud Geruinum Calenium, & haeredes Iohannis Quentel.

399 Johann Cochlaeus (Dobnek) (1611), *Joh. Cochlaei Historia Martini Lutheri: d.i. kurze Beschreibung seiner Handlungen, und Schriften, von 1517 bis 1546.* Dilingen.

400 Johann Mathesius (1570), *Historien, von des ehrwirdigen inn Gott seligen thewren Manns Gottes, Doctoris Martini Luthers, Anfang, Lehr, Leben vnnd Sterben: alles ordenlich der Jahrzal nach, wie sich alle Sachen zu jeder Zeyt haben zugetragen.* Nürnberg: Durch die Erben Johann vom Bergs.

401 Erasmus of Rotterdam Philip Melanchthon (1642), *Epistularum libri 31 et Melanchthonis lib. 4 etc.* Londini.

402 David Chytraeus (1578), *Historia Augustanae confessionis.* Francofurti ad Moenum: apud Paulum Reffeler, impensis Sigismundi Feirabend.

403 Rudolf Hospinian (1607), *Concordia Discors: De Origine Et Progressu Formulae Concordiae Bergensis Liber Vnus: In Quo Eius Errores Et Falsa Dogmata... demonstrantur.* Tiguri: Officina Wolphiana.

404 Leonhard Hutter (1614), *Concordia concors.* Witebergae: impensis Clementis Bergeri.

405 Petrus Suavis Polanus (pseud. of Paolo Sarpi) (1658), *Petri Suavis Polani Historiae concilii Tridentini libri octo.* Gorinchemi: Paulus Vink.

was given by the *Author of the Dissertation of the Three Historians of the Council of Trent*[406]. In an equivalent manner for all of these there is Jacques Auguste de Thou [1553–1617], a man who deserves the praises reserved to the ancient historians, the Livy of our age, in his admirable volume of *History*[407]. On the subject of Belgian History Emanuel van Meteren [1535–1612] [408] was excellent; and second to none of the ancient writers for value is the Tacitus of our century: Hugo Grotius [1583–1645], in the *Belgian Annals*[409]. Pietro Bizarri [1525–1585][410] described the war of Cyprus of the Federated forces against the Turks. With regard to our century it is of interest to read Gabriel Barthélemy de Gramond [c. 1590–1654][411] and the account of the German war *The Sacred Germany Restored*[412] by Carlo Carafa [1584–1644], and also the short, but very refined *Anonymous Author of the Compendium of German history*[413], who starting from the early Bohemian beginnings extended his narrative up to the capture of Leipzig by Lennart Torstensson [Swedish Field Marshall, 1603–1651]; nor

---

[406] Scipione Errico [1592–1670] (1662), *De tribus historicis* [*P. Sarpi, S. Herrico, S. Pallavicino*] *concilii Tridentini, auctore Caesare Aquilino* [*i. e. S. Herrico*]. Amstelodami.

[407] Jacques Auguste de Thou (1625), *Historiarum sui temporis libri CXXXVIII*. Francofurti.

[408] Emanuel van Meteren (1600), *Historia Belgica nostri potissimum temporis*. [S. l.].

[409] Hugo Grotius (1658), *Annales et historiae de rebus Belgicis*. Amstelædami: Ex typographejo Ioannis Blaev.

[410] Pietro Bizarri (1573), *De bello Cyprico et Pannonico*. Basilae.

[411] Gabriel Barthélemy de Gramond (1653), *Historiarum Galliae Ab Excessu Henrici IV, libri XVIII*. Amstelodami: Apud Ludovicum Elzevirium.

[412] Carlo Carafa (1639), *Commentaria de Germania sacra restaurata*. Coloniae Agrippinae: Apud C. ab Egmond.

[413] Could be: (1643), *Epitome rerum Germanicarum ab anno 1617 ad annum 1643*. [S. l.].

should one omit Bogeslaus of Chemnitz [1605–1678][414], if this is his real name, who broadly explained German history. Some of Gramond's writings on the previous century that were hitherto hidden will, from what I hear, be published when the danger has ceased. The history of these times by Vittorio Siri [1608–1685] is also recommended[415]. I will say nothing about the *Theater*, nothing about the great works *embodied in the European Diary*, which are constantly increasing[416]. On the other hand, attention should be paid to the collections of the public deeds, which come out in different forms: posters, pamphlets and other things from which a specific knowledge of the facts may be inferred. Hortleder selected these acts in the book *On the causes of war in Germany*[417], Michael Caspar Lundorp [1580–1629] in the recently reprinted *Public Deeds*[418] and his continuer, Martin Meyer[419]. Firstly, whenever the controversies of Public Law have

---

[414] Philipp Bogeslaus von Chemnitz (1647), *Dissertatio de ratione status in Imperio nostro romano-germanico.* Freistadii [*i.e.* Amsterdam]: Louis Elsevier, but see *infra* note 426.

[415] Vittorio Siri (1644–1682), *Il Mercurio Overo Historia De' correnti tempi.* 15 vols. Casale, Venice, Lyon, Paris, Florence.

[416] (1618–1718), *Theatrum Europaeum*. 21 vols., Francofurti; (1639) Philemerus Irenicus Elisius (pseudonym of Martin Meyer [1630–1670], founder) (1659–1683), *Diarium Europaeum*. 45 vols., Frankfurti.

[417] Friedrich Hortleder [1579–1640] (1617–1618), *Der Römischen Keyser- und Königlichen Majesteten... Von den Ursachen deß Teutschen Kriegs Käiser Carls deß V. wider die Schmalkaldische Bunds-Oberste , Chur- und Fürsten, Sachsen und Hessen, und Jhrer Chur- und ... Mitvervandte, Anno 1546. und 47*. Francofurti.

[418] Michael Caspar Lundorp (1621), *Acta publica inter Matthiam et Ferdinandum II Rom. imperatores atque Fredericum V electorem aliosque imperii ordines exterosque reges ac principes atque respublicas, ab initio Austrio-Bohemo-Germanicorum motuum huc usque ventilata.* Moeno-Francfurti: J.F. Weissius, continued by Martin Mayer with the title, (1637–1641) *Lundorpius Suppletus et Continuatus*, Francofurti

[419] See note 416.

been raised in published writings, one should make sure that the jurisconsult acquires an adequate knowledge of these issues, such as the Case of the Palatine, Donawerden, Brunswick, Erfurt guardianship, the institute of *Wildfagiatus*[420], the right of coronation between Mainz and Cologne; one should also consult others that have been made known publicly, which the esteemed Johann Theodor Sprenger [d. 1668] recently set out in an orderly fashion in *The Illustrious pretensions*[421] and in other works as a means of explaining public law. And although Dominik van Arum [1579–1637][422] and Johann Limnaeus [1592–1665][423] dissertated on Public Law in considerable books, they included so many extraneous topics, the former of private law, the latter of history and philology, that I do not doubt that all of the topics, which are properly of public law, can be summed up from those books in a booklet; therefore I plan to prepare a compendium of public law and from Van Arum and Limnaeus, which will not include anything of superfluous, and omit anything of essential. Meanwhile, it is important to read Jakob Lampadius [1593–1649][424], on which we are waiting for notes

---

[420] Charles Fresne du Cange [1610–1688] and others (1883–1887), *Glossarium mediae et infimae latinitatis*. Niort, *ad vocem Wildfangiatus*, "Ius et facultas, ex privilegio Electoratui Palatino competens, retinendi homines alterius domini, ita ut a propriis dominis repeti non possint"; see also Henricus Hildebrand (1741), *De Jure Wildfangiatus*. Altorfii.

[421] Johann Theodor Sprenger (1659), *Jurisprudentia publica: moderno usui, recessibus, actis & capitulationibus novissimis conformata*. Francofurti: Fickwirth.

[422] Dominik van Arum (1616), *Volumina dissertationum De Iure Publico*. 5 vols., Jenae.

[423] Johann Limnaeus (1629), *Iuris publici Imperii Romano-Germanici libri IX*. Argentorati: Sumptibus Pauli Ledertz.

[424] Jakob Lampadius (1640), *Tractatus de republica Romano-Germanica*.Helmestadii.

by the illustrious Hermann Conring [1606–1681][425]. Before the almost famous booklet by Hippolytus a Lapide *On the Reason of State*[426] against the House of Austria, one should take into consideration the *Commentary on the Reason of State*[427] by the illustrious Johann Wolfgang Textor [1638–1701] and the latest by Stefano de Mozambano[428], both worthy of reading.

§. 40. On this matter it would be helpful if an Irenical History were written [429], starting from the early beginnings of the schism to the present time. A conciliation was attempted by Erasmus of Rotterdam [1466–1536], Philip Melanchthon [1497–1560], Martin Bucer [1491–1551] [430], Julius Pflug [1499–1564] bishop of Nurem-

---

[425] Hermann Conring (1671), *Ad Jacobi Lampadii ... De republica Romano-Germanica annotata.*Helmestadii: Mullerus.

[426] Hippolytus a Lapide (1647), *De Ratione Status in Imperio Nostro Romano-Germanico*. Freistadii. It is believed [see the old and partial French translation of the *NM* by G. L. Maurin (1830), Paris, p. 68, n. 1; and AnnaVittoria Migliorini (ed.) (1982), *Bernardo Tanucci, Epistolario*, III, 1752–1756, Roma, Lettera n. 268, 223, n. 2] that Hippolytus a Lapide is the pseudonym of Bogislav Philipp von Chemnitz [1605–1678] (see note 414).

[427] Johann Wolfgang Textor (1667), *Tractatus iuris publici de vera et varia ratione status Germaniae modernae*. Altdorphi.

[428] Severinus, Comite & Barones de Mozambano (pseudonym of Samuel Pufendorf [1632–1694]) (1667), *Severini de Monzambano Veronensis De Statu Imperii Germanici ad Laelium Fratrem Dominum Trezolani Liber Unus.* Augusta Allobrogum.

[429] *I. e.* the history of the attempts to unify Christianity by using reason as an essential attribute; see about Brian Lugioyo (2010), *Martin Bucer's Doctrine of Justification. Reformation Theology ans Early Modern Irenicism*. Oxford: Oxford University Press.

[430] Martin Bucer [1491–1551] (1542), *De vera ecclesiarum in doctrina, ceremoniis, et disciplina reconciliatione & compositione.* Argentorati: Wendelin Rihel.

berg[431] and other writers whose intent, certainly good if it had been successful, was put forward in the Augsburg *Interim*[432]. Thence, the *Concordia* was prepared[433] and the reasons of its beginning were partly revealed by George Cassander [1513–1566][434], George Witzel [1501–1573][435], Andreas Fricius [1503–1572] [but Ericius (?) in

---

[431] Julius von Pflug (1549), *Formula reformationis per Caesaream Maiestatem statibus ecclesiasticis in comitiis Augustanis ad deliberandum proposita*. Mogunt.

[432] The Augsburg Interim, was a temporary (namely from Latin *interim*, meanwhile) doctrinal agreement between German Catholics and Protestants, proclaimed in May 1548 at the Diet of Augsburg (1547–1548), which became imperial law on June 30, 1548. It was prepared and accepted at the insistence of the Holy Roman Emperor Charles V, who hoped to establish temporary religious unity in Germany until differences could be worked out in a general council of the Catholic Church. Consisting of 26 articles, the first draft of the Augsburg Interim was written by J. von Pflug. It was not was fully accepted, and a German religious settlement was not brought about until the Peace of Augsburg (1555). On this, see Joachim Whaley (2012), *Germany and the Holy Roman Empire.* Oxford: Oxford University Press, vol. 1, 321–324.

[433] *I.e.* the *Book of Concord*, which is the historic doctrinal standard of the Lutheran Church, consisting of ten credal documents recognized as authoritative in Lutheranism since the 6th century. They are also known as the symbolic books of the Evangelical Lutheran Church. *The Book of Concord* was published in German on June 25, 1580. See Paul T. McCain (2007), *Concordia. The Luteran Confession*. St. Luis MO.

[434] George Cassander (1608), *De articulis religionis inter Catholicos et Protestantes controversis consultatio*. Lugduni.

[435] George Witzel (1650), *Via regia. Methodus ad concordiam.* Helmestadii.

Latin text edited in AA VI 1, e.n.] Modrevius[436], the Cardinal of Lorraine [1524–1574] in the *Colloquy with Théodor de Bèze* which is carefully examined by De Thou[437]; other important authors include Jacopo Aconcio in the book *on Satan's Stratagem*[438], Marco Antonio de Dominis[439], Parerus in the *Irenical*[440], De Thou himself in the *Preface of the Histories*[441], Grotius[442]; George Calixtus [1586–1656][443], in the University of Helmestedt, Christian Dreier [1610–1688][444], in the Academy of Könisberg [today Kalinigrad, e. n.]; the author, in no way

---

[436] Andreas Fricius Modrevius (1554), *De republica emendanda libri quinque*. Basileae [not included in AA VI, 2, sources directory]; Id. (1590), *Sylvae quattuor: I. De tribus personis et una essentia Dei, ... II. De necessitate conventus habendi ad sedandos religionis controversias, ... III. De Iesu Christo filio Dei, et hominis, ... IV. De Homousio, et de iis, quae huc pertineant.* Cracoviae: Rodecki [not included in AA VI, 2, sources directory].

[437] Chalres de Guise (1561), *L'oraison de Monseigneur le illustrissime & reverendissime Cardinal de Lorraine, faicte en l'Assemblée de Poyssi, le Roy y estant present, le xvi iour de Septembre, M.D. LXI*. Paris: G. Morel [not included in AA VI, 2, sources directory]; Théodor de Bèze [1519–1609] (1560), *Confessione della fede christiana*. [S.l.] : Appresso Fabio Todesco [not included in AA VI, 2, sources directory]; Jacques Auguste de Thou [1553–1617] (1620), *Historiarum sui temporis tomo secundus*. Genevae, *sub a.* 1561; Id. (1669), *Thuana. Sive excerpta ex ore Jac. Aug. Thuani per F.F. P.P. (Fratres Puteani)*. [S.l.].

[438] See note 60.

[439] See note 321.

[440] Pareus, pseud. of David Wängler [1548–1633] (1616), *Admonitio Christiana, De Irenico sive Libro Votivo*. Tubingae: Cellius.

[441] Jacques Auguste de Thou, see note 407.

[442] Hugo Grotius [1583–1645] (1642), *Animadversiones in animadversiones Andreae Riveti*. Lutetiae Parisiorum; Id. (1642), *Votum pro pace ecclesiatica contra examen Andreae Riveti et alios irreconciliabiles*. [S. l.].

[443] George Calixtus (1650), *Desiderium Et Studium Concordiae Ecclesiasticae*. Helmestadii: Typographeum Calixtinum.

[444] Christian Dreier (1651), *Gründliche Erörterung etzlicher schwerer Theologischer Fragen*. Könisberg.

acceptable, of *The Irenical of the Irenicals*[445] in altercation with John Amos Comenius [1592–1670][446]; the Scottish John Durie [1596–1680][447], the Swedish bishop Johann Matthiae [1592–1670] in *The Northern Olive Branch*[448]; finally, in a manner very similar to the Collocutors of Rinteln[449], also the Peace-makers of the Mark. These, as I will state again, are necessarily to be known by a jurisconsult so that he learns to distinguish among the various controversies, and ceases to hurl lightning over others due to any disagreement of opinion or rituals.

§. 41. From historical jurisprudence, I proceed to the exegetical. For although the exegetical is in some way historical, it describes what actually is likely to have been the idea of the law-maker, and since it has been produced in very large amount, it is rightly treated apart. It has two strands, the one from the text, the other on the text. The former is derived from various texts simultaneously, not according to the order of the texts, but by combining the one with the other, while the latter, namely the strand based directly on the text, is applied κατά πόδα [in Greek in the text, word for word, e. n.] to the texts themselves. The former belongs to the Philology of right in imitation of

---

445 Irenicus Irenicorum pseud. of Daniel Zwicker? [1612–1678] (1661), *Irenicomastix perpetuo convictus et constrictus, seu, Nova confirmatio infallibilitatis Irenici irenicorum per ostensam futilitatem criminosae comenianiae refutationis*. Amsterdami.
446 See note 77.
447 John Durie (1636), *De pace ecclesiatica inter Evangelicos procuranda sententiae*. Amstelodami.
448 Johann Matthiae (1656), *Ramus Olivae Septentrionalis primus et secundus*. Strengnesiae.
449 Perhaps, Sebastianus Curtius [1620–1684] and others (1662) *Brevis relatio de colloquio inter theologos quosdam Marpurgenses et Rintelenses habito Casselis 1661*. Wismariae.

the *Sacred Philology* by Salomon Glass [1593–1656][450]; the latter is in imitation of the Commentaries of Law.

§. 42. The Philology of Law consists in the application of the disciplines to jurisprudence; it is divided into grammar, didactics, rhetoric (to which poetics also belongs), history, ethical-political and logical-metaphysical issues, finally legal physics. We have dealt diffusely with these aspects in our *Essay of Philosophical Questions Collected from the Right*[451]. To this should be added *The Maniples of the Right*[452] by the illustrious Christian Woldenberg [1621–1674], jurist from Rostock. If we are allowed to carry out our thought, to which once we dedicated an essay at some point we will endeavor to achieve completeness up to the present with the title *Philology and Philosophy of Law*. In that matter we have considered many uncommon things.

§. 43. First of all, the Legal Grammar requires the juridical concordances. On this matter so far theologians have partly defeated the juriconsults. I would not, however, increase this matter up to the point of prolixity, on which the theologians are working now. The concordances, both theological and juridical, could be separable if we considered only the famous passages and the more specific use in those items: for what purpose, in fact, is there any need to collect thoroughly all of the similars? You should observe, instead, with regard to item 1) the meaning; 2) the derivation; 3) the words placed close together, when the substantives are joined: for example: it has been ob-

---

[450] Salomon Glass (1623), *Philologia sacra*. Jenae.
[451] See note 18.
[452] Christian Woldenberg (1665), *Micarum juris manipuli*. Rostochii.

served that *vis et potestas*[453] are often joined, as is commonly annotated in the definition of guardianship; 4) the epithets when they are joined to the adjectives; 5) the opposites; 6) the arrangement [of the words] or the declension, for example *vis* among jurists is used in the genitive: *huius vis*[454]. Therefore, these are the concordances of right, nothing but the word index.

§. 44. This is one of the aims of the Juridical Lexicon, which records under the item those also written in the Books of the Laws, which belong to the item, even if it is not mentioned, for example how many times is a synonym or the paraphrase of a term used, not the term itself; however, this cannot be recorded in the concordances, but in the lexicon, under that term. Here, the matter also includes the homonymies, which are to be collected from the various places of the laws. The lexicon, in fact, is not tied only to the books of right, but flies here and there through all kinds of interpretations, and displays the use of the terms according to these. For today the unanimous opinion of the Doctors in the controversies which are to be decided are often more influential than the ancient Law of the Romans. On the other hand, it is not so much necessary to make a new Juridical Lexicon, but to increase the ancients, which are the Latin Lexicons by Johann Oldendorp [1488–1567], Simon Schardius [c. 1535–1573], Johann Kahl [1554–1614], Johann Jakob

---

[453] Berger, see note 19, *ad vocem Vis*, "The power one has over a free person (*vis ac potestas*)".

[454] For example, in Ulpian, Paul and others. On this see also Marcus-Terentius Varro [116 BC–27 BC], *Marci Terentii Varronis de lingua latina fragmenta*, Lib. IX, "16. Vis et ipsa tertiae sunt declinationis et similem nominativo faciunt genetivum, hic civis huius civis, haec vis huius vis et plurali hae vis, sicut Lucretius et Varro: nam hae vires numero semper plurali declinantur".

Speidel [1600?–1666][455]; of these, the following has at most copied the previous and, without increasing enough the work of the latter, put his name on it with very little commendable ambition; then, the German Lexicons in the *Observations* by Paul Matthias Wehner [1583–1612], in the *Practical Treasury* by Christoph Besold [1577–1638], in the *Noteworthy Things* by Johann Jakob Speidel[456]. Speidel, in truth, increased with the supplements of all of the others, has been published *in folio* with the title of *Mirror*[457]; in addition, the illustrious Christoph Ludwig Dietherr von Anwanden [1619–1687] in Nuremberg has now set his hands on Besold, which he aims to revise and improve[458]. Because the items occurring in these lexicons are, for the most part, both German and Barbarian distorted from German in Latin, here what should be read are those who have written on German items, such as Johann Goropius Becanus [1519–1572] in various works, Johann Isacius Pontanus [1571–1639] in the *Origins*, Schottel in *The Art of Speaking German*, and many others quoted by Justus Georg Schottel [1612–1676][459]. Gerhard Johan Vossius [1577–1649] has col-

---

[455] Latin Juridical Lexicon: Johann Oldendorp (1548), *Lexicon juris*. Francoforti; Simon Schardius (1664), *Lexicon iuridicum*. Coloniae Agrippinae; Johann Kahl (Calvinus) (1622), *Lexicon iuridicum*. Coloniae; Johann Jakob Speidel (1657), *Speculum iuridico-politico-philologico-historicarum observationum et notabilium verborum etc.* Noribergae.

[456] German Juridical Lexicon: Paul Matthias Wehner (1615), *Practicarum Iuris Observationum Selectarum Liber*. Francofurti: Bringer; Christoph Besold, (1643), *Thesaurus practicus*. Noribergae; Johann Jakob Speidel (1634), *Notabilia juridico-historico-politica selecta ex legum sanctionibus*. Argentorati.

[457] See note 455.

[458] Christoph Ludwig Dietherr von Anwanden [1619–1687, edited Besold's book in 1666 (Nurberg) quoted in note 456.

[459] For the German items: Johann Becanus Goropius (1580), *Opera hactenus in lucem non edita nempe, Hermathena, Heiroglyphica,*

lected Latin-Barbarian items in the work *On the Defects of the Speech*[460]; Johannes Meursius [1579–1639] Greek-Barbarian in the *Glossary*[461].

§. 45. Other issues are to be considered according to the Legal Grammar, for example the *Legal Orthography*[462] by Paul Olinger [1517–…] has been published, and it is worth considering closely the method of writing in *Florentine Pandects*[463]. An admirably precise, accurate, preserver of the antiquity. Nor should one omit the abbreviations[464] of the ancient [authors], of which so far only fragments are left: I remember what seems to me to be the peculiar case of the booklet by a certain ancient author *On the Abbreviations*. To this can also be added the elegant *Epistle on the Abbreviations*[465] by Justus Lipsius [1547–1606], and the comment on the same by Michael Meisner [fl. 1623–1647][466], rector in Meissen. Nor should one neglect some singular methods of expression in Law carefully examined

Vertumnus, Gallica, Francica, Hispanica. Antuerpiae: Excudebat C. Plantinus; Johann Isacius Pontanus (1616), *Originum Francicarum libri VI*. Hardervici: Ex officinal Thomæ Henrici; Justus Georg Schottel (1641), *Teutsche Sprachkunst, darinn die allerwortreichste, prächtigste, reinlichste*. Braunschweig: Gruber.

[460] For the Latin-Barbarian items: Gerhard Johannes Vossius (1645) *De Vitiis Sermonis*. Amstelodami: Elzevirius.

[461] For the Greek-Barbarian items: Johannes Meursius (1610), *Glossarium Graecobarbarum*. Lugduni Batavorum.

[462] Paul Olinger (1555), *Orthographia Legalis Nova*. Argentorati.

[463] *Pandectae Florentinae, Ms., Codex Florentinus*.

[464] I.e., *latine* "notae", Charles Fresne du Cange, see note 420, *ad vocem Nota*, "notae sunt *signa* quaedam literarum quibus vox integra intelligitur".

[465] Justus Lipsius (1660), *De notis sive siglis antiquorum Justi Lipsii epistola 27. centur. 1. ad Belgas, observationibus quibusdam ipsarumque notarum catalogo ex variis auctoribus contracto illustrata a M. Joanne Pretenio*. Cizae: Cellarius.

[466] Michael Meisner (1622), *Syntagma philologicum de adnotamentis criticorum sive de notis sententiarum: cui adnatum Apospasma*. Hofii Variscorum: Pfeilschmid.

by Lorenzo Valla [1407–1457][467], supported by Guillaume Budé [1467–1540][468]. Moreover, Anton Matthaeus, in the *Compendium of the Foundations of the Law*[469] believed that he observed Priscianisms in Law[470]. Likewise, certain other ridiculous derivations do not differ from this observation[471], for example [the derivation] by Marcus Terentius Varro [116 BC–27 BC] on *fundus,* since it can be thrown with a *funda* [sling, e. n.][472]; by Accursius [c. 1182–1263] on the *Irenarchi* [Irenarchs, e. n.], since they *arceant iram* [prevent the anger, e. n.][473]; I do not know to whom one should attribute the derivation of the *Ecclesia Laterana* [Lateran Church, e. n.], said to derive from a *Latens Rana*

---

467 Lorenzo Valla (1499), *De linguae latinae elegantia libri VI*. Venetiis.

468 Guillaume Budé (1557), *Forensia*. Basileae.

469 Anton Matthaeus, see note 135.

470 *I.e.* the rules of the Priscian's Grammar; Priscianus Caesariensis (fl. 500 AD), was a grammarian of the VI cent.

471 *I.e.* "it belongs to this matter too expounding false derivations"; the Latin text is, "Nec abludunt ab hoc loco derivationes quaedam riduculae (…)"; here L. seems to paraphrase Horace [65 BC–27 BC.], *Saturae*. 2, 3, 320, "Haec a te non multum abludit imago".

472 From the homophony between *fundus* (a plot of land) and *funda* (sling); the quote from Varro seems, however, wrong, since the derivation mocked by Leibniz in the text, appears, instead, in Quintilian, see note 85, 6, 6, 76, which attributes it to a playful booklet (*joculari libello*) by Cicero, now missing.

473 As for the Irenarchs (whose name derives from the Greek ἐιρήνη, peace, and ἄρχω, to govern), they were officers of the urban police, whose presence is also ascertained as from the II cent. AD even in the towns of the Byzantine empire; one can read the false Latin derivation of the same noun (criticized by L. in the text) in (1627) *Corpus Juris cum Glossa Accursii*. Lugduni, t. V, col. 119. On this, see, Antonio de Nebrija [1441–1552] (1537), *Lexicon Juris Civilis adversus quosdam insignis Accursii errores*. Lugduni, *ad vocem Irenarca*, "In Codice Iustiniani titulus est de Irenarchis: quos Accursius [c. 1182–1263] interpretatur iram arcentes, quasi irenarchia nomen esset latinum".

[hiding frog, e. n.], which Nero is said to have vomited there[474], etc.

§. 46. It is of interest, especially for rhetoricians, to leaf through the works of the ancient jurists in order to collect issues which should not be neglected in the field of rhetoric. We are aware that Bartholomaeus Westhemer [1499–1570] wrote *On the Tropes of Scripture*[475], but I am surprised that so far no one has written *On the Tropes of the Laws*, except for certain metaphors of law, adages, and lines of the *Glossa*, which the illustrious Woldenberg[476] collected. It would be worthwhile also to collect formulas from Right, for example how you should begin, end, criticize, refute, reprove, refute, praise. This might enable the juriconsult to avail himself of the legal style in writing, as well as theologians of the sacred, and this would be of great distinction. To this sphere of investigation belong the Adages of Right: consider for instance what Mr. Johann Martin Brandes [1617–1668] recommends in the *Treaty on the true Jurisprudence*[477]: an essay has been composed by Mr. Woldenberg, and Martin Delrio [1551–1608] and Joachim Zehner [1566–1612] wrote *Sacred Adages*[478], just as Aloisio Novarini [1594–1650] drew up the *Adages of the Fathers*[479]. With regard to the issue of

---

[474] This unfounded etymology of the word "Lateranus" derives from a medieval legend, on which see Arturo Graf [1848–1913] (1915), *Roma nella leggenda e nella immaginazione del medioevo*. Torino, I, 215.

[475] Bartholomaeus Westhemer (1561), *Troporum, Schematum, Idiomatumque communium Liber*. Basileae: per Joh. Hervagium.

[476] See note 452.

[477] Johann Martin Brandes (1668), *De Vera Et Simulata Jurisconsultorum Philosophia*. Francofurti: Impensis Joh. Davidis Zunneri, Bibliop. Typis Johannis Andreae.

[478] Martin Antonio Delrio (1612), *Adagialia Sacra Veteris et Novi Testamenti*. Lvgdvni; Joachim Zehner (1601), *Adagia Sacra*. Lipsiae.

[479] Aloisio Novarini (1637), *Adagia Ex Sanctorum Patrum Ecclesiasticorumqve Scriptorum Monumentis Prompta*. Lugduni: Durand.

the style and form of legal language there are many aspects that should not be neglected; some are in the Digest and in the Constitutions of the ancient Emperors; others are examined far more broadly and in a more loquacious manner in the Constitutions of the Emperors of the Greeks. There it is narrated that illustrious men, with a keen hearing like that of the Arcadian herd, and by careful examination of the style, have discovered Tribonian hidden under the name of the ancient Jurisconsults. According to the observations of the Poetics, the casual verses, that is those which unintentionally escaped the authors' attention, likewise belong to this topic. Conrad Bachmann [1572–1646] and Christoph Helwig [1581–1617] have observed several of this kind in *The Giessen Poetics*[480]. Similar observations hold for Denis Godefroy [1549–1622], also sometimes in the *Notes*[481], Von Barth in the *Adversaries*[482], and Gerard Johannes Vossius [1577–1649] in the *Oratorical Institutes*[483].

---

480 Conrad Bachmann, Christoph Helwig (1624), *Poetica: Praeceptis, Commentariis, Observationibus, Exemplis*. Giessae Hassorum.

481 Possibly, Denis Godefroy (1602), *Auctores Linguae Latinae in unum redacti corpus…Adiectis Notis Dionisii Gothofredi*. S. Gervasii: Apud I. Chouet [not included in AA VI, 2, sources directory].

482 See note 236.

483 Gerard Johannes Vossius (1630), *Commentariorum rhetoricorum, sive Oratoriarum institutionum libri sex*. Lugduni Batavorum: J. Maire, in particular, lib. IV, tit. III, *Metrum in prosaculpari: historicis tamen, imo et Ciceroni, et aliis, saepe hemistichia, atque adeo totos versus excidisse*, therein, "Ac plurimos quoque e veterum jurisconsultorum scriptis collegit Scipio Gentilis lib. II, Παρέργα cap. ult. […]. Et apud Othonem Frisingensem lib. IV, cap XVIII: *Qui eius fautor erat, semel mergendo necavit.* Multa huius generis tam ex antiquis, quam posterioris aevi scriptoribus, annotavit Caspar Barthius in Adversariis suis *d.* Sed subinde mirificos nobis versus adfert. Ut e Sallustiano illo *e*: *Res Romana plurimum imperio valuit, Servio Sulpicio, et M. Marcello coss., omni Gallia cis Rhenum, atque inter mare nostrum, et Oceanum, nisi quae a paludibus fuit in via, perdomita.* Unde versum elicit *f.*

§. 47. Juridical Didactics is precisely what we are writing, whereby we are presenting the method of setting out, teaching, and learning law, to which there belongs the Art of Memory of various kinds. Memory can be obtained and trained either through verses, such as *The Juridical Memory*[484] by George Bucksulber; or through figures and paintings, [and] some have imagined a young girl with a colorful dress, with the Concordant Titles of the Law according to the proper order of the law woven into the hems of her dress and intertwined with her ornaments. There were also some writers who tried to represent all the topics of the law through the figure of a donkey; truly, you could call this the Bridge of Asses[485]. But the safest kind of Memory is a perfect and accurate Method. The Orders of the Laws likewise belong to the Didactics, on which not long ago a booklet, written with admirable pre-

---

Omnis Gallia cis Rhenum, atque inter mare nostrum.
Quasi non Sallustius in auferendi casu, *omni Gallia*, scripserit.".
It is worth remembering that alongside jurisconsults as "unintentional" poets there were jurisconsults who were known and appreciated even as poets, such as Hugo Grotius [1583–1645], who also wrote a "Paraphrasis Tituli Institutionum, *De Rerum Divisione et acquirendum earum dominio*", in Id. (1645), *Poemata Omnia*. Lugduni Batavorum; see James W. Binns (2010), "Diritto e Poesia nell'opera di Alberico Gentili ", in *Atti dei convegni nel quarto centenario della morte*. Vol II, Milano: Giuffrè, 181, who points out that there were many schools of poet-jurists in the XVII and XVIII cents.

[484] George Bucksulber (1652), *Memoriale juridicum*. Francofurti.

[485] http://www.britannica.com/EBchecked/topic/724634/The-Bridge-of-Asses [accessed 4 may 2015], "Euclid's fifth proposition in the first book of his *Elements* (that the base angles in an isosceles triangle are equal) may have been named the Bridge of Asses (Latin: Pons Asinorum) for medieval students who, clearly not destined to cross over into more abstract mathematics, had difficulty understanding the proof—or even the need for the proof. An alternative name for this famous theorem was Elefuga, which Roger Bacon [1214–1292], writing circa AD 1250, derived from Greek words indicating 'escape from misery.' Medieval schoolboys did not usually go beyond the Bridge of Asses, which thus marked their last obstruction before liberation from the *Elements*.". (John Lewis Heilbron).

cision, was published in Heidelberg. Its author, having carefully perused and weighed up the laws, has distributed all of those which are found in the whole *Corpus Juris*[486] according to 5 orders of necessity and utility. This work can be of extraordinary benefit to one who is getting ready to read the *Corpus Juris* in its entirety, for the booklet contains a δακτυλοδείκτην [in Greek in the text, index, e. n.] of the most useful and especially necessary [provisions]. It would be worthwhile if certain signs were added in the new edition of the *Corpus Juris* to indicate each order of the laws, so that the reader would understand at a glance every time what should be read, or omitted. In addition to this work, we also have the catalog of the difficult laws, and as he calls them "of the candidates", in the *Maniples*[487] of the illustrious Woldenberg.

§. 48. Legal History was touched on a little while ago in §. 28, where on the occasion of External history, which is more a requirement than a part of jurisprudence, we also treated Internal history: here, however, it is necessary to add the issues that definitely belong to the Exegetic, the cohesion of the laws in the Digest according to its authors. The latter work was prepared, on the basis of τῶν ἐπιγραφῶν [in Greek in the text, of the titles, e. n.] with great zeal by which by Jacques Labitte [d. 1603] in his *Index*[488], and his work was instrumental in ensuring that Paul[489], Ulpian[490], Gaius[491], and Modestinus[492] could be

---

[486] See note 19.

[487] See note 452.

[488] Jacques Labitte (1557), *Index Legum Omnium Quae In Pandectis Continentur.* Parisiis: Cavellat; see also Id. (1616), *Indicis usus quadruplex. Jac. Labitti ....ex recensione et cum notis Wilhelmi Schmuccii*, Angeb [not included in AA VI, 2, sources directory].

[489] Berger, see note 19, *ad vocem Paulus Iulius*, "A famous jurist whose prolific literary activity (about 320 *libri*) gave Justinian's compilers the opportunity to excerpt his writings very extensively for

regarded not as fragmented but, rather, continuous. Labitte demonstrated with examples four uses[493] thereof [of the index, e. n.]; the most prominent is that by which, this method having been learned through συναφείᾳ [in Greek in the text, the connection, e. n.] of the text, the law will explain the law, and the ἐναντιοφανείαι [in Greek in the text, the contradictions, e. n.] will be eliminated [494]. The

---

Digest. The dates of his birth and death are unknown. He was a member of the imperial council under Septimius Severus and Caracalla and Praefectus Praetorius under Alexander Severus [...]".

[490] Berger, see note 19, *ad vocem Ulpianus, Domitius*, "A jurist whose works were excerpted in a large measure by the compilers of the Digest; nearly onethird thereof originated from Ulpian's pen. He was born in Tyre (Phoenicia). He held various imperial office, was prefect of Praetorians from A.D. 222 and died in 228, assassinated by his subordinates [...]".

[491] Berger, see note 19, *ad vocem Gaius*, "One of the most renowned Roman jurist of the middle of the second century after Christ (born under Hadrian). His origin, full name and personal whereabouts are unknown [...]". His standard work is *Institutiones Gai* on which Berger, see note 19, *ad vocem*, "An introductory textbook of legal institutions in four books (called *commentarii* by the author) written by Gaius about A.D. 161. The system adopted by Gaius is tripartite: law of persons, law of things (including succession) and law of actions (civil procedure). The work, discovered in 1816 in Verona (hence called *Gaius Veronensis*) in a manuscript of the (late) fifth century, is preserved nearly in full. Some of the lacunae have been fulfilled by a few parchment sheets, found in 1933, seemingly of the late fourth century (now in Florence, hence called *Gaius Florentinus*). The new text confirmed the reliability of the *Veronensis* to a large extent [...]".

[492] Berger, see note 19, *ad vocem Modestinus, Herennius*, "One of he last representative of theclassical Roman Jurisprudence, a pupil of Ulpian, and high official in the administration of Rome about A.D. 240 [...]".

[493] See note 488.

[494] Enantiophanesis is also the name by which is known the unknown author of a work on the contradictions (VII cent.) contained in the Justinian *Digest*. Probably, this author also wrote the index of contradictions widely used in the *Basilici* (see note 276).

Catalog of the Repealed Laws[495] by Philibert Bugnyon [1530–1590] likewise belongs to the history of the laws. And the αμαρτήματα μνημονικά [in Greek in the text, the mnemonic errors, e. n.] was not avoided by several eminent men; Pomponius[496], or rather Tribonianus concealed under that name, as Hotman prefers, left many such errors in the title *On the Origin of the Right*.

§. 49. There follow the sections on Ethics and Legal Politics; on this topic see Paul Olinger [1517–...] in *Legal Ethics*, Vincentius Turturetus [fl. 1621] in *Ethical-Juridical Parallels*, Adam Keller [16th to 17th cent.] in *Juridical-Political Duties*, Liborius von Bodenstein [pseud. of Wawrzyniec Goślick, 1530/35–1607] in *Political Jurisprudence*. Furthermore, many topics relevant to ethics and politics are investigated and illustrated by Rutger Rulant [1568–1630] in his *On Commissioners*. Even Jacques Godefroy in his *Handbook* has extensively collected ethical-political axioms from the *Corpus Juris*, which lacks only a certain systematic order that can easily be added. We should also include the Ethical-Political Sentences [which are] in the *Maniples* of the illustrious Woldenberg[497]. Forensic medicine [liter-

---

[495] Philibert Bugnyon (1563), *Traicté des loix abrogées et inusitées en toutes les Cours du royaume de France, diligemment recueillies de tous bons autheurs practiciens, par M. Philibert Bugnyon*. Lyon.

[496] Berger, see note 19, *ad vocem Pomponius Sextus*, "A prominent jurist of the time of Hadrian and Antoninus Pius (around the middle of the second century). He is the author of three tretise on civil law written as commentaries on works of earlier jurists (ad Quintum Mucium, ad Plautium, ad Sabinum), of an extensive Commentary on the praetorian Edict (known only from citations by later jurists), and of a series of monographs on various topics (on *fideicommissa*, on stipulations, on *senatusconsulta*). [...]".

[497] Ethics and Legal Politics: Paul Olinger (1555), *Ethicorum Legalium Liber Primus*. Argentorati; Vincentius Turturetus (1629), *Parallela ethica & juridica*. Parisii; Adam Keller (1607), *De officiis juridico-politicis chiragogici libri tres*, Constantiae; Liborius von

ally in the text, the natural sciences, e. n.], on the other hand, is comprehensively expounded in the *Medical-Legal Questions* by Paolo Zacchia [1584–1659] and in the *Method of Demonstrating in the Questions Submitted to the Physicians* by Giovan Battista Codronchi [1547–1628][498]. We have composed an essay of Legal Geometry on calculating [literally, on giving account, e. n.] the distance of ditches between boundaries of lands, regarding the last law [in the title of Digest, e. n.] on determining boundaries between adjoining lands in *Essay of Philosophical Questions from the Law, question 3*[499]. The harvest of the Juridical Arithmetics is abundant, and the following should also be added: *On the As* by Budé and the *Treatise on the Share and Instalment*, by Jean Baptiste Lacoste [d. 1637?], as well as our own work in the *Combinatorial Art, problem 3, n. 16.*[500]

§. 50. But, firstly, we must not omit the Logic and Metaphysics of Right, that is, certain philosophical rules that are to be respected in right, but which commonly are inappropriately mixed with the rules of right. Several authors of Juridical Logics have devoted study to these rules: François Hotman [1524–1590] in *Dialectical Institutions*, Johann Thomas Freige [1543–1583] in *Logic of the Jurisconsults*, Martin Schickard [1579–1636] in *Ju-*

Bodenstein (1609), *Jurisprudentia politica*. Basel; Rutger Rulant (1617), *Tractatus de Commissariis et Commissionibus Camerae Imperialis*. Francofurti; Jacques Godefroy, see note 205; Woldenberg, see note 452.

[498] Forensic medicine: Paolo Zacchia (1621), *Quaestiones medicolegales*. Romae: Sumptibus A. Brugiotti; Giovan Battista Codronchi (1597), *De Vitiis Vocis: Libri Duo ... Cui accedit Consilium de Raucedine, ac Methodus testificandi, in quibusvis casibus medicis oblatis*. Francofurti; Id., in Clemente Puccini and others (eds.) (1987), *Methodus testificandi*. Sala Bolognese: Forni.

[499] See note 12.

[500] Juridical Arithmetics: Guillaume Budé, see note 233 Parisii: Badius; Jean Baptiste Lacoste (1667), *De Quota [et] Rata*, Noribergae; Leibniz, see note 54.

ridical Logic; Nikolaus Vigel [1529–1600], Matthias Stephani [1570–1646] and Daniel Otto [fl. 1606–1620] in *Dialectics of the Right*, Nicolaas Everaerts [c.1461–1532] in *Common Places of the Legal Arguments*, and Georg Adam Brunner [1580–1652] in *Synopsis of Everaert Topics*, and Johann von Felden [d. c. 1668] in *Handwritten Notes to the Aristotle Topics*, where he illustrates with chosen examples almost all of the rules, which number over a thousand. This is a noteworthy work, to which should be added a final correction by the hand of the author and an appropriate printing format at public expense. These authors, therefore, by profession paid attention to the philosophical rules that must be excluded [literally, dragged away, e. n.] from right[501]. The same approach, one may add, was adopted–and without order–by the jurisconsults of that barbarian age in their commentaries on the laws: no small number of such jurisconsults took care to derive general rules from the law, to such a point that, in the end, their zeal was excessive and almost superstitious. What is more incorrect than drawing from the *Law Barbarius*[502] *in Digest, Duties of Praetor*, the rule: *Common error makes right?* However, these moles of ancient

---

[501] Juridical Logics: François Hotman (1573), *Dialecticae institutionis libri iiii*. Genevae: Ex Officina Iacobi Stoerij; Johann Thomas Freige (1582), *De logica iureconsultorum libri duo*. Basileae; Martin Schickard (1615), *Logica iuridica*. Herborn; Nikolaus Vigel (1581), *Dialectica juris civilis libri III*. Basileae: off. Oporiniana; Matthias Stephani (1610), *Dialectica Iuris Exactissima Et Absolutissima*. Francofurti: Saurius; Daniel Otto (1621), *Dialectica juris libri duo*. Jenae; Nicolaas Everaerts (1516), *Topicorum seu de locis legalibus liber*. Louanii: T. Martinus, impensis cum H. Eckert communibus; Georg Adam Brunner (1555), *Synopsis locorum legalium*. Magdeburg: Kirchn; as direct reference to Aristotle found only Johann von Felden (1654), *Analysis librorum politicorum Aristotelis*. Francofurti.

[502] So called after Philippus Barbarius, a runaway slave who stood as candidate for the praetorship at home and became praetor designate, see *D*.1.14.3.

times should not cause us to abandon completely the study of the rules and brocardica, which Jacques Cujas [1522–1590] and Claudius Cantiuncula [c.1496–1560] very strongly advised[503]. To this Logic of Right there belong the methods of Jurisconsults in defining, dividing, presenting a case through combinatorial art; such activities are known by the name of *ars casuandi* in the *Handbook*[504] by Jaques Godefroy, as well as in the *Finenesses of Right*[505] by Paul Buys [1531–1594]; likewise Anton Matthaeus collected the Logical παροράματα [in Greek in the text, errors, e. n.] of the laws and the *petitiones principii* [begging the question, e. n.], some of them with the specific line of argument inserted in the *Collection of the Foundations.*[506] We have observed, also, that many of these syllogisms are incorrect in their form. To this topic there additionally belongs the Method on whatever matter has been treated or has been observed according to the title; in the Digest [such a method] is fairly good, but it is absent in the Code, where Tribonian did not follow the order of the subjects, but the time [*scil.* of issuing of the laws, e.n.].

§. 51. Similarly, the Reconciliation of the Antinomies [*i.e.*, the conflict of laws, e. n.] belongs to Juridical Logic. Hence, the most vexed question: are antinomies perhaps allowed in law? In this regard, I no longer nurture any doubt about Horace's sentence *In a long work it is allow-*

---

[503] Jacques Cujas (1595), *Recitationes ad Titulum Digestorum De Justitia et Jure.* Spirae Nemetum; Claudius Cantiuncula (1522), *Oratio apologetica in patrocinium Juris Civils.* Basileae; Id. (1520), *Topica.* In Inclyta Basilea: Apud Andream Cartandrum.

[504] See note 205.

[505] Paul Buys (1626), *Subtiliorumexercitationum legaliumlibri septem.*Coloniae Agrippinae.

[506] Anton Matthaeus, see note 135.

able for sleep to steal upon us[507], especially since it is not believable that many associates of an *opus* always followed the same advice. On the contrary, whoever claims that traces of ancient law can be detected in the Digest thereby admits antinomies. In fact, Justinian ordered and Tribonian declared that all of the old [laws] were to be considered as repealed. What should I say about the schools of jurisconsults, which are in conflict? There are also certain laws, where in terms the one alleges that the other is dissenting, whose dissent can then be found expressly in a different passage of the Digest. The most distinguished jurisconsults, introduced by the others as a long army, teach the same thing: that is to say, only Holy Scripture can claim to be consistent everywhere. The art of solving antinomies consists in being careful so that the one be the subject or predicate in this law or proposition, the other be [the subject or predicate] in that law or proposition, and both remain the same. In this manner Aristotle shows it is possible to prove diversity and identity, thereby revealing many ways in which antinomies can be unravelled. We intend to demonstrate this in a more comprehensive manner with a specific *Commentary on the Art of Solving the Antinomies*. Before or around [the age of] Accursius, the ancient glossators had already proceeded to collect numerous and very considerable antinomies, though not so many as were discovered and added to by later jurisconsults; but more recently, a complete reconciliation was achieved, for the most part. Accursius abounds in reconciliations; however, they are very uncertain, as he himself with his continuous: *vel dic* [or say, e. n.] admits. But those great reformers of jurisprudence François Douaren [1509–1559], Jacques Cujas [1522–1590], François Hotman [1524–1590] cut these

[507] Horace [65 BC–27 BC, *Ars Poetica*, 360, "verum opera longo fas est obrepere somnum".

numerous Gordian knots. From their writings Hubert van Giffen [1534–1604] gathered the reconciliations into a single book[508], Giulio Pace [1550–1635] the *Centuriae of the* ἐναντιοφανειῶν[509] [in Greek in the text, of the contradictions, e. n.], Nicolaus von Salis in *Aftermath of Right*[510], Niccolò Passeri [1585–1615][511] in the book where he claims to have solved all of the antinomies; and the remaining mostly unknown multitude [of the authors]. We lack a short assessment of the antinomies which consist of four sheets of paper, where only a primary and complete solution is inserted, and the writer is alleged to have been its first inventor; moreover, if the antinomy is incontestable, even this observation is to be concisely brought to attention on the basis of the authority of some eminent man. When we have some peace and time to work, we will prepare this work, which, though short, will be very useful to students, with the title *Antinomicus minor*, in contrast to the *maior*, i.e. to that which broadly describes the various solutions and explanations of the authors and the related difficulties.

§. 52. We have summed up the Philology and Philosophy of the Law almost as preliminaries. There follows the actual interpretation of the laws, which is either simultaneous interpretation of one law with the other, or solitary interpretation of a given law according to itself. It is simultaneous when either the series of laws, or the es-

---

[508] Hubert van Giffen (1666), *Antinomiarum juris civilis disputationes* XI. Francofurti: Zunner.

[509] Giulio Pace (1596), *Enantiofanon seu legum conciliatarum Centuriae (VII)*, Tertia ed. recognita et aucta, Spirae: B. Albinus.

[510] Nicolaus von Salis (1614), *Sicilimenta ex toto jure civili collecta.* Hanoviae.

[511] Niccolò Passeri (1596), *Conciliatio cunctarum legum quae in toto corpore iuris civilis invicem quasi ex diametro sibi contrariari videbantur*. Venetiis.

sential parts, are made clear, or when *Paratitla* are composed[512]. The series of the laws cannot be obtained if it was not arranged according to the series of the titles[513]: a series derived from many of the titles has been outlined in *Economies of Right*[514], such as in the works by Matthaeus Wesenbeck [1531–1586] and Hubert Van Giffen [1534–1604]; although many others, later, were to neglect them, Wilhelm Schmuck [1575–1634] made use of tables in an effective [literally, vigorous, e. n.] *Synopsis of Civil and Canon Law*[515]. In works by more recent authors, appreciation is expressed both for the tables of the illustrious Iohann OttoTabor[516], and the series of titles inserted in the excellent *Handbook*[517] by Jacques Godefroy, where he unravelled many knots through the history and order of the Perpetual Edict. The series of laws of various titles in the *Digest* and *Decretum* was taken from this subject-matter for some specific purpose, and therefore can also be reduced to tables; in contrast, such an approach is not allowed by the *Code* and the *Decretals*, because the rescripts are arranged according to the sequence of time [scil. of issuing, e. n.]. But even if the problem of time is disregarded, were any man to have proceeded to this point, so that the very laws in question were reduced into the tables, such a development would be superseded by the diligence of the theologians, who have continuously

---

512 See *infra* §. 59.

513 The titles (*titla*) indicate the matter ruled in the books of the Digest and Code.

514 Matthaeus Wesenbeck (1579), *Commentarius iuris Oeconomia iam olim dictus*. Basileae: Episcopius; Hubert van Giffen (1611), *Oeconomica iuris*. Argentorati.

515 Wilhelm Schmuck (1629), *Synopsis juris civilis*. Lipsiae; Id. (1630), *Synopsis juris canonici*. Lipsiae [maternal grandfather of L., e. n.].

516 Johann Otto Tabor, see note 163.

517 See note 205.

created their own tables and analysis for the same verses [of the Holy Scriptures, e. n.]

§. 53. There follows, at this point, the Series entitled the Essential Part, which is either General or Particular. The general part of all of the books of law consists of the Pandects, the Code, the Novels, Feudal Law, and Canon Law, such as the Decisions of the Diet. I refer to the Essential Part as the General Institutes of Right: which differ from the Elements of Right described in §. 22 and ff., because here a brief treatment is also given of the repealed rules and ancient law–in accordance with the approach also adopted by Justinian in his *Institutes*—which are excluded by the practice of today. Meanwhile, the method will be the same as in the Elements. We assess what must always be observed, so that the students will not be confused by the variety of methods. I do not remember who, so far, has composed Institutes of General Right.

§. 54. The Essential Particular Part is either of the books or works, or of the titles. The essential part of the books varies according to the books of Right. A fine compendium of Justinian's Institutes has been used as an introduction in Denis Godefroy's [1549–1622] *Corpus Juris*[518]. However, as it preserves the order of titles and laws, it should be called the essential part of the laws in the Institutes, rather than of the Institutes themselves. Arnold Corvinus van Belderen [d. 1680?] is an illustrious figure, with distinct *Aphorisms*[519] excellently summed up

---

[518] *Epitome Institutionum*, in Denis Godefroy (1583), *Corpus Juris Civilis in IIII partes distinctum*. [Augusta Allobrogum] Lugduni: Jacobus Stoer, 115 [not included in AA VI, 2, sources directory]; see also note 19.
[519] Arnold Corvinus van Belderen (1649), *Digesta per aphorismos strictim explicate*. Amsterodami: Elzevir.

the Digest and the Code. Pierre Goudelin [1550–1619][520] has collected the Newest Right, that is, of the *Novels*, in a single book. The *Institutes of Canon Law* was composed with a personal study, firstly by Giampaolo Lancelloti [1511–1591]; after his death, upon the arrival of public approval, they were inserted into the *Body of Canon Law*. There also exist the *Institutes* by Marco Antonio Cucchi [1506–1567] and the *Aphorisms* by the above cited Arnold Corvinus van Belderen[521]. Among many, Hermann Vulteius [1555–1634] gave the best *Institutes of Feudal Right*, which he summed up again toward the end through a very concise synopsis[522]. We feel the lack, so far, of the *Institutes of Imperial Right*, that is, a *Compendium of the Rescripts of the Diet and of the Regulation of the Chamber*. Likewise one feels the lack of the Institutes of Saxon Right methodically collected from the Body of the Saxon Right. I am always amazed that so far no scholar has embarked on such a project. "But since while the one is waiting for the other, all of them desist, we shortly, if God helps us, will prepare the Institutes both of the Imperial, and of the Saxon Right, unless in the meantime someone readier, will preceed us. "[quotation marks in the text, e. n.]. Meanwhile, as far as Imperial Right is concerned, one can read primarily the material that concerns the trial, the *Pandects of the Chamber*[523] by

---

[520] Pierre Goudelin (1643), *Commentariorum de jure novissimo libri 6*. Arnhemii: Biesius.

[521] Institutes and aphorisms of Canon Law: Giampaolo Lancelloti [1511–1591] (1606), *Institutiones iuris canonici*. Lugduni: Apud hæredes Gulielmi Rovillii; Marco Antonio Cucchi (1565), *Institutiones iuris canonici*. Papia; Arnold Corvinus van Belderen (1648), *Jus Canonicum per aphorismos strictim explicatum*. Amstelodami.

[522] Hermann Vulteius (1602), *De Feudis eorundemque jure libri II*. Marburgi.

[523] Wilhelm Roding (1598), *Pandectae iuris cameralis*. Spirae: Apud B. Albinum.

Wilhelm Roding [1549–1603]. As for Saxon Right, it is certainly worth reading the *Synopsis of Justinian's Institutes*[524] by Georg Schultze [1612–1634], to which he has added the parallel places of the Saxon Right.

§. 55. The Essential Part of the Titles that can be found in *Glossed Body* is flawed, incomplete and redundant[525], just as even the edition of Godefroy is superfluous and disorderly, inasmuch as the title claims to examine the series of the laws, and flawed insofar as it considers only single terms, not the whole proposition. Excellent for this purpose is the *Analysis*[526] of Giulio Pace of Beriga [1550–1635], recently increased and printed in Belgium. We plan to compose an essay whose title will summarize the titles both of the *Digest* and *Code*, and also of the *Novels*. This kind of Essential Part of all of the titles is especially indispensable in the *Code* and in the *Novels*, which collected the Constitutions issued by successive Emperors, as their loquacity, long preambles, and a whole host of rhetorical arguments not only distract the reader's attention, but are also confusing.

---

[524] Georg Schultze (1655), *Synopsis Institutionum Imperialium*. Lipsiae: Berger.
[525] See note 518.
[526] Giulio Pace (1605), *Institutionum Imperialium Analysis earundem institutionum Epitome*. Lugdunum.

§. 56. The title 3, *Procurators*[527] *and Defenders*[528], of book 3 of the *Digest* (*D*.3.3), encompassing 78 laws, written in a very concise kind of language, seemed appropriate. By abstracting the universals, we have summarized them, so that by means of our rules one may deduce all the laws of the title. The Procurator is he who assents to administering the businesses of another, who grants his consent. Firstly, in this step, attention will focus on the judgments. A person who is allowed by right to be in control over his own things may appoint a procurator *l.* 8. 33. 35. §. 1, *l.* 43. §. 1 [529], provided that such a person is

---

[527] Watson, see note 179, vol. 3, *Glossary, ad vocem*, "This term has a number of meanings. (a) The representative of a party in a civil trial. (b) A general manager of another person's businesses or other affairs. This position was often given to a freedman [*libertinus* q.v.] or a slave. Occasionally, the term was applied to an agent for a single transaction. An earlier type of business manager [*institor*] come to be considered a kind of procurator. See *D*.3.3.; *D*.14.3. (c) Many imperial officials were called procurators, for example, *a procurator Caesaris*, originally a fiscal agent but later given many administrative duties. See *D*.1.19".

[528] Watson, see note 179, vol. 3, *Glossary, ad vocem*, "A person who defends another's interests at trial, often because of his legal relation to him, for example, as *tutor*. See *D*.3.3".

[529] Those are the laws from the entire *D*.3.3 *Procurators and Defenders*, summed up by Leibniz in the text (For the related references in this paragraph, I will utilize x, the translation made by Watson, see note 179): *D*.3.3.8, "A son-in-power can also appoint a procurator for any action which he has the right to bring himself, and not just a son with military *peculium*, but also any son-in-power."; 33, "They say that a slave and son-in-power can also have a procurator. As far as the son-in-power is concerned, it is correct, but with regard to the slave, we are doubtful. Certainly, we allow that someone can conduct business connected with slave's *peculium* and in these circumstances be his procurator (this is Labeo's opinion too); but we rule out bringing an action"; 35.§1, "A patron can prosecute his freedman through a procurator, and the freedman can answer the charge through a procurator"; 43.§1, "When it is asked whether somebody is allowed to have a

not legally forbidden from holding the position of Procurator *l.* 43. pr. §.1[530]. No soldier is allowed [as procurator] (unless he is acting in the name of his comrades or in his own interest, *l.* 8. §. 3[531]), nor a woman (unless she is acting on behalf of her parents in case of need) *l.* 41[532], or two in favor of only one *l.* 31. §. 1. 2, *l.* 33[533], or only one in favor of many adversaries in the same trial, *l.* 43. §. 6[534]. [A procurator] is appointed by mandate of the principal, *l.* 27.47[535], with the consent of the procurator, *l.* 1.

---

procurator, we should look to see whether he is not prevented from appointing a procurator, because the edict is prohibitory".

530 *D*.3.3.43. pr., "The deaf and the dumb are not forbidden to appoint a procurator by any method which can be of service. They may also be appointed themselves, not indeed for legal proceedings but for administration."; §.1, see above note 529.

531 *D*.3.3.8.§.3 [but 2, e. n.]., "Veterans can become procurators, but soldiers cannot be appointed procurators even if the other party agrees, unless at the time of joinder of issue this has been overlooked through some circumstance or other. An exception is made for the man who has been appointed procurator for his own interest, or who is to conduct or undertakes a case has in common with all his comrades".

532 *D*.3.3.41, "Women will sometimes be permitted to take legal action on behalf of their parents, if, say, their parents are prevented by illness or age and do not have a man to do so".

533 *D*.3.3.31.§.1, "There is no rules against several procurators being appointed for a single lawsuit in which several people are concerned"; 2, "Julian says that a person who has appointed two procurators at different times is held to have excluded the first by appointing the second"; 33 [but 32, e. n.], "Where several procurators with general powers have been appointed at the same time, the first to act will be given preference, so that a later one does not have the status of procurator in respect of the object of the earlier one claim.".

534 *D*.3.3.43.§.6, [but is 42.§.6, e n.] "If there are several heirs and an action is brought for dividing an inheritance or common property, several heirs should not be allowed to appoint the same procurator, since as regards assignments and impositions, a settlement would be impossible. Obviously, the appointment should be allowed if several heirs succeed one of the co-heirs".

535 *D*.3.3.27, "(...) But this is only the position if the procurator acted on a mandate from a principal. If there is not mandate, since he has

§. 2. *l.* 3. 5. 6. 7. 8. §. 1[536], or by *litis contestatio*[537], after the proper time for *exceptio procuratoria*[538], *l.* 8. §. 3. *l.* 40. §. 3. *l.* 57. §. 1[539], in all civil trials, except the follow-

---

brought no special power into the case and you have not given your approval to do it, acts done without your permission are no impediment to you, and consequently you do not need the transference of these lawsuits to avoid being incommoded by someone else's action. (…); 47, "If a person who has left two procurators with general powers over his estate has not expressly directed one to claim money from the other, he is considered not to have given a mandate to either of them".

536 *D.*3.3.1.§2 [but 1 e. n.], "A procurator may have appointed either for all his principal's business or only for one item of it, either in his principal presence or by message or by letter; although certain people, as Pomponius writes in his twenty-fourth book, do not consider that a person taking on a mandate for only one item of business is a procurator, just as man who has undertaken to convey a thing or to convey a letter or message is not properly called a procurator either. But it is more reasonable to consider a person appointed for one piece of business only also a procurator."; 3, "Likewise, he can be appointed for an impending law suit, for a future date, conditionally and until a certain date, [4, "and for indefinite period", e. n.]"; 5, "A person is considered to be present when he is in the garden,"; 6, "when he is in the forum, and when he is in the city and in adjacent buildings;"; 7, "and for this reason his procurator is considered to have his principal present"; 8.§.1, "It is not customary to appoint an unwilling procurator. We should take the word unwilling to include not only the man who refuses but also the one for whose consent there is no evidence".

537 Du Plessis, see note 125, 68, "Whatever the form of procedure used in the preliminary stage, the critical moment was reached when issue was joined (*litis contestatio*). This occurred on the completion of the parties' assertions, i.e. on the formulation of the issues between them (…)"; more in deep, Berger, see note 19, *ad vocem*.

538 Berger, see note 19, *ad vocem*, "The counterpart to the *exceptio cognitoria* in the case that the creditor is represented in a trial by *a procurator*. Through this *exception* the defendant objects that the plaintiff's representative has no right to act as a representative (*procuratorio nomine*)".

539 *D.*3.3.8.§.3, "The praetor says: 'I will compell a procurator appointed to undertake lawsuit, on whose behalf and with whose consent his principal has arranged to satisfy judgement, to accept

ing: *actio popularis*[540], unless it personally concerns the plaintiff, *l.* 42. 45. §. 1. *l.* 74[541], and generally *actiones famosae*[542], l. 39. §. 7[543]. There follows: 1) the obligation of the procurator towards the principal, of mandate, *l.*

---

trial'. But he should not be compelled if they are good reasons for not doing so. Suppose for example, a deadly, personal enmity has arisen between the procurator and his principal. Julian writes that an action against the procurator ought to be refused. Likewise, if the procurator has gone up in rank or is going to be absent on public business."; 40.§.3, "Security for ratification is taken from a procurator before joinder of issue. Once joinder of issue has taken place, he will not be compelled to give a guarantee."; 57.§.1, "If anyone has foregone the procuratorial defense, he will not be able to change his mind and raise it as an objection".

540 Watson, see note 179, 1 vol., Glossary, *ad vocem*, "A penal action which could be brought to any person to protect the public interest in certain circumstances".

541 *D*.3.3.42, "Although a procurator cannot be appointed in actions in the public interest, it has however, rightly been said that a person who goes to law about public right of way and suffers personal loss from its closure can appoint a procurator for an action that is in some sense private. With even more reason will the person concerned appoint one for an action for the violation of a tomb."; 45.§1, "Persons who, in bringing an action in a matter of public interest, are also protecting their private interest, are allowed, after examination of the case, to appoint a procurator and anyone else trying to bring an action later on will be barred by a defense (*exceptio*)."; 74, "The advocate of a state cannot perform public business through a procurator".

542 Watson, see note 179, 1 vol., Glossary, *ad vocem Infamia*, "A condition of disgrace resulting from certain types of immoral or wrongful conduct. It followed, for instance, on conviction of crime, or condemnation in delictal actions and those involving breach of trust called *actiones famosae*. Many legal disabilities resulted from this condition".

543 *D*.3.3.39.§.7, "Likewise, he says that at the arraignment of a suspect tutor his defender also ought to guarantee ratification, that he will not want to reopen the case on his return. But permission will not lightly be given for one suspect to be accused through a procurator, since the case involves *infamia*, unless it is agreed that he was expressly given a mandate by a tutor, or if also, in the absence of the tutor, the praetor was going to treat the case as undefended".

42[544], in order to administer *l.* 15[545], and return the things obtained from this lawsuit, *l.* 46. §. 4[546]; toward the opponent, in order to undertake a lawsuit in the following circumstances: if, with his consent, the principal has given surety to satisfy judgment, *l.* 8. §. 3. *l.* 17[547], unless he has been absolved, due to necessity on both parts *D. l.* 8. §. 3. *l.* 9. 19. 21[548], or due to his greater advantage, *l.* 10. 20[549], or due to enmity with the principal, *l.* 14. 21[550],

---

[544] *D.*3.3.42[.§.2, e. n.; Leibniz cannot be precise in quoting, because he is writing this book during a journey, without books, see §. 42, of the first part], "The obligations which usually exist between a principal and his procurator gave rise to an action on mandate (…)".

[545] *D.*3.3.15, "If principal has died before joinder of issue, after entering into a Stipulation for satisfaction of judgement on his procurator's behalf, the procurator should be compelled to accept trial only if the principal did this with the knowledge and not against the express wish of the procurator. For otherwise, it is very much against the spirit of law for the procurator to be held liable, and the section of the stipulation for failure to defend becomes operatives."

[546] *D.*3.3.46.§.4, "In a lawsuit too, a procurator must present his accounts in accordance with the principle of good faith, just as in the conduct of other business also. Therefore, in action on mandate he is obliged to make over what he has obtained from a lawsuit, whether directly and expressly on account of the case or indirectly because of it, so much so that even if he has obtained something not due through a mistake or injustice on the part of the judge, he is obliged to make over too".

[547] *D.*3.3.8.§.3, see note 539; 17, "After joinder of issue a defendant who has appointed a procurator can certainly change him or transfer the suit from him to himself, even while the procurator is still alive or living in the state, but only after examination of the cause.".

[548] *D.*3.3.8§.3, see note 539; 9, "or if he pleads ill-health or unavoidable absence from home"; 19, "Likewise, if the procurator should be of doubtful character, in prison, or in the power of the enemy or robbers"; 21, "or exile, or if he should evasive or later become personal enemy".

[549] *D.*3.3.10, "Or coming into an inheritance keeps him busy or for any other adequate reason. Furthermore, a procurator should also not be put under compulsion if his principal is present"; 20, "or occupied with criminal or civil proceedings, his health, or more important business of his own".

or because he has been elevated to public office, *l.* 8. §. 3[551], or on account of the presence of the principal, *l.* 10. 11[552], and unless in these cases there is danger in delay, *l.* 12[553], and he is obliged by the opponent of the judgment; if he acted in his own interest, if he came forward knowing that no guarantee had been given, *l.*61[554]. Hence, from these considerations there follows: 2) the obligation of the opponent to contend in a lawsuit, with the procurator or the principal, see nevertheless *l.* 29. 43. §. 5[555], if [a procurator], giving surety on ratification, is [acting] as plaintiff, *l.* 39. §. 1[556], unless he comes from sons, par-

---

[550] *D.*3.3.14, "If after the appointment of procurator a deadly enmity has arisen, he should not be compelled to accept trial, and the stipulation for failure to defend does not become operative since the circumstances of the case have changed"; 21, see note 548.

[551] See note 539.

[552] *D.*3.3.10, see note 549; 11, "provided that constraint can be put upon the principal".

[553] *D.*3.3.12, "But it is said that for the following reasons (also) a procurator should sometimes be compelled to accept trial, for example, if his principal is not present and the plaintiff asserts that with lapse of time the suit is going to be lost".

[554] *D.*3.3.61, "Plautius says: 'All are of the opinion that a procurator who has suffered condemnation should not be sued, unless he was appointed in his own interest or came forward although he knew no guarantee had been given. The same principle will apply also if he has come forward with security as defender in a lawsuit'".

[555] *D.*3.3.29, "If a plaintiff prefers to sue the principal rather than the person who is procurator in his own interest, he should be told that is free to do so."; 43.§.5, "If a procurator brings an action and a slave of his absent principal is present, Atilicinus says the slave must be given security, not the procurator.".

[556] *D.*3.3.39. §.1, "Anyone bringing an action in someone else's name must guarantee that the person the matter concerns will ratify it. But sometimes, even though a procurator proceeds in own name, he will be obliged to guarantee ratification, as Pomponius writes in his twenty-fourth book. For example, suppose that an oath has been offered back to procurator and he has sworn that conveyance is due to his absent principal. He is acting in this case in his own name because the oath is his own (for this procedure could not have been available to this to his principal), but he will be obliged to guarantee

ents, brothers, relatives by marriage, freedmen[557], *l.* 35. pr. *l.* 40. §. 4[558], or the principal states that he will deem as ratified his acts, l. 65, or gives surety to satisfy judgment if in favor of the defendant, *l.* 39. §. 4[559]. Moreover, the mandate contains the necessary means for the goal, l. 56. 62[560], but the general mandate does not cover a compromise, *l.* 60 [561]. Hence, there likewise follows the

---

ratification. Again, if the arrangement to pay (constitutum debiti) has been made with the procurator and he brings an action rising from it, there should be no doubt that a guarantee of ratification is required, and so Pomponius writes".

557 Watson, see note 179, vol. 1, Glossary, *ad vocem Libertinus, Libertus* (Freedman), "A former slave who, on manumission [*manumission*], became a freeman and a Roman citizen, though with extensive public law disabilities. He had many duties toward his former master, his patron [*patronus*]. An imperial freedman [*libertus Caesaris*] manumitted by the emperor often obtained high governmental office in the early empire".

558 *D.*3.3.35 pr., "But the following classes of procurators who are allowed to sue without a mandate will also be under an obligation to defend, for example, children, even though they are in power, likewise parents, brothers, relations by marriage, and freedmen."; 40.§.4, "As regards those procurators who do not require a mandate, it should be said that they ought to be debarred if it is clear that they come to court contrary to the wish of those on whose behalf they are intervening. So we do not require that they have consent or a mandate but that there is no proof of a wish to the contrary, even though they offer a guarantee of ratification".

559 *D.*3.3.39.§.4, "If a father brings an action on his son's account, since there are two actions, one for the father and one for the son, a guarantee of ratification is not required".

560 *D.*3.3.56, "A procurator appointed to bring a claim for a movable will be entitled to bring an action for production,"; 62, "If a procurator appointed to claim a legacy makes use against the heir of the interdict for the production of a will, he is not stopped by a procuratorial defense, made on the ground that he has not also been given a mandate for this".

561 *D.*3.3.60, "A general mandate does not also cover a compromise introduced to effect a settlement, and for this reason, if the mandatory has not afterward ratified the compromise, he cannot be barred from bringing actions".

obligation of the opponent or the sureties (*fideiussores*) toward the principal so that the latter has an *actio utilis*[562] against them, *l.* 27. §. 2, *l.* 28[563], unless the procurator is acting in his own interest, *l.* 56[564]. Therefore: 3) the obligation of the principal toward the procurator [gives rise to an action] on mandate, *l.* 42. 46. §. 5. 6[565], unless the

---

[562] Watson, see note 179, vol. 1, Glossary, *ad vocem Actio in factum*, "An action given originally by the *praetor* on the alleged facts of the case alone, where no standard civil law [*ius civile*] action was directly applicable. The expression *actio utilis* is also found, referring to a praetorian action which extended the scope of an existing civil law action, for example, by means of a fiction. The exact difference, if any, between this and the *actio in factum* is not known".

[563] *D*.3.3.27.§.2 [but §.1, e. n.], "If transference of suit takes place on the part of the plaintiff, the opinion we give is that the stipulation entered into by the defendant for satisfaction of judgment is operative. Both Neratius and Julian support this, and it is the law today, certainly if the principal has received security. But even if the procurator has received security and the case is transferred to his principal, it is fairer for the stipulation to be operative and for an action on stipulation to be transferred from the procurator to his principal. But even if the case is transferred from a principal or from a procurator to a procurator, Marcellus has no doubt that the stipulation is operative. This is the law. And even though it is the procurator who has brought the stipulation into play, still his principal should be given an *actio utilis* on stipulation, though a straightforward (*directa*) action would be completely out of the question."; 28, "If my procurator has received security for satisfaction of judgment, I have an *actio utilis* on stipulation, just as an action on judgment is granted to me. (…)".

[564] *D*.3.3.56 [but it is 55, e. n.], "If a procurator has been appointed in his own interest, the principal is not to be given preference over the procurator in bringing an action or receiving money; for a person having *actiones utiles* available in his own name is entitled to bring them.".

[565] *D*.3.3.42.[§.2, here is the proper passage, e. n.], "The obligations which usually exist between a principal and his procurator give rise to an action on mandate. (…)"; 46.§, "5. On the other hand, he is likewise entitled to recover what he paid out as the result of judgment, but he is not entitled to recompense for a penalty he incurred because of his own wrongdoing. 6. Fairness suggests that a procura-

procurator (who is not acting in his own interest by necessity, *l.* 33. §. 5. *l.* 34, add *l.* 79[566]) has refused to defend *l.* 33. §. 4, *l.* 35. pr. §. 2[567], any other thing, *l.* 43. §. 4[568]. Everyone who is [in turn], easy to sue *l.* 54[569], can defend, *l.* 34. §. 2[570], with sure effectiveness, *l.* 51[571], the

tor of either the plaintiff or the defendant should be reimbursed for expenditure on a lawsuit which has been incurred in good faith.".

566 *D*.3.3.33.§.5, "If anyone comes into a case as procurator in his own interest, it should be said that he is still under an obligation to defend, unless his appointment happens to have been the result of necessity"; 34, "If anyone sues as procurator in his own interest, for example, the buyer of an inheritance, is he obliged to defend the vendor? The answer is: If the transaction was in good faith and not to defraud those who might want to sue in their turn, he is not obliged in turn to defend."; 79 does not exist and 78 does not seem properly related to the matter.

567 *D*.3.3.33.§.4, "The praetor has decided that it is right for the same person who sues as procurator in someone's name also to undertake his defense"; 35.pr., see note 558; §.2, "A procurator will be obliged to defend his absent principal before the appropriate court and in the same province if an application is made not only for an action against him but also for a preliminary enquiry (*praeiudicium*) or interdict, or if security is required by stipulation against danger of loss (*damnum infectum*) or for legacies. But it would be harsh for him also to be compelled to leave Rome for a province or the other way round or one province for another and defend.".

568 *D*.3.3.43.§.4, "The penalty for a procurator who will not defend is this, to be refused an action.".

569 *D*.3.3.54, "Neither a woman nor soldier nor a person who is going to be away on public business or suffering from a chronic disease or about to take on magistracy or unable to submit to trial though willing is thought to be suitable as defender.".

570 *D*.3.3.34.§.2 [but 33.§.2, e. n.]. "It is in the public interest for anybody to be able to defend absentees; for the right to defend is granted even in capital crimes, Therefore, in alla cases where anyone can be condamned in his absence, it is right to give a hearing to anyone speaking on his behalf and defending his innocence, and it is customary to allow him to appear. This is also clear from a rescript of our emperor.".

571 *D*.3.3.51, "A person offering himself as defender below the age of twenty-five, which can be a reason for awarding him *in integrum*

absentee, *D. l.* 34. §. 2, *l.* 64[572], if he gives surety on ratification, *l.* 39. §. 7, *l.* 40. §. 2, *l.* 76[573], and to satisfy judgment, *l.* 28. 46. §. 2, *l.* 53. 76[574], and even if this is done later, he is forced to defend *l.* 43. §. 6[575], unless an

---

restitution, is not a suitable defender, because he himself and his *fideiussores* receive help through *in integrum restitution.*".

[572] *D*.3.3.34.§.2, see note 570; 64, "If a person in whose name a defender has come forward has appeared in court before joinder of issue and applies to take on the suit in his own name, his request should be granted after examination of the case.".

[573] *D*.3.3.39.§.7 [but 6, e. n.], "There are also circumstances in which both ratification and satisfaction of judgment need to be guaranteed. (…)."; 40.§.2, "Furthermore, a person who is taken to court as a defender in an action *in rem* also has, in addition to the usual security for satisfaction of judgment, to guarantee ratification as well.(…)"; 76, "When Titius was defending an absent principal, he furnished security; and before he accepted trial, the defendant became insolvent. Because of this, the defender objected than an action should not be granted against him. The question is whether this should be agreed to, Julian replied: 'Once a defender has furnished security, he should be considered as in position of his principal. And the praetor is not going to help him much if he does not force him to accept trial, since recourse can be had to his *fideiussores* and whatever these pay out, they are going to get from the defender'".

[574] *D*.3.3.28, "If my procurator has received security for satisfaction of judgment, I have available an *actio utilis* on stipulation, just as an action on judgment is granted to me."; 46.§.2, "Someone who defends another person has to give security; for no one is considered an adequate defender in an action against someone else unless he gives security."; 56, " is not considered to be offering a defense, unless he is prepared to give security."; 76, see note 573.

[575] *D*.3.3.43.§.6, "A procurator who is not compelled to defend an absent principal, should, however, be compelled to accept trial if he has given security for satisfaction of judgment in order to bel allowed to defend the absentee, to prevent the person who accepted security from being misled; for those who are not compelled to defend a case are compelled to do so after the giving of security. Labeo says that a ruling should be given after examination of the case, and if the passage of time bring disadvantage to the plaintiff, he should be compelled to accept trial. But if a marriage relationship has been ended or enmity has arisen or possession has been taken of the property of the absent

adequate reason comes up that otherwise exonerates him from the commitment as procurator, *l.* 43. §. 6, *l.* 44[576]; when defending, on the other hand, he undergoes the same fate as the defendant, *l.* 35. §. 3, *l.* 51. §. 1[577]. The charge ceases with the exemptions of the procurator, as mentioned above: freely, by the principal before joinder of issue, *l.* 16[578], or by other ways, or if [the principal] is appointed with general power, subsequently or at the same time as another, who acted first, *l.* 31. § .1, *l.* 32[579]. After joinder of issue a procurator can be excused only by decree of the praetor for reasons other than those, likewise for suspicion, from *l.* 17 to *l.* 27[580]; clearly, on the other hand, [a principal] cannot remove a procurator, if the latter has been

---

principal [44, or if he is going to be a long way or some other adequate reason has come up, 45, he should not be forced up.(…), e. n.]."

576 See note 534.

577 *D*.3.3.35.§.3, "(…) Apart from the giving of security, a procurator is considered to offer a defense if he accepts trials. (…)"; 51.§.1, "However, since to defend means to undergo the same fate as the defendant, the defender of the husband should not be condemned to pay a larger sum then the husband is able to.".

578 *D*.3.3.16, "Before Joinder of issue the principal has the right either to change his procurator or to accept trial himself.".

579 *D*.3.3.31.§.1, "There is no rules against several procurators being appointed for a single lawsuit in which several people are concerned."; 32, "Where several procurators with general powers have been appointed at the same time, the first to act will be given preference, so that a later one does not have the status of procurator in respect of the object of the earlier's claim.".

580 For example, *D*.3.3.17, "After joinder of issue a defendant who has appointed a procurator can certainly change him or transfer the suit from him to himself, even while the procurator is dtill alive or living in the state, but only after examination of the cause. (…). §.2, "In examination of cause the relevant facts are not only those we mentioned above in connection with not compelling a procurator to undergo trial, but also age" (…); 19, "Likewise, if the procurator should be of doubtful character, in prison, or in power of the enemy or robbers"; 20, "or occupied with criminal or civil proceedings, his health, or more important business of his own"; 21, "or exile, or if he should be evasive or later become a personal enemy (…)".

appointed in his own interest, or wishes to avail himself of the right of retention, *l.* 25[581].

§. 57. From *Codex* we transfer the title 50 [but it is 51, e. n.], l. 6, *On abolishing lapses* (*escheats*[582]) (*De caducis tollendis*[583]) which was rendered cumbsersome by the difficulty of the issues and the long-windedness of Justinian. In such a way we have extracted its kernel (the remaining words are shells): if the bequests left by the

---

[581] *D.*3.3.25, "(…) Obviously, if he says he has been appointed in his own interest and has succeeded in proving this, he should not be refused a special action. Likewise, if the procurator wishes to avail himself of some right of retention, the suit should not lightly be transferred from him.".

[582] For the translation of the passages of the Codex quoted in text, I will avail myself of Fred H. Blume, *Annotated Justinian Code*, in http://www.uwyo.edu/lawlib/blume-justinian/ajc-edition-1/book-6.htm [accessed May 2015]; with one clarification: Blume translates *fideicommissus* with "trust", but this is not correct; on this, see Carey Miller, note 121.

[583] Berger, see note 19, *ad vocem Caduca*, "Testamentary dispositions made in favor of persons who, according to certain statutes (*leges caducariae*), were incapable of acquiring under a will. The term indicates also the inheritance itself or the legacy which became vacant because of other reasons (death of beneficiary before the opening of the testament or his refusal to accept the gift). Dispositions which became void during the testator's life are styled *in causa caduci*. The treatment of *caduca* and the things *in causa caduci* was identical: they were assigned to persons who benefited by the testament if they had children. If such heirs of legatees were lacking the *caduca* went to "the treasury of the Roman people" (*aerarium*, later *fiscus*). Already in later Empire some case of *caduca* were abolished. In an extensive constitution Justinian abrogated the whole institution of *caduca* (*"De caducis tollendis", C.6.51.1*), and fixed new general rules concerning testamentary dispositions which became vacant for any reason. A fundamental rule in the law of *caduca* was that the person who benefited by them received them with all charges (*cum onere*) imposed by the testator, such as legacies, or manumissions.".

deceased become extinct §. 14[584], that is to say, they become impossible due to death, namely, of the noured[585], or due to non-fulfillment of a condition[586] (in fact, such clauses from the very beginning or from the time of the testament are treated as if they were not written), and if this happens while the testator is living, such circumstances were once styled *in causa caduci*[587], or if they occurred after his death, they were properly called *caduca*[588], [if the clauses of the bequest become impossible] before the day the bequest falls due[589] (under the old right the day was regarded as falling on the day of opening of the testament). These are the rules according to §. 2[590]. But

---

[584] *C*.6.51.14, "All these provisions shall apply in (case of lapses arising out of) testaments, written or verbal, codicils, every last wish, every intestate succession, and gifts in anticipation of death. 14a. For so great is our clemency that we knowingly let our fisc be the very last to claim any lapses, and give it no advantage; nor do we exercise our imperial prerogatives, but believe that what is for the common benefit should have preference over our own private interests, deeming any benefit to our subjects to be identical with that to the emperor.".

[585] Berger, see note 19, *ad vocem honoratus*, "In the law of succession a person 'honoured' by a legacy in a testament".

[586] Berger, see note 19, *ad vocem Condicio*, "A condition, i.e., a clause added to a transaction or a testamentary disposition which makes the validity thereof dependent upon the occurrence or non-occurrence of a future event; the clause is introduced by *si* or *nisi* (*si non*). (…)".

[587] See note 583.

[588] See note 583.

[589] Berger, see note 19, ad vocem *Dies cedens* (*legati*), "The day on which the legatee becomes entitles to legacy. (…)".

[590] *C*.6.51.2, "And since bequests left in last wills were held to lapse in three different ways, it is proper to state the times and the names thereof, so that it may be known what is abolished and what is reformed. 2a. Now these bequests were made to those who, without the testator, perchance, knowing it, were not in existence at the time of the making of the last will. These bequests were, by the laws, considered as though not made. Again, a person who received something under a testament, while the testator was living, but died after the testament was made, or some bequest was defeated because some

Justinian gave analogous guidelines in the case of the testator's death; except that, if bequests are left on condition of the presence of a given circumstance which in turn depends on the arrival of an uncertain day, then the such bequests become the property [of the beneficiaries] only when the day arrives §. 7[591]. Inheritance left to those who died earlier, §. 5[592], and the manumissions[593], §. 6[594],

---

condition failed under which it was left. This was by the ancients considered the same as a lapse. Or a bequest terminated after the testator's death, which was more clearly called a lapse.".

591 *C.*6.51.7, "If any bequest is left on condition, which either depends on chance, or on the will of the donee, or is mixed, that is to say, the outcome of which depends on a chance-event of nature, on the wish of the person honoured, or on both, or on the arrival of an uncertain day, the outcome of the condition under which it was left or the arrival of the uncertain day, must be awaited, so that it may vest when the condition is fulfilled or the uncertain day arrives. And if he too who receives a benefit under a testament dies in the meantime, or if the condition fails during his lifetime, such bequest which on that account did not remain in force, we direct, become the property of those who were directed to pay it, unless a substitute or joint beneficiary, whether that is an heir or legatee, has been appointed; for in such event, the latter will receive it, since the law is certain that a substitute may be appointed in instituting heirs, giving a trust or making gifts in anticipation of death.".

592 *C.*6.51.5, "In the last class of cases, that of lapses proper, according to what we have previously said, the heirs, whether appointed for part or all of the inheritance, shall be considered as such while the will is still unopened, and may enter on the inheritance, at the time of the testator's death, and, as we have previously stated, the legacies and trusts shall vest at the time of the decedent's death; but an inheritance, unless accepted, could not, according to the ancients, be transmitted (to heirs), nor do we permit such transmission, except, of course, in the case of descendants, as stated in the Theodosian law (C. 6.52.1), introduced for such cases, and (further) the provisions made by us (*D.* 6.30.19), concerning those who die while deliberating (whether to accept an inheritance or not), shall remain in full force.".

593 Berger, see note 19, *ad vocem Manumissio*, "The release of a slave from the power of his master by the latter, i.e., 'giving freedom, *datio libertatis*' (*D.*1.1.4).".

[could be obtained] by means of the *aditio*[595], which Justinian also admitted before the opening of the testament, §. 1[596]. In contrast, according to the ancient law

---

[594] *C*.6.51.6, "Manumissions, of course, which, on account of their nature, have to wait the acceptance of the inheritance by the heir, and bequests left to slaves manumitted in the will or to slaves bequeathed to others, vest from the time that the inheritance is accepted.".

[595] Berger, see note 19, *ad vocem Aditio hereditatis*, "The acceptance of an inheritance by an heir appointed in a last will or inherithing under the law. Only certain categories of heirs was obliged to declare expressly their willngness to accept the estate, whereas the nearest relatives belonging to the family of the testator acquired the inheritance automatically under the law (*ipso iure*) without any particular formality.".

[596] *C*.6.51.1, "We have thought it necessary conscript fathers, to banish from the Roman empire, in the peaceful times of our reign, both the name of escheats, as well as the grounds therefor, which arose from, and increased by, civil war which the Roman people carried on among themselves, so that what was introduced by the calamities of war may be banished by the blessings of peace. 1. And as the Papian law was, in many respects, corrected by former emperors and at last fell into desuetude, so, too, it shall lose its hateful vigor in its application to escheats (*caduca*) by us, inasmuch as it was displeasing even to the great jurists who found many ways to avoid the occurrence of lapses (caduca). 1a. And adherence to the rule of lapses was seen to be burdensome by testators themselves, and they introduced substitutes, so that no lapses would occur, and if they did, directed that the property should in such case go to other persons, thereby avoiding the conditions under which bequests were declared to be lapsed by the Papian law. And we permit that to be done. 1b. And since the Papian law surrounded the ancient law, which was applicable to all alike, with difficulties and artifices, but blushed to impose its yoke on the ascendants and descendants of the testator to the third degree, if they were appointed heirs, leaving the ancient law applicable to them, we do this for all our subjects without distinction. 1c. since, therefore, the Papian law found the material for, and the beginning of, lapses, in connection with entrance on inheritances, the senate decrees enacted in connection with the Papian law, not permitting the vesting of property as of the time of the testator's death, but as of the time of the opening of the will, so that property lapsed which the beneficiary thereof was in the meantime found to be unable to take, we, in correcting this and restoring the ancient law,

Papia Poppea, under Augustus, *caduca* were returned to the fisc to cover lack of funds in the public treasury due to wars, §. 1[597]. But Justinian directed that the goods covered by provisions considered as not written, those *in causa caduci* and the *caduca* were all to be transferred to the *substitutus*[598] or to the *coniunctus*[599], §. 3. 4. 5[600], to the

---

ordain, that all heirs shall have the right to enter an inheritance at the time of the testator's death, and legacies and trusts, unconditional or payable at a future time, shall vest at the death of the testator.".

[597] See note 596.

[598] Berger, see note 19, *ad vocem Substitutio*, "The appointment of another heir by a testator in the event that the heir first instituted did not take the inheritance either because he would not or could not do so. The heir instituted in the second place (...).".

[599] A co-heir or co-legatee with equal shares; Berger, see note 19, *ad voces Coniunctim and Coniunctio*, "An institution of several heirs for the same estate or of several legatees for the same thing in common. The estate (or legacy) became common property of the coheredes (or collegatarii). The heirs or legatees thus awarded are termed coniuncti.".

[600] C.6.51.3, "The rule as to the first class, namely when bequests, which had been left to persons already deceased at the time of the making of the testament, were considered as not made, was that such bequests remained the property of those who had been directed to pay them, unless a substitute for, or a joint beneficiary with, such deceased person, had been provided; for in such case no lapse took place, but the bequests went to such substitute or joint beneficiary, and the burden charged upon such gift, considered as not made, seldom went with it."; 4, "But as to the second class to which belong all terminated bequests which are the equivalent of lapses, we correct the laws which led to such result, and ordain that such bequests, in like manner, shall remain the property of those who were directed to pay them, such as heirs or legatees, or others who may be burdened with a trust, unless in such case, too, a substitute or joint-beneficiary has the preference. But all persons who are benefited in this class of cases must bear the burden, which was annexed to the bequest from the beginning, whether that consists in giving or doing something, or is intended for a certain purpose, or to fulfil a condition, or is imposed for any other reason; for it would be intolerable that he who receives a benefit should be able to reject the burden annexed thereto.; 5, "In the last class of cases, that of lapses proper, according to what we have previously said, the heirs, whether appointed for part or all of the inheritance, shall be considered as such while the will is still unopened,

substitutus, to the *coniunctus verbis*[601] and to the co-heir, §. 11[602], with burden (*cum onere*)[603] not bound to the person [of the first designated], but borne by the substitute, §.

---

and may enter on the inheritance, at the time of the testator's death, and, as we have previously stated, the legacies and trusts shall vest at the time of the decedent's death; but an inheritance, unless accepted, could not, according to the ancients, be transmitted (to heirs), nor do we permit such transmission, except, of course, in the case of descendants, as stated in the Theodosian law (C. 6.52.1), introduced for such cases, and (further) the provisions made by us (*D.* 6.30.19), concerning those who die while deliberating (whether to accept an inheritance or not), shall remain in full force.".

[601] *I.e.*, the person designated as co-heir, in the same will and in the same provision which contemplates others co-heirs, with equal share or without any indication of share for all of the co-heirs. See *D.*50.16.142 in Watson, note 179.

[602] *C.*6.51.11, "When there are, perchance, two or more legatees or trust-beneficiaries, to whom anything was bequeathed, and this is left to them jointly and all accept, each one receives his proportion. 11a. And if the part of one of them lapses, it, with its burden, goes to all in proportion to their bequest, if all want to accept; if none want to accept, then it remains the property of the party directed to pay it in the first instance; if some want to accept and other not, then the whole goes to those who want to accept. 11b. If the property was left severally and all can and wish to accept, each receives his proportional share and they need not expect one of them to take the property, while the others should receive their proportion of the value thereof. When such avarice appeared, antiquity treated it variously, permitting it in connection with some legacies, but rejecting it in connection with others. But we do not permit it at all, and treat all legacies and trusts alike, creating harmony out of ancient discord. 11c. These provisions shall apply, if the testator has not clearly and expressly provided that the property shall go to one, and the proportionate value thereof to the others severally. 11d. If all the legatees, to whom property has been left severally, do not concur in accepting the lapsed portion, but one of them, perchance, accepts, the whole shall belong to him; because the provision of the testator appears, prima facie, to give all of it to each, but in also providing for and joining others, diminishes the portion of the first to that extent. So if no one else accepts or can accept, no one's part lapses or accrues to anyone.".

[603] Imposed by the testator, such as legacies, or manumissions, see above note 583.

9[604], the co-heir certainly and necessarily if he wishes to be co-heir, for his share (not, as at another time, *virilis*[605], §.

---

[604] *C*.6.51.9, "In order, moreover, that we may not over what Ulpian, a man of the greatest genius, elegantly and with acumen stated in this connection, we shall make that plainer by this law. 9a. For since we have already decided, that a person who benefits by a bequest must take it with all its burdens, we ordain that if a condition or a burden directing something to be given is annexed thereto, all the parties who are benefited must bear the burden in proper proportion. 9b. If the burden consists of something to be done, even though this can be done by another, each beneficiary must, in like manner, do his part; as, for instance, where the person honoured is ordered to construct a lodging house, monument or other structure, or the heir, legatee or some other person for whom the testator wished it to be constructed, or to purchase certain property from the heir of the testator or to make a lease or become a surety, or to do anything else similar to this; for it makes no difference in such case whether this is done by the person named by the testator or by another who succeeds to the bequest. 9c. But if the meaning of the direction given and the nature of the act to be done, are such that what was directed to be done cannot be done through another, then through the benefit accrues to such other, the burden, nevertheless, does not follow, since the nature of the act does not permit it and the testator did not wish it. For how could it be otherwise if the testator, for instance, had ordered a party to go to a certain place, or to devote himself to the liberal arts, or to build a house with his own hands, or to paint, or to marry? The testator must be considered to have intended all these things for the person only to whom he left his bounty in the first place. 9d. The general rule in all these cases is that all the parties who are benefited shall bear their proportionate burden, when the duties imposed are possible to be carried out. 9e. And this shall apply to situations which give rise to lapses proper an terminations equivalent to lapses, as stated above; but this shall apply to bequests (of the first class above mentioned) which are considered as not given at all only in certain cases. Some of them, though considered as not given at all (*etsi talia sunt*), are, nevertheless, taken over with the burdens annexed thereto. We have ordered such cases to be specially enumerated in our new compilation of laws, so that no one may reintroduce the prolixity of the ancient law as necessary on the subject or for the purpose of study thereof.".

11[606]) but of the inheritance, §. 10[607]. Rather than *coniunctus re*[608] without burden, §. 11[609], *coniunctus verbis*[610] is to be preferred, §. 10[611]. In the absence of these, [the be-

---

[605] Berger, see note 19, *ad vocem Portio Hereditaria*, "(...) *Portio virilis* = a fraction of the inheritance which an heir on intestacy receives equally with other heirs of the same degree of relationship.".

[606] See note 602.

[607] *C.*6.51.10, "Now this being settled, we find that in the preceding part of this constitution we made mention in several places of joint beneficiaries, and we have thought it necessary to consider this subject with greater care and treat it in greater detail, so that this subject, too, may be clear to all. 10a. Bequests are left not only jointly but also severally (disjunctivo). When coheirs have all been appointed or substituted jointly or all severally, a lapsed bequest consisting of a part or parts of an inheritance, belongs, subject to all of its burdens, to the other coheirs in proportion to the parts inherited by them, even though some of them are already deceased. 10b. And this applies even to those who are unwilling to accept the lapsed portion, if they have accepted their portion for which they were originally appointed, since it is absurd to accept part and refuse part, as has also been provided by decisions of our majesty. C. 6.30.20. 10c. If the heirs and substitutes are mixed in kind, some having been appointed jointly and others severally, and the portion of one of those appointed jointly lapses, this portion, with its burden, shall go only to those who were appointed jointly with him, in proportion to the amount inherited by each. 10d. If, however, a portion of one of those who were appointed severally lapses, this portion, with its burden, goes not only to those who were appointed severally, but to all alike, those who are appointed jointly and severally, in proportion to their inheritance. 10e. The distinction is made because those who are appointed jointly constitute one person, as it were, on account of the unity in the appointment, and hold the portion of the joint heirs with them as their own, but heirs appointed severally have, by reason of the very words of the testator, been separated and have indeed their own, but cannot alone claim another's property, but receive it jointly with all their coheirs.The foregoing provisions are made only for heirs.".

[608] *I.e.*, the designation as co-heir concerning the same thing, but the co-heirs were not designated in the same provision. See *D.*50.16.142, in Watson, note 179.

[609] See note 602.

[610] See note 601.

[611] See note 607.

quests] remain attributed to him[612] by whom they were abandoned, §. 8[613], and only if the latter is also lacking do such bequests pass to the fisc (escheat), §. 13[614].

§. 58. From the *Novels*, we have summarized the *third on the monks*[615]. Any man can be a monk if he has been in a monastery for three years, without attire, as a layman, so that it is evident if the monastic life is to his liking or not; but the master during this time may bring back a fugitive slave to the monastery because of crimes, c. 2[616]. After a

---

[612] *I.e.*, to the intestate successor (see the subsequent *C*.6.51.13, note 614) of the person benefited (Berger, note 583).

[613] *C*.6.51.8, "But in order that it may be made clear in what proportion the bequest which failed shall become the property of those who are directed to pay it, we ordain that if the benefit accrues to the heirs, distribution shall be made according to the proportions inherited, since, had the bequest remained valid, it would have been paid in like manner—unless it was directed to be paid by one or more of the appointed heirs; for if one or more would have paid it, so they shall, in such case, also be the gainers. 8a. But if (the persons directed to pay it) are legatees, trustees, persons honoured with a gift in anticipation of death, or other persons who may be burdened with a trust, and the trust fails, we ordain that it shall become the property of the enumerated persons, according to each one's proportion, that is, according to the number of persons.".

[614] *C*.6.51.13, "Since, moreover, we have provided in a preceding portion of this law (§. 5), that an inheritance not accepted cannot, except in certain cases, be transmitted to heirs, it follows that if anyone fails to accept the whole inheritance, it falls to his substitute, if there is one, and he wishes to and can accept. If there is no substitute, it will fall to the intestate successors, or if there are none of these, or they are not willing to or cannot accept, or they for any reason do not take it, then it falls to our fisc.".

[615] In actual fact it is Novel 5, *Concerning Monasteriens, Monks and Abbots (De monasteriis et monachis et praesulibus)*; for this Novel I will likewise follow *infra* the translation of Blume, see note 268.

[616] *Nov*.5.2, "After that we also must give consideration to each of the monks; in what becoming manner they should be made such, and whether only free persons or, perchance, slaves also (may become monks), since the divine mercy receives all equally, expressly declar-

ing, that, so far as the worship of God is concerned, there is no male or female, free or slave; for in Christ, they all are justly considered the same. We therefore ordain, following the sacred canons, that those who devote themselves to a monastic life, shall not inconsiderately and immediately receive the monastic attire from the reverend abbots of the venerable monasteries, but they shall remain, whether they are free or slaves, for a full term of three years, without as yet being considered worthy of the monastic attire, but they shall be tonsured as, and wear the dress of, the so called laymen, remaining to learn the word of God. And their reverend abbots shall interrogate them, whether they are free or slave, whence they received the desire for a monastic life; and when they have learned from them (the applicants) that they have been led thereto by no vicious occasion, they shall be accepted among the number of those who are instructed and admonished, and they shall prove their perseverance and honour. For a change in life is not easy, if not made with a mental struggle."; 1, "And, if they, indeed, sustain the manner of life through the three years, proving themselves noble and persevering to the remaining monks and to the abbot, they shall be considered worthy of the monastic attire and tonsure, and if they are free, they shall remain subject to no wrongs, and if they are slaves, they, who have passed over into the common worship of all–we mean the celestial -shall no longer be troubled, and they shall receive their liberty. For if that takes place in many cases or through the law, and liberty of that kind is given, why is the divine favor not able to liberate them from such chains? But if anyone comes during the three years, and wants to claim one of those who devotes himself to monastic practice—a happening recently reported to us from Lycia by the God–beloved Zosimus, a man celebrated in (monastic) practice, and who, nearly 120 years old, flourishes in mental and bodily strength—if any one, therefore, as already stated, comes within three years, to claim one of those who desires to become a monk and who perseveres therein, into slavery, and asserts that such person has stolen property and for that reason betook himself into a monastery, he shall not, we ordain, do so immediately, but he must first prove that such man is in fact a slave, is guilty of theft, perchance, or dishonest life or grave crimes, and has fled and come to the monastery on account of such crime. And if it is shown that he told the truth, and such man is found to have taken up monastic practice for such a reason, or, indeed, perchance became a fugitive on account of a life of turpitude, without in truth loving the (monastic) practice, he shall be returned to his master with the things which, forsooth, he stole, provided they also are in the monastery. But he who is shown to be the master must pledge, lapse of two years he begins to be a monk and the goods which he once had now belong to the monastery, c. 6[617], provided that, however, the fourth part comes to the children, c. 5[618]. The erected monastery will be so conescrated: the bishop has to raise his hands to the sky and consecrate the place with a prayer and the sign of the Cross, c. 1[619]. Monks of a monastery shall have only one upstairs dining room and only one dormitory, c. 3[620]. The

---

what is called his faith, that he will not wrong him (the slave), and will receive him and take him home.".

617 *Nov*.5.6, " But if he leaves the monastery and takes up imperial service or other manner of life, his property shall also in such case, as previously stated by us, remain in the monastery (…)".

618 *Nov*.5.5, "We further direct that, the person who wants to enter a monastery, shall have the right, before he does so, to dispose of his property in whatever manner he wishes. For his property follows him in his entrance, although he has not expressly stated that he was bringing it, and he will no longer be its owner. If he has children, and he has, perchance, already given them some property, either as a prenuptial gift or as dowry, and in an amount of a fourth of his property (which they would have received) in case of intestacy, the children shall have no part in remaining property.".

619 *Nov*.5.1, "It is, first of all, to be decided, therefore, that all the times in every part of our empire, whenever any one wants to build a venerable monastery, that shall not be permitted to be done, till he has called the God–beloved bishop, and he has consecrated the place to God with prayer and hands stretched out to heaven,
affixing in it the sign of our Saviour — we mean the cross worthy of adoration and the only one to be honoured —and he may then, after laying such beautiful and becoming foundation, commence the building. This, then, shall be the beginning of piously building venerable monasteries.".

620 *Nov*. 5.3, "(…) For we want no monastery under our sway, whether having many or few men, to separate the monks, who are there, from each other, using separate houses; but we ordain that they shall eat together and all sleep in a place common to them all, each of them, indeed, sleeping in his own bed, but all of them placed in one house; or if one house has insufficient capacity, to hold them all, (they may be placed) in two houses or more, not by themselves and alone, but together, so that they may be witnesses of each other's honourable conduct and purity and so that they may not indulge in

abbot shall be chosen by the bishop from among the group of monks, c. 9[621]. Whoever voluntarily returns to secular life ceases to be a monk (but as a punishment he shall be placed among the officers of the judge of the province), c. 6[622]. Likewise, whoever takes a wife, which is lawful for one who failed to rise beyond the degree of cantor or reader, shall as a punishment be excluded from public office or military service, c. 8[623]. The transfer from one monastery to another is banned, c. 17[624].

---

indolent sleep, giving offense to those who see, but may be modest therein; except that those of them who lead a life of contemplation and perfecti on, who are usually called anchorites and hesychasts, may have their own cottage, as though, excepted from a life in common, reserved for something better.(…).".

[621] *Nov*.5.9, "If a monastery is in a need, at some time, of an abbot shall not be made, according to the rank occupied by the reverend monks, and the person who is next in rank shall not at all be made abbot (by reason of that fact), nor the person who is the second or third after him, or others—as also stated in another of our laws–but the God–beloved bishop of that place shall thereafter look them all over—time and rank, consequent thereon, not being disregarded of course—and the person who appears to be the first—best among the monks and worthy to be over the other shall be chosen, since human nature is so made, that not all are either placed in the highest or in the lowest position. (…)".

[622] *Nov*.5.6, "But if he leaves the monastery and takes up imperial service or other manner of life (…), he himself shall be compelled to join the order of the provincial apparitors [Berger, see note 19, *ad vocem Apparitores*, " Subordinate officials preforming auxiliary serevices in the offices of magistrates and imperial officials, such as secretaries *(scribae*), messengers (*viatores*), heralds (*praecones*). (…)"of the honourable president of the province, and the result of the change shall be, that as he despised the divine service, he shall remain in the service of a worldly judge.".

[623] Nov.5.8, "If one of those who profess monastic practice is considered worthy of ordination as clergyman, he shall also in such case persevere in the purity of such practice, so that if he abuses the freedom of the clergy and dares to marry—occupying a grade as clergyman which permits him to marry, namely, that of singer or reader—for we forbid all others, according to the divine canons, to marry or have a concubine, or in any way give themselves to a life of

§. 59. The *paratitla*[625] are a system of laws summarized from different titles concerning the same topic. These *paratitla* do not have the function of the principal matter, but sometimes they are by no means inferior in importance compared to the same books of the laws. And they are either general or particular. The *paratitla* classified as general are those derived from the whole body of the law, but I believe they are few. Among them, here it is particularly appropriate to mention Hugues Doneau's *Commentaries of the Civil Law*[626] and the very useful and well-ordered book *The Method of the Civil Law*[627] by Nikolaus Vigel [1529–1600]. Particular *paratitla* are those of Wesenbeck[628], Jacques Cujas [1522–1590][629] on *Di-*

---

luxury—he shall be expelled from the order of the clergy, as one who has dishonoured the monastic practice and life; he shall thereafter be a private person and shall not dare to aspire to any imperial service or to any office, unless he wishes to incur the penalty previously threatened; be he shall live the life of private person and see what account he is to render to God in this matter.".

624 *Nov.*5.7 [17 does not exist; it may be a printing mistake, e. n.], "If he leaves a monastery in which he engaged in (practice) monastic and goes to another monastery, in that case, too, his property shall remain with and be claimed by the former monastery, where he, renouncing (the world), left it. The reverend abbots, moreover, ought not to receive a person who does this. For such a life is a vagrant one, not at all that of monastic perseverance, nor that of a firm and constant mind, having the mark of a wandering life, seeking one thing in one place, another in another. Hence the God-beloved bishops and the so-called abbots should also prohibit this, persevering monastic dignity according to the divine canons.".

625 Watson, see note 179, I, *Confirmation of Digest*, lxxi, n. 50, translates as "explanatory notes".

626 Hugue Doneau, see note 140.

627 Nikolaus Vigel (1565), *Iuris civilis uniuersi absolutissima methodus*. Basileae: per Ioannem Oporinum, & haeredes Ioan. Heruagii.

628 Matthaeus Wesenbeck, see note 185.

629 Jacques Cujas (1570), *Paratitla in libros quinquaginta Digestorum, seu Pandectarum imperatoris Iustiniani*. Coloniae

gest and *Code* separately, and Meier's very accurate *Collegium Juridicum*[630], only on the *Digest*, which, however, was plowed in no small part by Vigel's heifer. We have Antonio Perez [1583–1672] on the *Code*[631]: Reinhard Bachoff von Echt [c. 1575–1640] and Heinrich Hahn [1605–1668][632] added supplements to Wesenbeck. I do not intend to enumerate the similar studies of the almost numberless authors, because it is certain that only by naming them, I would have been induced necessarily to utilize their works.

§. 60. There follows the sole interpretation of the text itself, of any part according to it, or to put it better, the Commentaries. Of such kind are countless writings on the *Institutes*, or even those sufficient for covering up the Denmark Strait. François Hotman [1524–1590][633], François Baudouin [1520–1573][634], Bachoff Von Echt[635], Arnold Vinnius [1588–1657][636], Wilhelm Ludwell [1589–1663][637] are recommended. But, if we love the truth, Cujas wisely [thinks that] the Institutes hardly need an

---

Agrippinae: Apud Gualtherum Fabricium; Id. (1579), *Paratitla in libros IX. Codicis Ivstiniani repetitae praelectionis*. Parisiis.

630 Justus Meier, see note 134.

631 Antonio Pérez (1651), *Ant. Perezii Praelectiones in duodecim libros codicis Justiniani*. Lovanii.

632 Heinrich Hahn (1650), *Henrici Hahnii observata theoretico practica ad Matthaei Wesenbecii in L. libros digestorum et in hos editas Reinhardi Bachovii notas et animadversiones*. Helmaestadii.

633 François Hotman (1560), *Commentarius in 4 libros Institutionum juris civilis*. Basileae.

634 François Baudouin (1554), *Commentarii in libros quatuor Institutionum Juris civilis*. Parisiis.

635 Reinhard Bachoff Von Echt (1643), *In Institutionum Iuris Divi Iustiniani Libros Quatuor Commentarii Theorici & Practici*. Francofurti [not included in AA VI, 2, sources directory].

636 Arnold Vinnius (1655), *Commentarius ad Institutiones*. Amstelodami.

637 Wilhelm Ludwell (1656), *Commentarii in IV libros Institutionum Justiniani*. Altdorfii Noricorum.

interpreter, unless he be a concise marginal and purely textual annotator, just as it was done with a small edition either by Jean Crespin [c. 1520–1572] [638] and Pace[639], or by Arnold Vinnius[640].

§. 61. On the *Digest* and the *Code*, we have the great Commentaries of the ancient authors, Bartolo [1313–1357][641], Baldo [1327–1400][642], Guillaume Budé [1467–1540] [643], Giasone [1435–1519][644], Filippo Decio [1454–1535][645], etc. In their manure many valuable things lie hidden, which are to be unearthed with shrewd talent. With renewed doctrine there appeared the annotations of Budé[646], Ulrich Zasius [1461–1536][647], François Douaren [1509–1559][648] on the majority of Laws. Jacques Cujas

---

638 Jean Crespin (1591*), Notae ad Institutiones*. Francofurti.
639 Pace, see note 526.
640 Vinnius, see note 636.
641 Bartolo da Sassoferrato (1493), *Lectura prima et secunda parte Codicis*, Venetiis; Id. (1477–1478) *Lectura prima et secunsa parte Digesti Veteris*. Venetiis; Id. (1478), *Lectura prima et secunda parte Infortiati*. Venetiis.
642 Baldo degli Ubaldi (1572–1577), *Commentaria in primam et secundam Digesti veteris partem...Commentaria in primam et secundam Infortiati partem. In Digestum novum Commentaria. Commentaria in Codicis libros XI*. 9 vols. Venetiis.
643 Guillaume Budé (1528), *Annotationes ad XXIV Pandectarum libros*. Parisiis.
644 Giasone del Maino (1569), *Commentaria ad Digesta*. Lugduni; Id. (1569), *Commentarium in partem primam et secundam Codicis*. Lugduni.
645 Filippo Decio (1595), *In Digestum vetus et Codicem commentarii cum doctissimorum juriconsultorum adnotationibus*. Venetiis.
646 Budé, see note 643.
647 Ulrich Zasius (1537), *Commentarium ad Pandectas*. Basileae.
648 François Douaren (1579), *Omnia quae quidem hactenus extant opera, nunc demum plurimis in Digesta seu Pandectas et Codicem commentariis*. Lugduni.

[1522–1590][649], by another method, picked up in a single text the responses of many a jurisconsult and made a comment about them, such as on Paulus[650], Papinianus[651], Modestinus[652] etc. The following authors rarely comment on the text, but they exercise either with paratitla or disputes. An exception is the case, very recently, of the illustrious Johann Brunnemann [1608–1672][653], with his extraordinary example of diligence expounded in order with regard to all the rules of the *Code*, and the same is promised in connection with the *Digest*. On other matters, the diligence of Denis Godefroy [1549–1622], a man of immense merit in Roman jurisprudence (as expressed in Caspar von Barth's[654] epitaph referring to him) made sure that we hardly need new Commentaries on text, for he singled out with the most admirable zeal the most revered works not only of the glossators and ancient commentators, but also of the men of greatest doctrine of the previous age. Whence, no longer was it so urgent for new commentaries to be composed, as supplements to Gode-

---

[649] Jacques Cujas [1522–1590] (1558), *J. Pauli receptarum sententiarum ad filium libri V. In eosdem J. Cujacii interpretations. Parisiis*; Id. (1573), *Ad Africanum reliqui tractatus*. Lugduni; Id. (1673), *Ad Universa Papiniani Opera recitations accuratissimae et utilissimae* (in *Opera Posthuma*, vol. I). Parisiis; Id. (1637) *Ad Julii Pauli libros ad Edictum, et libros Quaestionum recitations exactissimae; Responsa Pauli, et Horatii Ulpiani, Modestini et Scevolae; libri IX differentiarum Juris Modestini* (in *Opera Posthuma*, vol. II). Parisiis.

[650] See note 489.

[651] Berger, see note 19, *ad vocem Papinianus, Aemilius*, "A Roman jurist of the second/third century after Christ. He was praefectus praetorio from 203 until 205. He died in A.D. 212 executed by order of the emperor Caracalla.[…] Papinianus is one of the most remarkable figures among Roman jurists. […].".

[652] See note 492.

[653] Johann Brunnemann [1608–1672] (1663), *Commentarius in XII libros Codicis Justiniani*. Lipsiae.

[654] Caspar von Bart [1587–1658] was a German philologist and writer.

froy were announced firstly by the jurisconsults of this century, but also because in the Dutch edition of the Godefroy's *Corpus* the title itself embodies this very promise. However, neither do I approve that the observations of others are to be inserted in new editions of Godefroy, so that either the previous ones become useless or the subsequent edition not bought by those who own the earlier version. It was fitting, rather, that in imitation of Hugo Grotius' [1583–1645] *Scattered Flowers*[655], separately, merely as supplements of Godefroy, reflections not present in the latter were printed according to the order of the texts. Before I stray from this point, I must observe that although theologians have defeated us, Denis Godefroy made sure that, at least sometimes, we stand on a higher level. For not even the Holy Scriptures had such continuous notes, so complete yet so concise at the same time. Antonius Walaeus [1573–1639] has begun something in regard to the New Testament[656], but he is still far from the end. Conversely, those [theologians] have *Numbered Bibles*, of which first and foremost the *Dorschean* manuscripts[657] are in the hands of many today. We, in truth, do not yet have *numbered Laws*, that is to say, a text in which, for every single law, there is an annotation indicating the authors who expounded that law or title, or book, with the exception of the Great Man, Johann Cristoph Marci [1614–1672], Chancellor of Martinsburgh and Elder Echevin of Leipzig, who owns a numerated Code.

[655] Hugo Grotius (1642), *Florum sparsio ad Jus Justinianeum*. Parisiis.
[656] Antonius Walaeus [1573–1639] (1647), *Notae marginales ad Novum Testamentum* (in *Opera*, 2 vols.). Lugduni Batavorum.
[657] That is, with an index of the Old and the New Testament for each chapter of each book; see Sigismondo da Venezia [1777–1847] (1842), *Bibliografia universale sacra e profana*. Venezia, 319.

§. 62. As far as the interpretation (*interpretatio*[658]) of some text is concerned, it is either real or textual. It is real when it deduces certain propositions from the law, and perfectly treats them, demonstrating and objecting, and untying objections, if this seems apposite. In some cases this is done by using the law to make a claim; elsewhere, to build a defense. The proof (*probatio*[659]) is given either through authorities or through arguments. The authorities are other laws, *i. e.* parallel passages; similarly, the opinions of the jurisconsult doctors, as it were universal authorities, are likewise invoked; mention should also be made of the stories or the sentences [passed] in the different ministries, therefore they also pertain to the counsels (*consilia*[660]). The objection is put forward in the same manner; moreover, conflicting laws on the same case constitute an antinomy. In both cases, the reasons pro and con are different.

§. 63. The textual interpretation is κατά πόδα [in Greek in the text, word for word, e. n.] on the text of the law, and it is either total on the whole law, or partial on the single words; the total deals with the connection of the law with other laws, the principal matter and the subdivision of the law, the author and the history of law and the occasion in which it was proposed. To this matter belong the inscription and subscription, of which the former brings in the author, the latter the place and the date. Also belonging to the history is the description of the outcome which proceeded from that law, since it has been in force, other remarkable outcomes linked to it, in what way some experienced practitioner cunningly abused of the law in

[658] Berger, see note 19, *ad vocem Interpretatio*, "The explanation of significance of a legal norm or term".
[659] Berger, see note 19, *ad vocem Probatio.*
[660] Berger, see note 19, *ad vocem Consilium*.

question; to what extent other noteworthy aspects are involved, e. g., where in the laws consideration is given to the three rules of the law: living honestly (*honeste vivere*), causing no injury to others (*neminem laedere*), rendering to everyone his due (*suum cuique tribuere*); here it is worth recalling that sagacious bon mot of John Barclay [1582–1621] in *Euformio*[661]; where he states that he aims to prepare a list of repealed rules, among which he would include first and foremost these three. Likewise, in the law it is stated that it is lawful for a servant to act cruelly on his body; from this, many invoke this statement to prove that suicide (*autochiria*) was lawful under Roman law. In this connection it can be mentioned that a distinguished man of Nuremberg, not so many years ago, submitted this text to a theologian, who was comforting his grief and melancholy. Seeking to prove the lawfulness of αυτοχειρίας [in Greek in the text, suicide, e. n.], and noting that the theologian had given no answer with regard to the text but had said that another rule was dictated according to divine and natural law, the questioner was heartened in the intention, and shortly thereafter inflicted death on himself.

§. 64. Thus far, we have dealt with the total interpretation. The partial consists in ascertaining a text and in expounding the ascertained text. The definition of the text is achieved by analyzing different texts and, specifically, by the so-called textual criticism, on which there is a notable study by Caspar Schoppe [1576–1649], setting out the rules to ascertain a text[662]. The explanation of the ascertained text is performed either through another language or by translation; or in some other suitable manner. The Greek version of our laws is very useful for interpretation.

---

[661] John Barclay (1609), *Euphormionis Lusini Satyricon*. Parisiis.
[662] Caspar Schoppe (1597), *De arte critica*. Noribergae: Fuhrmann.

Greek paraphrasts and scholiasts had copies older than ours, and had perfect knowledge of the history of the laws. Hence, the Theophilus version of the *Institutes* is highly recommended. The *Basilica*[663], in truth, are a definitive Greek version of the remaining right. However, I will not go deeply into *Novellae*[664], whose original text is in Greek. These are commonly believed to have been the source for the collection of the *Authenticae*[665] by Irnerius [c. 1050–after 1125][666], but the great jurist Johann Strauch [1612–1679] demonstrated the opposite in the dissertation *Irnerius doesn't make mistakes*[667], written in opposition to Johann Jakob Wissenback's [1607–1665] *Mistakes of Irnerius*[668]. Not long ago, illustrious men prepared a German version of Right, and ERNEST, Sasso Prussian Prince, celebrated for loyalty and wisdom, strongly promoted the project. This involved much hard work, firstly on the *Digest,* because of the almost inimitable concision of the style, in such great simplicity. But, how often I think that the most rapid of historians and even the most acute in their opinions, Sallust and Tacitus, not inconveniently tried

---

[663] See note 276.

[664] Berger, see note 19, *ad vocem Novellae Iustiniani*, "Justinian's constitutions (= Novels) promulgated after the second edition of his Code, in the period between A.D. 534 and 536.".

[665] Berger, see note 19, *ad vocem Authenticum*, "A collection of 134 Novels promulgated by Justinian between a.d. 535 and 536, after the publication of the second edition of his Code. The Greek Novels are translated into Latin therein, not always quite correctly. The date (eleventh century?) and place of origin of the *Authenticum* are unknown. It was first considered a forgery, but the Law School in Bologna established its authenticity (hence the name *Authenticum*)".

[666] Referred also as *lucerna juris* ("lantern of the law"), was an Italian jurist, and founder of the School of Glossators and thus of the tradition of Medieval Roman Law.

[667] Johann Strauch (1662), *Irnerius non errans*. Brunsvigae.

[668] Johann Jakob Wissenback (1640), *Sylloge errorum Irnerianorum*. Franckerae.

to penetrate the mentality of the Germans, for it is clear that the thing is vast more than difficult. This is particularly true because the *Vetus Speculum Saxonicum* and *Suevicum*, the Rescripts of the Diet and the present *Stylus Curiarum* offer an admirable expression in German words concerning the majority of Latin legal terms. Moreover, I know that in some famous ministries they purposely avoided inserting any Latin word in the sentences.

§. 65. The interpretation by means of whatever language, whether the original or a different version, either expounds the meaning, and it is defined as a paraphrase, or applies the grammar, rhetoric and dialectics to the words, and this is defined as analysis. The paraphrase, therefore, is to speech as the definition to the word. In fact, it is not sufficient for a paraphrase to be made by means of synonymous words, if it is not made through clearer words. To this pertains, inter alia, the formation of the legal problem (*casus*), for which Accursius [c. 1182–1263][669] is rightly recommended. On other matters, the rules for deriving the true meaning (this is the main purpose of exegetical jurisprudence) are widely known. In this regard, see in particular Justus Brawen [1615–1665] in *The calling to mind of logic*[670], edited in Rostow by Gerhard Boddenius [1620–1697] and Bernhard Gossmann [1622–1691], where, under the guise of teaching logic, nothing but hermeneutics is expounded, but too briefly and without the illuminating presence of examples. On the same subject, accurately, the work by the anonymous author

---

[669] Accursius (1549), *Digestum vetus, infortiatum et novum ad Florentinas Avenionensesque Pandectas exploratum et Codex Divi Justiniani, cum Accursii Glossa*. Lugduni. On the birth of *Ius Commune*, see extensively, John W. Cairns and Paul J. du Plessis (eds.) (2010), *The creation of the* Ius Commune. *From casus to Regula*. Edimburgh.

[670] Justus Brawen (1643), *Commonefactio logica*. Rostochii.

Arminianus, in *Philosophy as Interpreter of Scripture*[671], was recently published in Belgium. Nor should one disregard the lessons that Stephanus de Phedericis [d. 1497?] bequeathed us in the book *The Method of Interpreting Laws*[672] and Andrea Alciato [1492–1550] in *The Meaning of the Words*[673]. It would also not be useless to consult the Rhetoricians, where their teachings focus on the judicial method περὶ ρητοῦ καὶ διανοίας περὶ αντινομίας[674], [in Greek in the text, about the literal meaning and purpose, about the antinomy or conflict of laws, e. n.], and in other similar passages.

§. 66. Briefly, it seems to me that the source of the whole of hermeneutics can be addressed in this way. The paraphrase, as we said, is to the speech as the definition is to the word. Therefore, in order to compose a paraphrase or to interpret, the first step is to give the definitions of all the words; and when a word may be homonymous or have different definitions, an attempt should be made to

---

[671] It is the essay by Ludwig Meyer [1629–1681] (1666), *Philosophia S. Scripturae Interpres*. Eleutheropoli; see about Francesco Piro (2003), "Derive semantiche e psicologie cognitive in Leibniz. Discutendo con Lia Formigari", in Stefano Gensini, Arturo Martone (eds.), *Il linguaggio, Teoria e storia delle teoria. In onore di Lia Formigari.* Napoli.

[672] Stephanus de Phedericis (1536), *De Interpretatione Iuris*. Lugduni.

[673] Andrea Alciato (1547), *De verborum et rerum significatione*. Basileae: Isingrinus.

[674] Here Leibniz is quoting Quintilian, see note 85, 3, 6, 46, "They the created species of these, subordinating to the Legal Issue both definition and other Issues deriving from a written text, namely a Conflict of Laws (*antinomia* as it is called), Letter and Spirit or Intention *(kata rhēton kai dianoian) metalepsis,* which we call variously 'translative', 'transumptive', or 'transpositive', Inference (syllogism which we call 'ratiocinative' or 'collective'), and Ambiguity, *amphibolia.* I mention these because they too are called Issues by many writers, though some prefer to regad them as Legal Questions.".

ascertain its possible combinations with other words or to determine how many useful combinations of definitions may be made in a single paraphrase, or which of these are possible single [definitions]; those that prove to be useless are to be rejected. In order to choose the true [definitions] from among those preserved up to now, attempts should be made to propose a combination with the previous and following words, or the parallel passages, also taking into account the history, place, time and purpose. For in case of doubt, the author is assumed – unless proven otherwise – to have made correct statements; and if he is a sacred author, it is certain that any interpretation that contrasts with his avowed purpose, or with history or truth, is to be rejected. The same procedure should, in truth, be applied, to the highest degree possible, to the mind, to feelings, nature, and the aim pursued by the author: for example, it cannot be assumed that the author purposely constituted something vain and devoid of sense, or having no consequence in a testament. Accordingly, a deed is to be interpreted as valid rather than rendered null and void. Besides, it is the mind of the author that talks sometimes obscurely, sometimes clearly. For example, the Oracles, the ancient Pythagoreans, the authors of puzzles, the alchemists spoke obscurely on purpose. Whenever their statements are to be explained, the obvious sense is to be avoided. Likewise attention should be paid to the accent of whoever is talking and to the hand of whoever is writing, for if it so happens that with these folds [of the text], no useful meaning can be put upon a paraphrase, then it is necessary for letters to be transposed, no matter what are the rules of the stenographic or cryptographic technique; moreover, careful observation is required in order to determine whether the text or a detached sentence is damaged, or if it is necessary to make an inversion of the words, or whether some are omitted or superfluous or other tropes need to be employed[675], or other whether it is necessary to perform probable and possible transposition (*immutatio*[676]) not so much of the way of saying (*dictio*), but in the sequence of the words (*oratio*)[677]. If either the paraphrase or the sense is not passable, the oration is called obscure. If, in the other hand, many interpretations are passable at the same time, [the oration] is ambiguous; generally, however, only one, worked out, in some sense, according to the principle of the combinations with all the circumstances[678], is the most likely. From this it is clear that, briefly, the source of hermeneutics is twofold: 1) combination of the various modes of expression (*dictio*), different styles (*phrasis*[679]), parenthetical clauses (*comma*[680]), types of period (*periodus*)[681], all of which are to

---

675 Quintilian, see note 85, 8, 6, 1, "A Trope is a shift of the word or phrase from its proper meaning to another, in a way that has positive value".

676 A synonymous of trope in Quintilian and Cicero, according to Heinrich Lausberg [1912–1992], (David E. Orton, R. Dean Anderson eds. 1998), *Handbook of literary rhetoric: a foundation for literary study*. Leiden, 248.

677 Cicero, see note 79, 2, 270, *dictiones oratoriae*, the way of speaking of the orators; 3, 167, *oratio, id est continuatio verborum*, oration, that is the sequence or the words.

678 Quintilian, see note 85, 5, 10, 104, "Anyway, let us call this type of Argument one 'based on circumstances' (there is no other way of translating *peristasis*) or 'on special features of the individual Cause'".

679 Quintilian, see note 85, 8, 1, 1, "What the Greeks call *phrasis*, we call *elocutio* in Latin".

680 Quintilian, see note 85, 9, 4, 122, "(…) He says that there are Commata, Cola, and Periods. A Comma (in my view) is a complete thought without completeness of Rhythm; most people define it as a part of a Colon. Here is Cicero's example: 'You needed a house? But you had one. You had money to spare? But you were in need'. But a comma may consist of a single word: in 'We spoke (*diximus*): we are willing to provide witnesses', *diximus* is a Comma".

be tested in a range of combinations and in accordance with the diverse circumstances, in order to ascertain which version is possible, whether multiple forms are possible and which arrangement is the most likely one; 2) a probable paronomasia (*levis immutatio*[682]) or trope of the oration to be interpreted, if, in truth, no single passable meaning appears from the combinations examined.

§. 67. The analysis is the application of any of the rules from the arts of speaking to the current language. That is the grammar, the rhetoric, and the logic. Grammar deals with the words in themselves, their orthography, prosody, etymology, syntax, the distinctions concerning the syntax and its punctuation or the marks (such as the accents are the marks of prosody). In considering the words in themselves, however, it describes their meaning, derivation, appropriacy, epithets, synonyms, periphrasis. See above §. 43, 44, 45. Rhetorical analysis concerns speech forms that express tropes, figures of speech and everything of which above in §. 46; it likewise examines motions of the affections. Logical analysis considers the definitions (*definitiones*[683]), subdivisions (*divisiones*[684]), propositions

---

[681] Quintilian, see note 85, 9, 4, 124–125, "For 'Period' Cicero has a number of different names: *ambitus, circumitus, comprehensio, continuatio, circumscriptio*. There are two types, one simple, when a single thought is deployed in a Period of some lenght, and one made up of Cola and Commata, which contains several thoughts: *Aderat ianitor carceris, carnifex praetoris*, and so on. A Period contains al least two Cola. An average number seems to be four, but it often allows more. Its extent is fixed by Cicero either by the length of four senarii or by the compass of a single breath. It must comprise a complete thought; it must be open and intelligible, and not too long to be retained in the memory".

[682] Slightly altering a word or expression to obtain a remarkable change of meaning; Lausberg, see note 676, 286.

[683] Quintilian, see note 85, 3, 6, 89, "*Definitio* also belongs to both classes of questions, namely those concerned with consideration of the facts and those concerned with the letter of the law"(here transl.

(*propositiones*[685]), syllogisms and word order (*ordo*[686]) that one finds in language; moreover, each one of them takes into consideration not only the method of invention (*inventio*[687]) or the topics (*loci*[688]) concerned, but also the

---

by Harold. E. Butler (1927), (1927), *The Institutio Oratoria of Quintilian.* London, New York; Lausberg, see note 676, 52, "Of a legal term's content and range of meaning".

[684] Quintilian, see note 85, 5, 10, 63, "Cicero also points out that Division is an aid to Definition, and that it differs from Partition, inasmuch as Partition breaks up a whole into parts, while Division breaks up a Genus into Forms: the number of parts (on his view) is uncertain ('what elements make up the state?') whereas the number of Forms is certain ('how many species of states are there? We are told there are three. Namely those governed by the people, by few, by one man'). He does not of course use these examples, because, writing to Tebatius, he preferred examples from law; I have substituted plainer ones."; Lausberg, see note 676, 185, "the subdivision of the concepts defined".

[685] Quintilian, see note 85, 4, 4, 1, "Some put the propositions immediately after the Narrative, as being a part of the matter before the court. I have already answered this view. My own opinion is that a Proposition is the initial stage of any Confirmation, and is found not only when we set out the principal Question, but sometimes also the individual Arguments, especially those which are called *epicheirēmata.* I am now speaking only of the former kind."; Lausberg, see note 676, 185, "intellectual core component of the content of the narrative".

[686] Quintilian, see note 85, 9, 4, 23, "First, Order. This has to be considered in relation to words taken singly and in context".

[687] Quintilian, see note 85, 3, 3, 1, "The system of oratory, as a whole, according to most authorities, and the best of them, consists of five parts: Invention, Disposition, Elocution, Memory, and Delivery or performance (both terms are in use).", 5, "Some have added a sixth dividion, making Judgement come after Invention, because one has to 'invent' first and then 'judge'. For my part, I cannot believe that a person who has not made a judgement has performed the acr of 'invention' either; we do not say that a speaker has 'invented' inconsistent, ambivalent, or foolish arguments, but only he has 'failed to avoid' them."; Lausberg, see note 676, 119, "*Inventio* is the 'discovery'of ideas".

[688] *I.e.*, of the general forms of argument employed in probable reasoning; Quintilian, see note 85, 5, 10, 20, "Let us now investigate the Places where Arguments are found, though some hold that these are

method of judgement (*iudicium*[689]) or the accepted opinions (*maximae*[690]) according to which the things are to be considered. It is no wonder that some precepts, of which *supra* in the philology of right, can be found again here, because there they are collected from various texts whereas here they are merged into a single text. Similarly in the *Antinomics,* all of the antinomies are collected, but e more comprehensively into a single text, and in particular those which are to be interpreted, so that by means of that book can be understood in a text at least the size of a finger. By the same token, it is very helpful that the passages of the laws are brought to attention and collected in the philology and philosophy of law, but they are not treated extensively, an aspect which is to be reserved to examination of the actual text of the individual laws.

---

identical with the topics I have just been discussing. By 'Places' I do not mean what are nowadays commonly meant by *loci*, namely set pieces against luxury, adultery and the like, but the areas in which Arguments lurk and from which they have to be drown."; Harold. E. Butler, see note 676, 213," (…) in the sense of the secret places where arguments resides and from which they must be drawn forth."; Lausberg, see note 676, 171, "[*loci*] the formal analysis and classification of the *argumenta* presupposes the content of the arguments. It is precisely the task of rhetorical *invention*, however, to provide instructions for the discovery of ideas that correspond with the issue and the party, that is, for the discovery of the content.".

[689] Quintilian, see note 85, 3, 3. 5 as well as 6, 5, 3, "There is not much differences, in my opinion, between Judgement and Strategy, except that the former deals with matter which manifest themselves, and the latter with matters with are hidden, and either as yet entirely undiscovered and doubtful. Again, Judgement is most often certain, and Strategy is a sort of reasoning which has deep roots, generally weighs and compares various, possibilities, and contains in itself both Invention and the power of judging."; "discernment" for Lausberg, see note 676, 502.

[690] Charles Fresne du Cange, see note 420, *ad vocem Maxima*, "Recepta sententia, regula (…)".

§. 68. Thus, briefly, but clearly – I hope – and we have given a penetrating overview of the sources of interpretation (the sources are recommended for their clarity and breadth of vision, their magnitude creates lakes and rivers): by means of this approach, as I hope, we have lit up the way for those who, more modestly impregnated with philosophy, take their first steps toward some text that needs to be explained, according to the custom of the universities. In fact, the common formula:

Praemitto, scindo, summo, casumque figuro,
perlego, do causas, connoto and objicio,[691]

on which they usually base their method in the case of texts that are to be interpreted, is illustrative of our method. *Praemitto* concerns the total textual interpretation §. 63. *Scindo* the logical analysis §. 67. *Summo* is a kind of simultaneous interpretation §. 53 and ff. *Casumque figuro* the paraphrase §. 65, 66. *Perlego* the grammatical analysis and the rhetoric §. 67. *Do causas* and *objicio* the main proposition of the text, *connoto* the secondary propositions according to the text, in both cases by means of real interpretation §. 62. In the end, we now remember when it is necessary to make use of these principles. And I believe that logical analysis, grammar or rhetoric should be used only when something unique and worthy of observation occurs. For instance, a special case concerns the education of children, who have yet to be imbued with the most basic principles of grammar,

---

[691] This is a famous couplet by Gribaldi Mofa, see note 153, I, c. XIV, 95–98, "I state beforehand the topic (*praemitto*), divide it into his constitutive parts (*scindo*), synthesize it (*summo*), represent an actual case (*casumque figuro*), read over all (*perlego*), investigate the rational bases of judgement (*do causas*), define (*connoto*), expose the ojections (*objicio*) [e. transl.]". L. revises conceptually the couplet, see above in the text.

logic, rhetoric. It is to be hoped that those who approach jurisprudence have learned grammar, logic, and rhetoric from the books of law; theologians from Sébastien Châteillon's [1515–1563] *Bible*[692], the books of the truths of the faith of any Church; physicians from Galen [129–c. 201], Aulus Cornelius Celsus [c. 25 BC–c. 50 AD] and also from more recent authors, because even their style is not to be despised. As for the real interpretation it is necessary to distinguish between various different situations: either, a commentary is written only about a text, for example Joachim Von Beust's [1522–1597] *Reading on Old Digest Title about Oath*[693], Martin Antonio Delrio's [1551–1608] *Recapitulation on Compromise*[694], on Jacques Godefroy's [1587–1652] on *Lex Rhodia de jactu*[695], Christoph Philipp Richter's [1602–1673] *Explanation of the Authentica ne filius pro patre*[696]; in which case it is allowed due to lack of things to say, to include more extensive and far-reaching observations on matter that is contained in the text, thereby treating it fully and in depth: once this kind of interpretation was made with legal apparatus; a different kind of situation is faced when a commentary is written about the whole book, in which case, due to the amplitude of the things to say, the only permissible approach is to infer propositions from the text, annotating controversies which have been raised because of the text. On the other hand, when the method of

---

692 Sébastien Châteillon (1551), *Biblia interprete Castalione*. Basileae.

693 Joachim von Beust (1576), *Lectura in Digestum vetus de Jurejurando*. Wittembergae.

694 Martin Antonio Delrio (1589), *Repetitio ad L. Transigere C. De Transactionibus*. Lugduni.

695 Jacques Godefroy (1637), *De imperio maris... de lege Rhodia de jactu*. Augusta Allobrogum.

696 Christoph Philipp Richter (1661), *Expositio omnium Authenticarum Codici imperatoris Justiniani insertarum*. Jenae.

propositions is adopted, only two approaches are permitted as a means of illustrating the proof: the approach based on bringing up parallel passages, and that of defending through solution of the controversial passages. In truth, in either of these two methods – invoking propositions, or controversies – the interpreter can only refer the reader to the authors who have treated the question completely and in depth, with the exception of the controversies on the meaning of a law, which properly concern the interpreter's task and are to be dealt with accurately by the latter. Dissolution of the antinomy is to be performed for laws in cases where conflicting in interpretations of particularly obscure points creates severe difficulty. In other cases, no more than a reference to it is needed.[697]

§. 69. We have thus finally crossed the sea of exegetical jurisprudence; but it seems to us that we have reached the Straits of Gibraltar, which opens up the passage from the Mediterranean to the ocean. Polemical jurisprudence is so enormously widespread that it cannot be exhausted, because new cases emerge daily. Meanwhile, a service must be given by the jurist, so that he examines at least the known regions, that is, collects cases already raised and examines the decisions; so that when he is subsequently dragged to new shores by a storm, that is, when he meets with new cases, with the help of the magnet, that is, natural law, he will easily give the best explanation.

§. 70. We will now deal with both the principles of decision-making, and the collection of decisions. The principles of decision-making are reason-based on natural law and similarity based on certain civil law. Indeed, if we carefully consider the matter, the whole of civil law is more a matter of fact than of right: because it is to be

---

[697] It seems a reminiscence of Cicero, *De inventione*. 2, 147.

proved not according to the nature of things, but according to history, that is, to fact. Effectively, it must be proved that the law was enacted, and the custom was introduced; therefore it must be proved that whoever introduced the bill obtained the power of doing so by deed and agreement. Hence, it is evident that the law receives its validity from an agreement of the people. And since one of the elements of certainty on which we rest our case is respect for pure right in all of the cases where no agreement is reached, then it is evident that in those situations in which the law has gaps [literally, does not express itself clearly] the case must be judged according to natural law. Just as in the case of missing statutes the judgement must be given according to the *Jus commune*[698]. If decision makers observed this, the more easily they would disentangle themselves; but in truth, they prefer to look back at similar issues, which were decided in accordance with the civil law, and from those they draw conclusions that produce great perplexity: amid a myriad similarities, one appeals to this, another resorts to this or that other similarity. Therefore, I think it is safer to refer to pure and immutable natural law. And, equally, it seems to me not unlike the idea of someone wishing to apply to donkeys the rules that here and there in the statutes were established on the *evictio*[699] of the horses. But whether

---

[698] Leibniz (June 1668), *Ratio Corporis Juris Reconcinnandi*, in AA, VI, 2, "§. 1. We call Roman Law that which comes from Roman Emperor Justinian, as that which comes from Roman Pontiffs; the first is called Justinianean, the latter Papal. §. 2. Both have force in almost the whole of Europe, by spontaneous acceptance of the force of *Jus Commune*, and almost of *Jus Gentium Christianorum*, so that it is applied every time that it is not deviated by some special Law, Statute, or Custom of a certain State, Region, Province, Place." [italics added; ed. transl].

[699] Berger, see note 19, *ad vocem Evictio*, "Occurred when a seller sold a thing which did not belong to him and the buyer was later evicted by the real owner".

those rules can be applied to mules is doubtful. I would argue they cannot: the mule is more donkey than horse, because the offspring follows the womb and the mother is a donkey. Sometimes, however, we are indeed obliged to have recourse to other similar civil laws according either to the words or the intent of the legislator. According to the words, when the legislator, sometimes in general, or at other times on a specific matter, states that he regards a certain thing as desirable. Sometimes in general, for example, in Saxon law it was long held, according to the custom of the ministries (this custom counts as a law) that doubtful cases are to be decided according to the similarity with the other Saxon laws rather than the *Jus Commune*. On a specific matter, for example, it was decided according to the civil law that the rules relating to men are to be applied to women, unless it is prevented by a single law or reason. Furthermore, the intent of the legislator is also invoked as a reason in the absence of an explicit reason: for example the old Saxon law says: *Der Pfaff nehme Gerade* [in German in the text, the clergyman takes the *Gerade*[700], e. n.]. *Quaeritur*[701] if the clerics, who need not be properly qualified clergymen because it is not necessary for them to receive the sacrament of the Holy Orders, take the *Gerade*. And the answer is: that they do indeed take the *Gerade*, according to the intent of the law, because the *Gerade* is given in compensation (for balancing) to those who are not able [under the law

[700] Nils Jansen, "Testament formalities in Early modern Europe", in Kenneth G. Creid, Marius J. de Waal, Reinhard Zimmermann (eds.) (2011), *Comparative Succession Law*. I, Oxford, 31, "parts of the household that were regarded as the property of women and exclusively transferred to women".

[701] Berger, see note 19, *ad vocem Quaeritur* (*quesitum est*), "The jurists use these locutions to introduce doubtful cases in which 'a question arises' ('it has been questioned') about the legal solution of the question presented".

of succession] to take military equipment, such as women and ecclesiastical persons. From this it is evident that clerics are forbidden to engage in warfare, as the shedding of human blood results in an irregular state, in consequence of which the prebend (*praebenda*[702]) is removed. We thus have two principles of decision making: natural law and the law of the law similar: that is to say, in all circumstances in which the legislator was silent, a derived argument from one case applies to another case, because the purpose of the reasoning is held to be analogous; however, the reason and intent of laws also depends in part on the political, which is called nomothetic. Therefore it is evident that the two eyes of the jurisconsult in charge in some ministry are the science of the natural law and the nomothetic. Likewise, the cases already decided are known through the history of the acts and also through the exegesis of the laws, namely, all topics that we have treated *supra*.

§. 71. We will not describe any very minute topic of natural law, but only the principles. In the first place, those inferred from the opinions of other authors, and then ours. The other Authors who have philosophized on natural right are, in particular, the following: Plato [428/427 BC–348/347 BC], Aristotle [384 BC–322 BC], Epicurus [341 BC–270 BC], Cicero [106 BC–43 BC]. And in more recent times: Hugo Grotius [1583–1645], Pietro Sforza Pallavicino [1540–1598], Thomas Hobbes [1588–1679], Johann von Felden [d. c. 1668], Robert Sharrok [1630–1684]. Plato everywhere set up the foundation of the law τὸ κοινῇ συνφέρον [in Greek in the text, e. n.], i.e. the

---

[702] Rhidian Jones (2011), *The Canon Law of the Roman Catholic Church and the Church of England.* London, New York, 125, "prebend (*praebenda*). An ecclesiastical office to which is attached the income and other emoluments of an ecclesiastical living".

public utilty. Thrasymachus, in the books of the *Republic*[703] argues that justice is what is advantageous for the more powerful. Aristotle[704] and with him the Stoics asserted that the foundation of natural law is to live in accordance with nature[705] and all of the things of the nature, that is, everything which, according to the nature of things, is in accordance with what is optimal and most perfect for the creatures' condition, is right and just. Epicurus[706] stated that natural law is anything which could be useful to me, namely everything that produces pleasure of the soul and peace of mind. Cicero, in the book *On Duties*[707] and in other passages, was one of the first to

---

[703] Plato, *De Republica* (Πολιτεία) in G. R. F. Ferrari (ed.), Tom Griffith (transl.) (2000), *Plato, The Republic*. Cambridge: Cambridge University Press I, 338c, "Listen then, he replied. I say the justice is simply what is good for the stronger".

[704] Aristotle, Politica (Τὰ πολιτικά), in Benjamin Jowett [1817–1893] (ed.) (1885), *The Politics of Aristotle*. Oxford, 1325b 6–7, "For equals share alike the honourable and the just, as is just and equal. But that the inequal should be given to equals, and the unlike to those who are like, is contrary to nature, and nothing which is contrary to nature is good."; other passages on "natural law" in Aristotle's works are in *Nicomachean Ethics*, 1134b, 1135a5, 1790–1791; *Rethorics*, 1368b 1–10, 1375a 25–35, 2178, 2190; on this, see extensively, Tony Burns (2011), *Aristotle and Natural Law*. London, New York: Bloomsbury.

[705] It seems to be a quotation from Cicero; L. The Latin text is, "Aristoteles et cum eo Stoici statuere Juris Naturae esse fundamentum: Naturae convenienter vivere"; Cicero, *On Duties*. III, 3, 13, "Etenim quod summum bonum a Stoicis dicitur convenienter naturae vivere (…)".

[706] Epicurus, *Principal Doctrine*. http://classics.mit.edu/Epicurus/princdoc.html, [accessed may 2015], "31. Natural justice is a symbol or expression of usefullness, to prevent one person from harming or being harmed by another."; "17. The just person enjoys the greatest peace of mind, while the unjust is full of the utmost disquietude." (tr. by Robert D. Hicks).

[707] Cicero [106 BC–43 BC], *De officiis* in Walter Miller [1864–1949] (ed.) (1913), *Cicero, On Duties*. Cambridge MA, I, 7, 22, "But since, as Plato has admirably expressed it, we are not born for ourselves

base his beliefs on the following foundation: no one is born only for himself, but a man's country, parents and friends claim for themselves a part [of us].

§. 72. The more recent authors put forward the following appraisals: for Hugo Grotius[708], natural law is whatever would be appropriate to the nature of society in the interest of users or anything that is compatible with society; he therefore establishes as a principle what is denied by Hobbes, namely that man is naturally social. Sforza Pallavicino's fine book *The Good*[709], reaches the decision—after much debate—that: the just is what pleases nature. However by the term "nature" he means: the principle of motion and rest in the world, which is necessarily rational, since motion is so beautiful and well ordered. Thomas Hobbes, in the most subtle *On the Citizen*[710], proceeds in the following manner: in a civil state or a civil community, the condition of men is either without a superior or under a superior. In such a state, there exists the pure right of all people over all things, including the right of war; but since the state of war is destructive, anyone, by sound reason, most naturally disposes himself to peace, that is, to the condition of a single civic community, insofar as it is in his power to bring about such a community; once the civic community has been established, however, the right is only whatever pleases the state, and no other natural law prevails there. Johann von Felden in the *Elements of the Jurisprudence*[711] summarized the principles of Aristotle and perfected them. Robert Scharrok, in his book *On the Duties according to*

---

alone, but our country claims a share of our being, and our friends a share (…)".

[708] Grotius, see note 151.

[709] Pietro Sforza Pallavicino (1644), *Del Bene*. Roma: appresso gli eredi di Francesco Corbelletti.

[710] See note 101.

[711] See note 102.

the Natural Law[712], believes, in agreement with Epicurus, that the highest good, is the pleasure of the soul. Sins are thus to be avoided, because they are contrary to the pleasure of the soul, they are, indeed, comparable to incorporeal blows. From here comes the κριτήριον [in Greek in the text, e. n.] criterion for injustice, which comes about if something repugnant is done to the soul. Therefore, Scharrok believes that God created our soul, so that there is a certain natural ἀντιπάθεια [in Greex in the text, e. n.] antipathy between the soul itself and what are called sins.

§. 73. We will easily reconcile these opinions with one another, once we have clarified our opinion. Certainly the degrees of natural law are three: *jus strictum*[713], *aequitas*[714] and *pietas*[715]. Of these, each successive degree is

---

712 Robert Sharrok (1660), *De Officiis Secundum Naturæ Jus*. Oxoniae.
713 Berger, see note 19, *ad vocem Jus strictum*. "The rigid, stiff law. (…) Possibly it goes back to an earlier conception which started from the distinction that some actions were *bonae fidei* and others were not; therefore the judge had to pass his judgement strictly according to the law without making use of the liberties ha had *ex fide bona* or *ex aequo et bono*. Thus the *jus strictum* is conceived as a counterpart of *jus aequum*".
714 Berger, see note 19, *ad vocem Aequitas*, "Related to justice (*iustitia, iustum*), but distinguished from the positive law, *ius*. A law which is guided by *aequitas* is *ius aequum*, it antonym is *ius iniquum*. In the legal sphere *aequitas* may be realized either by interpreting the existing law or by supplementing it where an exact legal provision is missing. *Aequitas*, as the word itself indicates, implies the element of equality. Transferred into the province of the law it postulates equal treatment of all according to the conceptions nurtured in the social (common) conscience of the people with change, of course, when social and economic conditions undergo a change. (…)".
715 Berger, see note 19, *ad vocem Pietas*, "Dutifulness, respectful conduct, sense of duty, affection toward gods, parents, or near relatives; in general noblemindness, honest way of thinking. 'It is to be held that we are unable to commit acts which injure our dutiful (*pie-*

more perfect than the previous one and strengthens it; and in case of conflict it repeals the previous degree. The rigid or pure law derives from the intrinsic the definition of the terms, and if assessed, it can be seen to be nothing other than the law of war and peace. In fact, between person and person the law of peace is in force, as long as the other does not begin the war, or engage in harmful conduct. Between person and thing, however, there is a perpetual law of war, because a thing has no intelligence. And it is lawful for a lion to tear a man and for a mountain to crush a man by a landslide; equally, it is lawful for a man to restrain a lion, break down a mountain. But the victory of a person over a thing and the captivity of the thing is called possession. Thus, possession endows the person with a right over the thing, by law of war, provided that the thing belongs to no one. If, however, the thing belongs to someone, then no man is allowed to damage it or to appropriate it, any more than he is allowed to kill the slaves of others or give shelter to fugitives. Therefore, if one damages another either in his person or in his things, this gives him the same right as that which he has over a thing, namely, the right of war. And even malicious deception is counted among the species of damage, because the damage is inflicted on the mind, from which there derives the need for keeping promises. It is therefore clear that the only true precept of natural law is: never injure, hurt, or damage anyone (*neminem laedere*); in this manner you will ensure that no person can claim the right of war against you. To this belongs commutative justice, and the right that Grotius calls faculty.

---

tas), our reputation (*existimatio*), our way of thinking, and generally speaking, are contrary to the good customs. This saying is by Papinian (*D*.28.7.15). Although heavily criticized and frequently ascribed to Justinian's compilers, it expresses a late classical idea".

§. 74. *Aequitas*[716], or *aequalitas*, that is, the proper ratio or proportion, consists in harmony or congruence. It coincides with the principles of Aristotle, Grotius, and Von Felden, which require that when someone hurts me, I do not begin a murderous war: rather, *arbitri* are admitted[717] to restore justice. Furthermore, do not do to another what you do not wish to be done to yourself. Likewise to be punished is not so much imprudence, but rather deceit (*dolus*[718]) and wickedness; equally the deceptive points of a contract are to be annulled and those who have been deceived are to be assisted. For the remaining aspects, the *aequitas* itself dictates that rigid law be observed. To this matter belong Hobbes' arguments for peace. But equity provides law in a broad sense (*jus laxe*) or, according to the style of Grotius, an aptitude[719] to one part; the full obligation to another, *e. g.*, it is equitable that one who has removed a debt owed to me through subtle deceptions

---

[716] See note 714.

[717] In a more technical sense, according to the Roman Law, Berger, see note 19, *ad vocem Arbiter*, "In a judicial trial, in controversies which required specific professional or technical knowledge the magistrate could appoint an expert (*arbiter*), instead of a judge (*judex*), so that the judgement should be rendered by someone better qualified the the average Roman citizen listed in the panel of judges (*album iudicum*)".

[718] Berger, see note 19, *ad vocem Dolus*, "Defined by Labeo (*D.* 4.3.1.2) as follows, 'any cunning, deceit or contrivance used to defraud deceive or cheat another'".

[719] Neff, *Hugo Grotius On the law of War and Peace*, see note151, 25, "When the moral quality is perfect we call it *facultas*, 'faculty', when it is not perfect, *aptitudo*, 'aptitude'. To the former, in the range od natural things, 'act' (*actus*) correspons; to the latter, 'potency' (*potentia*). "; therein n. 8, "An aptitude in contrast to a faculty is an imperfect right, i.e., one which cannot be enforced by law of a legal action in a court of law. It is therefore in the nature of a moral claim or expectation. An example is the expectation of a person who has diligently cared for an aged man of receiving a legacy in the man's will (…)".

nevertheless still owes me, although I am not entitled to engage in a legal action to pursue him; indeed, the action or the exception, or any other instance derives from pure right (unless some law is added), but nevethless that person is still obliged to give me what is owed. Hence the precept: *render to everyone his due*. But the law or superior tends to *aequitas*, and from this sometimes grants action or exception.

§. 75. The third principle of law is the will of the superior. And here we recall what Thrasymachus pleaded in Plato: the just is that which is useful for the more powerful. However either there is a superior by nature, God (his will, on the other hand, is, again, either natural, hence the piety, or law, hence the divine positive right); or there is a superior by agreement, such as man, hence Civil Law. Piety is, therefore, a degree of natural law, and gives perfection and effect to the other. God, who is omniscient and wise, confirms the pure right and the equity; and since he is all-powerful he brings about these conditions. Here coincides the utility of humankind, indeed the beauty and harmony of the world, with the divine will. According to this principle it is not even permitted to abuse beasts and creatures. This leads back to the meditations of Sforza Pallavicino. On this basis, it is not even permitted to abuse oneself, because we ourselves belong to God, whose omnipotence distributes right into everything. Hence, that precept: to live honestly. And since strict right and equity are lacking of physical constraint, God makes sure that everything that which is publicly useful to mankind and the world is, by the same token, also made useful for the individual; accordingly, all that is honest is useful and all that is dishonest is harmful. It is certain that God, according to his wisdom, determines rewards for the just and punishment for the unjust: and the argument of omnipotence demonstrates that what He has decided will be accomplished. "Therefore, the existence of the wisest and most powerful Being, or God, is the ultimate foundation of natural law, the very existence, which through the demonstration given by us with mathematical certainty, when it appears in public, will be able to dissipate definitely the fog spread by the atheists on truth."[quotation marks in the text, e. n.]

§. 76. [77.] The other eye of the jurisconsult in deciding cases is the nomothetic, whose principle is the utility of the republic, which is to the republic as piety is to the world and the universal republic. On the nomothetic Hoppers gave a very clear discussion in *Seduardus*[720], Hermann Conring [1606–1681] partly in his preface to Hoppers, partly in *Civil Prudence* and *Propolitic*[*a*][721]. But, people's health (*salus populi*), the supreme law of the State[722], consists in the good of the citizens themselves in the substance and in the preservation of the regime as to the form. In fact, even Justus Lipsius [1547–1606] says that there are two aspects to be considered: the nature of the people and the nature of the kingdom[723], which Johann Heinrich Böckler [1611–1672] commends in his dissertation *On the Lipsian Politics*[724]. The good of the regime consists in Public Law and also in such a conformation of the laws that is appropriate to pre-

---

[720] See note 142.

[721] Hermann Conring (1662), *De civili prudentia*. Helmestadii; Id. (1663), *Propolitica, sive brevis introductio in civilem philosophiam*. Helmestadii.

[722] The phrase comes from Cicero, *De legibus*, III, 3, 8, "Ollis salus populi suprema lex esto".

[723] Justus Lipsius (1589), *Politicorum sive civilis doctrinae libri sex qui ad principatum maxime spectant*. Lugduni Batavorum [not included in AA VI, 2, sources directory].

[724] Johann Heinrich Böckler, (1642), *Dissertatio de politicis Justi Lipsii*. Argentorati.

vent a revolution[725]. The good of the citizens consists in ευδαιμονία [in Greek in the text, concord, e. n.] and in αυταρκεία [in Greek in the text, autarchy, e. n.], that is, in the goods of the soul and fortune. However, poverty makes men not only ridiculous, as the poet says[726], but wicked. To the eudaimonia, that is, to virtue belong all political systems, from which there derive, in the first place, education, conversation, as well as the principles of good and bad habits, likewise the rewards for virtue and the punishments for vices. To autarchy belong the laws of commerce, manufacturing, and public expenses, etc. To each of these belong at the same time the laws that organize private law and trials; thus if each man is assured of recognition of his own right, it will be possible to avoid the sins of those who hold back and the poverty of those who suffer the loss. We not only have to make sure that everyone is granted recognition of his own right, but also [that it is recognized] quickly. Such topics relate to the regulations of the process. On all these issues attention should be awarded to the splendid reflections of Ottavio Pisani in the *Lycurgus*[727], who taught how crimes may be eradicated through an organized manner of life and education; and how trials may be avoided if everything is managed and annotated in public records in the presence of a magistrate endowed with public authority, as in the *Banco* in Venice. We ourselves will not reach

---

[725] "Mutatio rerum", in Cicero [106 BC–43 BC], *Ad Atticum*, 8, 3, 4, means revolution. The word "rerum" is not present in the text, but I think that L. is using "mutatio" with this meaning.

[726] Juvenal [c. 50–after 127], *Saturae*. III, 152, in George Gilbert Ramsay see note 26, 42-43, *nil habet infelix paupertas durius in se/quam quod ridiculos homines facit* ["Of all the woes of luckless poverty none is harder to endure than this, that it exposes men to ridicule"].

[727] Ottavio Pisani, see note 144.

this point of perfection; however, the jurisconsult makes sure that he may approach it, as far as possible.

§. 78. So far we have spoken about the principles of decision/making: we will now turn to the issue of the collections of decisions, that is, of controversies. Here the matter is easier in words, as in exegetics, but more difficult in practice. It is not so much a question of the number of points to address or of books to compose, but rather, of the extent to which the field of enquiry should or should not be restricted, whether a limited number of books should be matched by a broader approach. The collection of controversies may have a limited or wide scope. Let us examine the case of a short collection, outlining how it was drawn up. The task must begin by creating a book, which can be called the Breviary of Controversies, as for instance in theology the *Handbook* of Martin Becanus [1561–1624][728] or the *Breviary* of Johann Hülsemann [1602–1661][729]. We will now examine the substance and the form of the Juridical Breviary. The substance consists in questions which are 1) doubtful, which thus exclude the Didactics part, the very questions, which are expressly decided by the laws; 2) juridical, thus excluding philological and philosophical questions; 3) in force, thus excluding the repealed rules; 4) rare, which, however, are reserved to the *Pandects* that are to be explained later. Here one should place the most illustrious issues, made famous by the diversity of opinions.

§. 79. Form consists in the order and manner of treatment. The order should be the same as the Elements §. 7 ff. up to § 26 and the Institutes §. 53. The manner of

---

[728] Martin Becanus (1622), *Manuale controversiarum huius temporis, in quinque libros distributum*. Monasteri Westphaliae: Sumptibus Michaëlis Dalii & Ioannis Volmari.
[729] Johann Hülsemann (1640), *Breviarium theologicum*.Vitebergae.

treatment consists in the reasons for doubt and decisions. In both cases, only the passages of the Elements and the Laws that seem either to oppose or to be in our favor should be addressed. It is worth noting that the Elements are to be composed according to mathematical usage, so that every question may be answered through these Elements. And just as Isaac Barrow [1630–1677], in his Cambridge edition of Euclid [fl. 300 BC][730], uses some signs of abbreviation: so in this place if the argument, according to the text of the Elements or the Laws, is based on a similar case (*a simili*), contrast (*a contrario*), cause, effect, gender, the whole, the part, or reference to other topics, then a symbol should be devised, so that anyone who looks through the text and notices the symbol can easily recognize the strength of the argument, and *eo ipso* exercise the mind, and will in no way be impeded by the conciseness. But, once such a breviary has been prepared, we will show these things in greater depth by means of examples and facts rather than in words. For example, in place of the argument from contrast, let the following symbols be used:)(; from similar case (); from cause O-; from effect –O; from gender ∩; from species ∪; from the whole ∩; from the part ∪. And whenever two laws or two combined passages of the Elements play a crucial role in showing the strength of the conclusion, one may use the symbol +, for example *l. 20 D.V.O. + l. D. de Leg*. Furthermore, quotations from other writings should include only authors who treated the questions in depth and collected very convincing arguments pros and cons. Likewise those that quote many others.

§ 80. We mentioned that a short collection of controversies should be composed; let us now examine how it can

---

[730] Euclid, *Elementa*, in Isaac Barrow (ed.) (1655), *Euclides Elementorum libri XV*. Cantabrigiae.

be made. We have many books of exercises, controversies, decisions, resolutions, questions, disputes, but none are fully suitable to our purpose, if we love the truth. If we simultaneously remove the philological questions, e. g. on the origin and the use of terms; and the historical issues, e. g. on the titles of Emperor Justinian, on the authors of the laws, on time, etc.; the philosophical issues on the correctness of definitions, subdivisions, method; the questions pertaining to a fact of nature, e. g. an eight months birth, the signs of virginity, the common purgations (*purgationes vulgares*[731]); likewise the rules that have long been abolished; what was in use at the time of Justinian [483–565], Theodosius [347–395], Constantine [272–337],—if, I say, we proceed in the above described manner, then half and more of the book itself [will be removed]. For what purpose is served by these arguments, which do not penetrate the substance of the right, or what is the purpose of in-depth examination of repealed rules, unless it be that we fear to become judges, legal advisers, professors of law, lawyers, under Arcadius [d. 408], Honourius [384–423] and Justinian, as if we were back in the Platonic year[732]. Therefore, I do not find authors whom I would recommend; a reader may choose, according to his likes, from among Valentin Wilhelm Forster [1574–1620][733], Bernard Sutholt [fl.1625][734], Wilhelm Ludwell

---

[731] It was a trial by ordeal, see Alexander Mansfield Burrill [1806–1869] (1870), *A Law Dictionary and Glossary*, 2. New York, *ad vocem Vulgaris Purgatio*.

[732] "The period of one complete cycle of the equinoxes around the ecliptic, about 25,800 years". http://www.hq.nasa.gov/office/hqlibrary/aerospacedictionary/aerodictall/g.html, sub *Great Year* [accessed 5 May 2015].

[733] Valentin Wilhelm Forster (1611), *Iustinianeae Tractationes*. Wittibergae [not included in AA VI, 2, sources directory].

[734] Bernard Sutholt (1633), *Dissertationes undeviginti: quibus universum jus Institutionum ex principiis explicatur, ea brevitate, ut instar*

[1589–1663][735], Treutler[736], ennobled by the attentions of Reinhard Bachoff Von Echt [c. 1575–1640][737] and Helfrich Ulrich Hunnius [1583–1636][738], the *Resolutions* of the Hunnius[739] himself, the *Illustrious Questions* of Leopold Hackelmann [1513–1619][740] appropriate for the authors who are extensively quoted. I say nothing with regard to Dominik Van Arum [1579–1637][741], Ortholp Fomann [1560–1634][742], Georg David Locamer [1588–1637][743] and others, who move back and forth the same saw, with continuous copying. Likewise, I shall conceal that there is a large number of authors who combine rules, exegesis, history and controversies, among whom I would recommend the *Syntagma* of the illustrious George Adam

---

compendii, ea item perspicuitate, ut in locis obscurioribus vice commentarii esse possint. Lugduni Batavorum: Ex officina Elzeviriorum.

735 Wilhelm Ludwell (1658), *Exercitationes XVIII ad IV Libros Institutionum Imperialium in Universitate Aldorfina*. Altdorfi Noricorum [not included in AA VI, 2, sources directory].

736 See notes 737, 738.

737 Reinhard Bachoff von Echt, Hieronymus Treutler [1565–1607] (1658), *Bachovius augmentatus i. e. Cl. V. Reinhardi Bachovii Echtii Notae et animadversiones ad Hieron. Treutleri*. Coloniae Agrippinae.

738 Hieronymus Treutler, Helfrich Ulrich Hunnius (1617), *Hieronymi Treutleri J. C. Selectarum disputationum ad jus civile Justinianaeum, quinquaginta libris Pandectarum comprehensum, resolutionum absolutissimarm volumina duo*. Francofurti: J. J. Porsius.

739 Helfrich Ulrich Hunnius (1646), *Variae resolutiones iuris civilis, libri IV*. Francofurti: Apud J. D. Zunnerum.

740 Leopold Hackelmann (1594), *Illustriores et selectiores quaestiones in vita communi vsum insignem habentes: ex omnibus iuris articulis collectae, ex iuxta seriem pandectarum*. Jenae.

741 Dominik van Arum (1612), *Decisionum et sententiarum liber primus*. Jenae.

742 Ortholp Fomann (1601),*Semicenturia Quaestionum miscellanearum, ex Iuris Civilis, Canonici, Feudalis & Saxonici varijs capitibus delibata*. Jenae.

743 Georg David Locamer [1588–1637] (1627), *Decas Quæstionum Iuris Controversarum*. Argentorati: Scher.

Struve [1619–1692][744]. Considerable esteem is awarded to the dissertations, published in Brunswick, of the illustrious Johann Strauch[745], *Proto-Syndacus* at this time, with which he has abandoned the method of Justinian, followed the natural approach and separated the Elements from the Disputes according to the shape of the types. I would recommend this especially with Ludwell and Treutler. Nor should one neglect Schnobel[746], who made a summary of Treutler.

§. 81. The broad and complete [collection] follows the short collection of controversies. And again, it is interesting to reflect both on how it was made, and how it should be made. How it was made is very evident. To this matter belong the great books of the decisions of the various ministries, *Rotae*[747], or parliaments, for example of the Roman, Genoan *Rotae*, of the Piedmontan, Toulousan, Frisian (by Frederik van den Sande [1576–1617]), Belgian (by Willem Grotius [1597–1662]) Senate, the Parisian *Customs* by Charles Dumoulin [1500–1566], the Lithuanian (by Pedro Ruiz de Moros [c. 1506–1571]), the Savoyard (by Antoine Favre [1557–1624]) *Decisions*, the *Camerales* by Andreas Von Gail [1526–1587], Joachim Müsinger [1514–1588], Adrian Gilmann [1583–1612], the *Customs* of the March by Joachim Scheplitz [1566–1634], the *Decisions* of the Lipsian Faculty of Law (in the *Observations* of Sigismondus Finckelthaus [1579–1644]) and of the Lipsian *Scabinatus* (in the *Various Writings* of the great Benedict Carpzov [1595–1666]).

---

[744] George Adam Struve (1658), *Syntagmatis Juris Civilis a libro ff. 39. usque ad finem*. Jenae.
[745] See note 667.
[746] Joachim Schnobel [1602–1671] (1658), *Disputationes juridicae ad quinquaginta libros Pandectarum ante aliquot annos*. Jenae: Nisius.
[747] The Catholic Church's judicial courts.

Philipp Richter [1602–1673] collected the Jenian *Responses*; in this connection one may also recall the *Advices* of the faculties of other universities, of Tübingen, Ingolstadt, Marburg, Altdorf[748]. And the *Advices* of private [jurists]: of Paolo di Castro [c.1360–1441], Marcantonio Natta [1568–1616], Christoph Coler [1570–1604], Caspar Klock [1583–1655], Petrus Wesenbeck junior [1546–1603], Georg Mundig von Rodach [1549–1647]: who, in talking, could include all of them[749]? And

---

[748] Wide Collections of Controversies: Frederik van den Sande (1637), *Commentarius in Gelrie et Zutphania consuetudines feudales*. Arnhemium; Wilhlem Grotius (1655), *Guilielmi Grotii Isagoge ad praxin fori Batavici*. Amstelaedami: ex typographia J. Blaeu; Charles Dumoulin (1613), *Commentarij in Parisienses totius Galliae Supremi Parlamenti consuetudines*. Coloniae Allobrogum: Excudebat Esaias Le Preux; Pedro Ruiz de Moros (1563), *Decisiones Petri Royzii Maurei Alcagnic. de rebus in sacro auditorio Lituonico ex appellatione judicatis*. Craccovve; Antoine Favre (1615), *De erroribus pragmaticorum et interpretum iuris. Chilias absoluta, ecc.* Coloniae Allobrogvm [Geneva]: Sumptibus Iacobi Crispini; Andreas von Gail (1578), *Practicarum observationum ad processum camerae Imperii libri II.* Coloniae; Joachim Müsinger von Frundeck (1666), *Decisiones camerales*. Francofurti; Adrian Gilmann (1603), *Decisionum seu rerum in camera imperali judicatarum libri 2*. Francofurti [not included in AA VI, 2, sources directory]; Joachim Scheplitz (1616), *Consuetudines electoratus et Marchiae Brandenburgensis*. Lipsiae: Gross; Sigismund Finckelthaus (1636), *Observationes practicae*. Lipsiae; Benedict Carpzov (1646), *Decisiones illustres Saxonicae rerum & quaestionum forensium*, 2. Lipsiae: Kühn; Christoph Philipp Richter (1663), *Centuria variarum iuris decisionum*. Jenae.

[749] Collections of Advices: Paolo di Castro (1582), *Consilia*. Francoforti: apud Ioan. Feyerab. impensis Sigismundi Feyerabendt; Marcantonio Natta (1558), *Consilia sive Responsa*. Lugdunum; Christoph Coler (1612), *Responsa Juris, sive consilia cum additionibus Saxoferati et Pontani*. Lipsiae; Caspar Klock (1649), *Consiliorum libri III*. Francofurti; Petrus Wesenbeck (1607), *Tractatus et responsae quae vulgo consilia dicuntur*. Francofurti; Georg Mundig von Rodach (1664), *Consiliorum sive tractatuum juris volumina II.* Jenae.

the opinion of Hugo Grotius in the preface to the book *On the Law of War and Peace*[750] can certainly be shared, when he states that the authors of counsels have adapted their responses more to the favor of the persons requesting the opinion, than to the substance of the good and equitable. I omit many others who have written on the whole of right, such as the *Works* by Prospero Farinacci [1554–1618][751], the *Questions Depending upon the Decision of the Judges* by Giacomo Menochio [1532–1607][752], and others; the *Common Opinions* by Juan Bautista de Villalobos[753], Francesco Vivio [1532–1616][754], and by those from whom Nicolaus Vigel [1529–1600]—the only one among others to be used—summarized his *Controversial Law*[755]; finally, one should not omit Petrus GregoriusTolosanus [d. 1597?] in the *Orderly Exposition of the Whole Law*[756].

§. 82. These authors are commendable for delivering to posterity new relevant cases and enriching the legal world with continuous growth, unlike the authors of exercises and commentaries, who content themselves with chewing over old things again. Consequently, according to those who are familiar with law and have expert knowledge, these authors should be read more seldom, while the others must be studied continuously. But in consideration of

---

[750] See note 151.
[751] Prospero Farinacci (1620), *Opera Omnia*, Antverpiae.
[752] Giacomo Menochio (1599), *De arbitrariis judicum quaestionibus*. Coloniae Agrippinae: Gymnicus.
[753] Juan Bautista de Villalobos (1564), *Opiniones in jure Communes*. Venetiis.
[754] Francesco Vivio (1611), *Sylvae Communium Opinionum Doctorum Utriusque Censurae in Tres Libros Distinctae*. Francofurti.
[755] Nikolaus Vigel (1579), *Methodus iuris controversi*. Basileae.
[756] Petrus Gregorius Tolosanus (1639), *Syntagma juris universi*. Coloniae Allobrogum: Typis Jacobi Stoer.

this argument I lament that they also mix well-known cases, for which decisions have already been handed down, with others that do not yet have a definitive solution; likewise to intermingle the obvious cases and those that are of certain right, determinable through the pure subsumption of the general principles. It would be appropriate to add only supplements to other authors, to avoid burdening the world with unnecessary repetition; or, if you disagree with them on some point or have some new reason and objection, this too should be recalled; not everything has to be copied again, neither is it appropriate to inflate, without the need, the costs for publishers and readers. In consideration of the form, I would choose for those collections an order which either is not widely in existence, or is not natural. Moreover, a question should not be treated too widely, as the authors of the counsels do, in order to make their work appear greater and more valuable, if it please God, and they engage in every proposition that incidentally comes to mind and they seek to treat it as the main issue. So it happens that in order to exert themselves on the most common and evident axioms, texts and opinion of the doctors, they leave behind the principal and, in truth, very controversial proposition, often without any proof, or strengthen it only with petty and silly rhetorical sophistries, not with accurate demonstrations. This is a feature that was already pointed out by Conrad Summenhart [d. 1502], in his book *On Contract*[757], and Jakob Thoming [1524–1576], of the Lipsian Faculty of Law, former ordinary dean, in his *Oration on the Study of law*[758]. Would that these present-day writers had imitated those whom they quote many times and al-

---

[757] Conrad Summenhart (1580), *De contractibus licitis, atque illicitis*. Venetiis: Zilletis.

[758] Jakob Thoming (1596), *De studio iuris recte instituendo Oratio*. Lipsiae: Grosius.

ways have on their lips, the ancient Jurisconsults, who with very few lines often compressed a large body of arguments. I do not doubt that through some response of Ulpian or Scevola, which occupies barely a page, those good *Decisionarii* of ours will fill more than ten sheets. Antoine Favre [1557–1624], however, in the *Savoyard Code,* stood out with distinction from among this flock of ordinary people[759], and he excellently showed to our men the torch of how one can exhaustively dissertate and at the same time write with concision. Equally commendable, and also adequate to the way of expounding of the old jurists, is the custom by which the faculty and Saxon Scabinatus, firstly in Leipzig, in their German Councils (called *Informat Urtheil*) examine the reasons on both sides with extreme conciseness and effectiveness.

§. 83. To this matter belong the Treatises of various authors on various subjects. Such works are either about a specific topic of right (for example on *fideicommissa*[760] by Marco Antonio Peregrino [1530–1616], on loan for consumption by Claude Saumaise [1588–1653], on pledges by Antonius Negusantius [1465–1508]; on contracts by Andrés [not Alexandro, as in the text, e. n.] de Exea [d. 1575], on marriage by Thomas Sánchez [1550–1610][761]); or they are about the terms of a fact connected

---

[759] Antoine Favre (1615), *Codex Fabrianus definitionum foresium et rerum in Sabaudiae senatu tractatarum*, Lugduni.

[760] See note 122.

[761] Monographs on specific subjects of law: Marco Antonio Peregrino (1599), *De Fideicommissis*. Francofurto; Claude Saumaise (1645), *Disquisitio de mutuo: qua probatur non esse alienationem*. Lugduni Batavorum; Antonius Negusantius (1549), *Tractatus de pignoribus et hypothecis*. Lugduni; Andrés de Exea (1584), *De pactis*, in Gregorius XIII [1502–1585], *Tractatus universi iuris, duce et auspice Gregorio XIII* vol. 6, Venetiis; Thomas Sánchez (1625), *De sancto matrimonii sacramento disputationum tomi tres*. Lugduni.

to the law (such as on the deaf and the dumb by Biagio Micalori [1621–1664], on women by Benedict Carpzov [1595–1666], on mills by Johann Hering [1599–1658] etc.[762]). Sometimes they treat not only some particular title [of the Digest], but something from various topics both of right and of fact taken from [Digest] (such as Antonio Corsetti [c.1450–1503], on the repetition of words, Jean Baptiste Lacoste [d. 1637?], *on the fictitious alienations*; as I shall conceal the innumerable disputes of the same kind, such as those that were collected in the volumes of *The Controversies of Basel*[763]). Almost all of the ancient treatises were collected in the *Treaty of the Treaties*[764], a vast work published several times. It has been expanded with the addition of a very complete and accurate index that fills an entire volume. However, I also lament many repetitions, which may occur even though the substance of the authors has not been inserted, but only their integers. Thus very often several different authors have been included on the same subject, one of whom says much same things as the others. I remember that sometime I read in the Treaty of Treaties two treaties on the games, one by Paride del Pozzo [1410–1493][765], I

---

[762] On terms of the fact applied to right: Biagio Micalori (1646), *Tractatus de coeco, surdo, et muto*. Venetiis: Apud Guerilios; Benedict Carpzov (1651), *De juribus foeminarum singularibus*. Lipsiae; Johann Hering (1625), *Tractatus singularis de molendinis, eorumqve jure*. Francofurti.

[763] Questions of fact and points of law: Antonio Corsetti (1584), *De verbis geminatis*.Venetiis; Jean Baptiste Lacoste (1606), *Tractatus de retrotractione seu de fictione traslativa*, Venetiis; (1653) *Disputationum iuridicarum inauguralium selectiorum in inclyta Basileensium universitate disquisitioni publicae ac solenni expositarum volumen novum*. Basileae.

[764] (1549) *Primum (-decimum septimum) volumen Tractatuum ex variis juris interpretibus collectorum*, 18 vols., Lugduni.

[765] Paride del Pozzo (1549), *Tractatus aureus in materia ludi*, in *Primum volumen Tractatuum ex variis juris*, see note 352.

do not remember the name of the other. One of these had copied the other word for word. Thus it happens that in certain subjects a work is too rich, in another extremely poor. This state of affairs gave Jerimias Drechsel [1581–1638] to believe, as he narrates in the *Gold Mine of the Arts and Sciences*[766], that this work [the Treaty of Treaties] was the model of all other books. It would be worth remoulding these Treaties of the Treaties, with irrelevant matters, the various authors on the same topics summarized in a single volume; and also with the addition of the kernel from many treaties, sometimes on different matters, chiefly those published in this century. This could easily have been done once, with the same attention by which an index was joined to a table of contents, and even now an index can be very helpful for that content. There are specific Treaties of the Treaties, for example The Treaties on Contracts published in a single volume, likewise on Testaments and so on. To the juridical Treaties of the Treaties there correspond in a certain sense the *Critical Anglican Bibles*[767] of the theologians, in which were collected selected theological treatises by various authors for the passages of the Scripture. And there is also another juridical work, not dissimilar from the Treaty of Treaties, which is called: *Repetitions*[768]. The English, as I hear, want to compose something similar in the Curious Philosophy that will be entitled *Philosophical Library*[769], in which philosophical, physics, mechanics, mathematics, on unusual cases and writings by various authors will be gathered, full of selected considerations

[766] Jerimias Drechsel (1657), *Aurifodina artium et scientiarum*. Antverpiae.
[767] I found, for example, Johann Freidrich Mayer [1650–1712] (1703), *Biblia critica Anglicana et Poli synopsis*. Gryphiswaldia.
[768] (1553), *Repetitiones seu commentaria in varia iuris consultorum responsa*. Lugduni.
[769] (1665), *Philosophical transactions of the Royal Society*. Londonii.

and experiments. But, coming back to the juridical treaties, once those Pandects of Right have been drafted, on which later, we can easily do without them. Especially because one often finds that only half the [part] regards the matter in question. One should read, for example, the treaty of Thomas Sagittarius [1577–1621], *On Counts*[770]; I will be amazed if a reader says that this book treats one tenth of the proposed matter.

§. 84. We have talked about the wide collection of controversies, and how they are made; we will now address the issue of how they should be written. In this regard, we will re-examine both the preparatory collections, namely the repertoires, and also the order of their presentation, Pandects of Right. Various repertoires were prepared by others whose opinions we have discussed. As far as the attempts of other [authors] are concerned, there is the *Repertoire of Civil Law* by Pieter Cornelis van Brederode [end 16th-cent.][771], as well as the Index of Justinian Law, which was undoubtedly useful for everyday use, indeed, I am surprised it has not been reissued. The opinions of the doctors were gathered in the *Repertoire* by Giovanni Bertachini [1448–15..?][772] as well as the *Conclusions* by Cardinal Domenico Toschi [1535–1620][773]. This [kind of work] also encompasses lexicons, such as the *Treasure* by Speidel, the *Common Places* by Arnald de Reyger [1559–1615], Brunoro da Sole [fl. 1596]

---

[770] Thomas Sagittarius (1619), *Disputatio inauguralis de jure et privilegiis comitum palatinorum Caesareorum*. Jenae.

[771] Pieter Cornelis van Brederode (1587), *Repertorium sententiarum et regularum, itémque definitionum divisionum ... ex universo Iuris civilis*. Francofurti.

[772] Giovanni Bertachini (1552) *Repertorium D. Joannis Bertachini*. Lugdunum.

[773] Domenico Toschi (1605–1608), *Conclusiones iuris practicae*. Romae.

with the Additions by Jacob Schultes [1571–1629][774]. Also belonging to work of this kind is the Library of Law, which more truly needs rebuilding rather than to be made stable by someone by virtue of an honorary office. In this context, it should be noted that what once Giovanni Nevizzano [d. 1540] and Johann Wolfgang Freymon von Randeck [1546–1610] attempted[775] is small and imperfect. The Juridical Libraries by[776] Paul Bolduan [fl. 1614–1622] and Georg Draud [1573–1635][777] (the work by the former being a separate composition, while that by the latter is inserted into the *Classical Library*) are composed according to catalogues of books, which review a great number of books, either never published or never to be published, never laid eggs, *ungelegte Eher* [in German in the text, e. .n.], as has been memorably said. Therefore, not having themselves carefully examined the books, but only the titles in catalogues, it follows that often they did not understand the subject-matter of the book; for not infrequently, the titles of the books are in fact too boastful and very discordant. Furthermore, both of the two above-cited authors were also inexperienced in Law, with the result that in many cases, although a given book genuinely existed, and the title corresponded to the book, they could not determine under which classification the book should be entered in their library. Hence, they believed that they would act very shrewdly if they recorded the book in question under the title ordered by

---

[774] Lexicons: Johann Jakob Speidel, see note 455; Arnald de Rayger (1604), *Thesaurus Iuris*, 2 T. Lipsiae; Brunoro da Sole (1607), *Loci communes juris cæsarei, pontificii et saxonici...aucti a Jac. Schultes*. Lipsiae.

[775] Giovanni Nevizzano, Johann Wolfgang Freymon von Randeck (1579), *Elenchus omnium auctorum sive scriptorum, qui in iure tam civili quam canonico vel commentando ... claruerunt*. Francofurtum.

[776] Not found a *Bibliotheca Juridica* by Paul Bolduan, but, among others, a (1620), *Bibliotheca historica*. Lipsia.

[777] Georg Draud (1625), *Bibliotheca classica.* Francofurti ad Moenum.

the author; but this was a very foolish manner of proceeding, as the authors' titles set on the front page of a book are typically more oratorical and pompous than technical and accurate. "Therefore It would be desirable for the Classical Library by Draud not only to be continued (so far, it has reached the year 1625), but also to be corrected" [quotation marks in the text, e. n.]. Joachim Meisner [1584–...], rector of Torgau, has prepared its continuation, but I think it has not yielded a single correction: he died and the work was left unfinished. Jacques Godefroy promised that he would insert a Practical Library in the practical part of his *Handbook*[778], yet to be published, but he did little more than make that vain promise. I am surprised that none of the Jurisconsults followed the example of Johann Antonides van der Linden [1609–1664], in *Medical Writers*[779], and Gijsbert Voet, in *Theological Library*[780]. Paul Buys [1609–1664] promised something similar in the *Preface* to his *Commentary on the Pandects*[781], but he also did not keep his promise. Meanwhile, here, *The Lives of German Jurisconsult*[782] by Adam Melchior [1575–1622] is worth noting. This completes our overview of the Library of Law. Connected to this is the appropriate place for each of the various subject-matters (*sedes materiae*). Jurists of the previous era used to treat some matters in certain laws in a comprehensive manner and with a solemn apparatus; therefore, it was worth having an index, that alleviated the fatigue of the search. Such an index, although too short, was inserted in

---

[778] See note 205.

[779] Johannes Antonides van der Linden (1651), *De scriptis medicis libri duo.* Amstelredami.

[780] Gijsbert Voet , see note 15.

[781] Paul Buys (1656), *Commentarius Pauli Busii IC. Zuollani In Universas Pandectas Domini Justiniani.* Daventriae.

[782] Melchior Adam (1620), *Vitae Jurisconsultorum Germanorum et Politicorum*. Heidelbergae.

the *Institutes*[783] by Julius [but Johannes, Jean e. n.] Crespin; another one, more comprehensive in alphabetical order is in the *Maniples*[784] by Woldenberg. It would be helpful to prepare such an index for the philosophers, so that one can easily ascertain which passages of Aristotle, the Master, and Thomas contain the questions that were treated professedly by commentators. The classical passages of theologians correspond symmetrically. These passages, in quotes, may be identified by some distinguishing characteristic, through some particular printing type or abbreviation, either in the theologians, or in the jurisconsults.

§. 85. We have seen the attempt of other authors to deal with the repertoires; we will now put forward our own opinion on the common places of the law[785] that must be prepared. Of these, we will examine the efficient cause, the mode of causing, the matter, the form, the goal, that is, the use or the effect. In general, Bartholomaeus Keckermann [c. 1572–1608] gave a very clear discussion on common places, but especially with regard to politics[786]. The efficient cause must be a society composed of many correspondents: for it is not the work of a single man, in the same way that in Italy the academies or societies of scholars act in unison; on this, see Philipp Jakob Sachs von Löwenheim [1627–1672] in the preface to the *Am-*

---

[783] See note 638.

[784] See note 452.

[785] *I. e.*, repertoires of juridical keywords arranged in alphabetical order with explanations of the concept, quotations from right and doctoral opinions; see for example, Johann Oldendorp [1488–1567] (1545), *Loci juris communes*. Lugduni.

[786] Bartholomaeus Keckermann (1609), *Apparatus practicus ....: in qua ostenditur studii practici dextrè conformandi, & locos communes colligendi, atque adeo tum politicos, tum historicos cum certo fructu legendi*. Hanoviæ [not included in AA VI, 2, sources directory]; Id. (1698), *Systema disciplinae politicae*. Hannoviae [not included in AA VI, 2, sources directory].

pelography[787] and Christoph Besold [1577–1638] in *Dissertations on Universities, Guilds, Academies*[788]; France is famous for that noble, and in more recent times silent, *College de l'esprit*; in England the London College of Physicians and that noble British Society in which every highly distinguished and most learned man of the whole kingdom participates, from which very recently there came the *Micrography*[789] by Robert Hooke [1635–1703], that is, on things that are not visible to the naked eye, but by means of the microscope; in Germany the College of Curious Physicians of the Nature[790], which corresponds in name to that Curious Frenchman whose meditations were recently translated into German[791]. By the same token, it would be highly desirable for jurisconsults in Germany, especially those who take delight in the academies, to act in unison in favour of that body of concepts which is as famous as the Universal Index of Right, namely, the Common Places of Law. One does not always realise how much can be achieved by united forces. Hence, the great advantage of the Roman Catholics in publishing excellent works: indeed, whole monasteries often work on one and the same book, which goes out

---

[787] Philipp Jakob Sachs von Löwenheim (1661), *Ampelografia sive vitis viniferae ejusque partium consideratio physico-philologico-historico-medico-chymica*. Lipsiae.

[788] Christoph Besold (1641), *Juridico-politicae dissertationes de jure rerum, (2) familiarum, (3) Collegiorum, (4) Academiarum, (5) aliarumque universitatum, (6) ac item territorio rum*. Argentorati

[789] Robert Hooke (1665), *Micrographia; Or, Some Physiological Descriptions of Minute Bodies Made by Magnifying Glasses, with Observations and Inquiries Thereupon*. London (repr. 1961, New York: Dover Publications).

[790] Could be the Academy of Sciences Leopoldina, founded in the city of Schweinfurt on 1 January 1652 under the Latin name *Academia Naturae Curiosorum.*

[791] I did not find the German translation of which L. talks in the text, nor it is mentioned in AA VI, 2, sources directory.

with the name of a single author. Thus, David von Doring [1577–1638], more with a laudable intention than with the aid of genuine facts, undertook a *Universal Library of the Law*[792], availing himself of the help of many, but he went no further than the letter A in his alphabet.

§. 86. The mode of causing consists in determining the method according to which the labor has to be distributed among them [the correspondents]. Some have decided that different arguments are to be assigned to different persons, with one collecting all the topics related to guardianship and supervision, another those related to intestate inheritance, another those related to substitutions etc. In this regard, note that once it was customary in Italy for some Doctor to excel in some certain matter, while in others his knowledge was quite elementary; similarly, one often hears of individuals who are said to know all the difficulties of the substitutions, yet would struggle and hesitate on other topics. And even today it would be helpful to distribute material to the professors not according to the books of Right, but according to the subject-matters dealt with, by giving to one the matter of successions, to another the question of the right inter vivos; and to another the issues concerning criminal, feudal, ecclesiastical and semi-public matters; to yet another, trials; and finally, to some other professor, the institutes or the synopsis of all of these. Indeed, I do not criticize these suggestions insofar as the method of distribution of the professions is concerned: even the physicians are so subdivided. But, I believe that [this method] is not proper for the collection of common places, because in this way all of the books would have to be read by each collector. It is more appropriate, there-

---

[792] David von Döring (1631), *Bibliotheca jure consultorum theorico-practica*. Francofurti ad Moenum.

fore, to distribute not so much the subject-matters among them, but the books. Thus according to this method, some are assigned the ancient authors Bartolo[793], Giasone[794], Alessandro[795]; others the most recent. Some are called upon to read the theoreticians, others the practitioners; some the Germans, others the Italians; some the counsels, others the decisions of the ministries; some the treaties, others the commentaries. To this should be added what was suggested by Janus Caecilius Frey in *The Road to the Sciences and to the Arts*[796].

§. 87. Matter or object are the authors and the passages that are selected from them. First of all, one should consult the authors who are used to quote others and fill the pages with quotes; from the latter it is helpful to transcribe allegations or at least make reference to them. Thence, one should turn to the authors who write miscellaneous books, for example *The Observations*[797] by Jacques Cujas [1522–1590], by Claude Saumasie [1588–1653] *On Roman and Attic Law*[798], *The Famous Questions*[799] by François Hotman [1524–1590], *The Corrections* [800] by Antonius Augustinus [1516–1586] etc. However, the good that is hidden in them is not easy to find. One should thus turn one's foot to the writers of treatises. And of these, when dealing with the matter they treat, nothing but the name of

---

[793] Bartolo, see note 641.
[794] See note 644.
[795] Probably Alessandro d'Alessandro [1461–1523], Italian jurist.
[796] See note 52.
[797] Jacques Cujas (1598), *Observationes*. Coloniae Agrippinae.
[798] Claude Saumaise (1645), *Miscellae defensiones: de variis observationibus & emendationibus ad ius atticum et romanum pertinentibus*. Lugduni Batavorum.
[799] François Hotman (1610), *Quaestionum illustrium liber*. Hanoviae.
[800] Antonius Augustinus (1591), *Emendationum, & Opinionum Lib. IIII*. Lugduni.

the author who wrote about this matter should be recorded under the title of the subject-matter; as for the rest, nothing that pertain to that specific matter should be selected, but rather the unconnected arguments which are interwoven. Similarly, from the Commentators nothing should be selected if at any place they annotate something in the text that does not concern it. On the remaining issues, what is important is to note, with regard to the numbered laws (on the latter, see *supra* §. 61), who in particular has written about that text. For instance, if a writer has composed a commentary on the whole book, this circumstance should likewise be mentioned on the title page of the entire book.

§. 88. The form [proper] is that of making excerpts so that firstly one reads the entire index of the author (or the table of the contents), which if it is well composed, should be excerpted and then the whole book can be read much more speedily. There is no need to annotate the books and the chapters of the author, this is too much, but the pages, provided you note down which edition you utilize. And later, another [correspondent] can easily take this into account in his edition. The utmost care should be taken in titles so that they are assigned accurately, but it will be quite possible if this is done according to the Elements, where the terms of the law are described in subdivisions by subject. To this should be added Bernard de Lavinheta [d. c. 1530], a monk of the order of the minors, in the *Commentary to Lull's Ars Magna*[801], where not inappropriately he reviews the legal terms: to avoid the need for titles to be assigned once again, it is very useful to have a separate empty dictionary [*charta pura*,

[801] Bernard de Lavinheta (1517), *Lulli Ars magna generalis et ultima.* Lugduni; Id. (1523) *Explanatio compendiosaque applicatio artis Raymundi Lulli.* Lugduni [not included in AA VI, 2, sources directory].

i.e., containing the sole letters of the alphabet, e. n.], so that annotations can be added in writing at the side of any word. Furthermore, every time that an author treats the whole matter, all that is necessary is to annote the topic under the word, for example, on Ownership. If some other subtitle is required, an annotation can be added under this, in order to draw attention to the fact: for example, on the ways of acquiring Ownership, that is, on the Causes, or on certain questions in another subtitle, for example, if the Donation is not a way of acquiring the ownership. When arranging these questions, very often the annotation must be set in relation to two topics, for example, the question of the ways of acquiring Ownership must be annotated under the cause of Ownership and under the effect of the Donation. Therefore, cross-references from one topic to another are introduced to avert the need to annotate the same topic twice. A question sign, A. or N. or D. should be added so that we know when the author affirms, denies (*negat*), or doubts. Likewise it is useful to add a sign which indicates that he does not provide a broad-based or accurate treatment of the issue in question, etc., a proposal Drechsel also suggests in *The Gold Mine*[802].

§. 89. The use, the goal and the effect of the Common Places is as follows: whenever any [author] has completed a task, the collection must be gathered together in a single [volume], but in such a way that it is made up of a number of books: this is to account for the fact that many persons will wish to use the same Pandects, which therefore should be composed of as many subdivisions [of the matters] as the potential number of users. But since the composition of the Pandects must reflect the distribution of subject-matters, it is advisable to assign,

---

[802] See note 766.

for example to one author the matter of the Institutes, to another that of the legacies, to others the codicils so that in one book you enroll the material collected from various sources on legacies, in another on codicils, etc.; thus once the authors have been consulted, it is relatively easy to collect from them the kernel, which is then to be reported in the Pandects.

§. 90. The same orderly exposition of the whole law, or Pandects, has to be carried out, as I said, according to the Common Places, in the same order in which [are composed] the Elements, the Institutes, the Breviary. It is important to introduce, as far as possible, the propositions having general application, and only the doubtful controversies and cases. Additionally, mention should be made of the demonstrative reasons from Elements, and if the objection is challenging, then it has to be solved, if easy it should be omitted. If the case has been decided in the Laws, no other author should be invoked, unless this constitutes another excellent reason for the decision, or dissolves the accusations. On the remaining issues, in whatever question or case is to be examined, only the author who first adduced and defined it should be taken into consideration, and only those who in [cases] adduced some new reasons or solved tricky points should be added. And the evidence [for the demonstrations] is to be added in the margin. Furthermore, it will be helpful to print the Elements, the Breviary and the Pandects in a single book, but with different typefaces. I am sure that such a book of Pandects will not fill more than two volumes *in folio*, because no other discipline and faculty has more books than concepts and has amassed repetitions so endlessly as can be observed in jurisprudence. Perfect Pandects will confer prestige on jurisprudence and such an outcome will now force into silence those loquacious imitators and sewers (*consarcinatores*) of treaties, because the index of these Pandects will have the value of all of the treaties. Only those who have observed some new doubtful case will dare to write something in the law. In fact, theoretical questions, which concern exegetical and historical jurisprudence, do not properly consider the right, and therefore are not to be inserted in the Pandects. On the other hand, with the Pandects having been completed, if some author composes a treatise on some aspect of the right, he will not repeat what is contained in the Pandects, but will publish only supplements and new observations. Those who disregard what diligence and order can achieve will mock our observations on the Common Places and the Pandects that I am planning to prepare. However, I am sure that 30 men can accomplish this work, although vast, in three years. But as Janus Cecilius Frey [c. 1580–1631] rightly observed with regard to another topic, it should begin in order of time from the oldest authors, so that the first author can always be taken into consideration and preserved in memory. If, in truth, the work does not begin as soon as possible, I fear that for the new and daily increasing harvest [of authors], the jurisprudence will be burdened and choked by an unnecessary amount of books, thus ultimately defeating all human diligence.

§. 91. We have outlined the idea of the perfect jurisprudence and we carried out the topic in its vastness, a goal which was very difficult to achieve even in the desires. It follows that we will trace the way to advance toward to its penetralia. Earlier we stated what would be necessary for a doctor, here we describe the task from the perspective of a student. Earlier was explained the knowledge required by a very skilful jurist who is destined to undertake important duties in a ministry; here we will describe the training that is called for and the rudiments of a good lawyer. As in the general didactic part, firstly we will address the subjects, causes, objects or species involved in the formation of a habit, as previously described up to §.

40, in the remaining 4 paragraphs up to the end we meditated more briefly on the method of learning; therefore, what remains to be explained more fully, toward the end, is the method of learning and teaching, according to the intention of each one, either tending toward perfection or contenting himself with going no further than the second or third level. Just as a man can frequently be a preceptor of himself, equally often he will not seek to proceed without a preceptor, considering the latter as a mentor, and thus even he will learn even the difficult notions more pleasantly and more easily. A curriculum built up in this manner will consist of three major strands, one being elementary, another other exegetic, and the third polemic.

§. 92. Here, it must be kept in mind that when we share a certain period, 1) the period will be defined not exactly but approximately, 2) this period applies to the mediocre intellects, I do not prevent, indeed, that neither slow-minded students may hesitate, nor that those with rapid learning abilities may learn earlier; 3) nobody should be too assiduous and too relaxed. It will be enough and more than enough if a daily maximum of six hours is dedicated to right. Of these, two hours should be spent with the preceptor, if there is one; two hours to repetition; the remaining two should be devoted to a lesson which focuses on a particular historical topic.

The historical lesson, which we will describe in greater detail, should ensure a thorough knowledge of the whole of history; this should be followed by knowledge of the history of our times, the latter being particularly important primarily for the institutional course; then, further, the contemporary history of religion, §. 34, 41, and dogmas, §. 3, of the empire, the state of nations in the world in our day §. 39. Roman history will be studied more carefully when the moment arrives for study of the compendium of the *Libri Authentici*[803] or at the time of the exegetical course, § 30, 31, 32, 33. Hence, when a breviary of the controversies – that is, a polemic course – has been obtained, attention will turn to study of the internal history of right or the laws of the various nations, §. 28, the ecclesiastical history of the government §. 37, German history and the Middle Ages, §. 39. Thereby, each will correspond accurately to each (*singula singulis*).

§. 93. We will now take a closer look at the curriculum for the study of right. The elementary course contains the history of law briefly, the most common terms, the most elementary precepts. As pointed out above in §. 68, we should make sure that children destined to jurisprudence learn the rudiments of Latin from the juridical books, for example from Justinian's Institutes, the title on the meaning of the words, and on the rule of law. But, since this procedure is usually not adopted, let us say a few words about the ordinary activities. We said in the general part, §. 42, that from the 12th to the 18th year in the primary course, practice and expertise in that profession must be acquired by those who are destined to it. However, in order to ensure that the other previously mentioned studies are not neglected, I propose, as I said in § 92, that no more than four hours daily should be dedicated to the study of law. Hence, not all of these three parts of the elementary course need be joined together: rather, they should be divided in the following manner. First of all, the history of law should be learned summarily from the foundation of Rome to the present day, through the example of the title *On the Origin of the Right*. This can be summarized in three pages and thus can be carefully learned in two weeks. In the meantime, in the absence of other suitable texts, students can read the *History* by

---

[803] See note 83 and *infra* §. 93.

Jacques Godefroy [1587–1652][804] and that by Whilelm Forster[805]. However, a recent history of law is lacking in the aforesaid texts. A student must thus be aware of the time, the authors and differences of the *Libri Authentici*. I define *Libri Authenthici*, as at least in general I would recommend, not only as the ancient books, but also as the recent treatments, such as the rescripts of the Diet, the Saxon body of laws, and the statutes or the reforms of each republic.

§. 94. The most commonly used terms follow the history of development of the subject: and what is amazing is that, as in any discipline, it is helpful to apply knowledge of the terms that mathematicians – not without reason – state beforehand. How these should be arranged; and which partitions should be adopted, was stated in §. 7 and 22. On the other hand, failing an adequate booklet, which we believe needs to be prepared, we may use the Hermann Vulteius' [1555–1634] *Compendium of Jurisprudence*[806], published in Belgium in book-face 12; but here too one notes the lack of the terms of German law in the Middle Ages and the more recent developments. In this circumstance, there is a need for a preceptor: the latter may in certain cases attempt to convey a better

---

[804] Jacques Godefroy, *Historia seu progressus juris civilis romani*, in Id. (1733), *Opera Juridica Minora.* Lugduni Batavorum [not included in AA VI, 2, sources directory].

[805] It seems a quote error: Valentin Wilhelm Forster did not write a *History* such as his father Valentin: see note 204; he only edited a posthumous edition of his father's *History*, Valentin Wilhelm Forster, Karl Forster (eds.) (1610), *Valentini Forsteri,... de Historia juris romani libri tres, nunc quartum hac elegantiori forma recusi et ex authoris jam pie defuncti autographo correctiores editi [a Valentino Guilielmo Forstero et Carolo Forstero]* Helmaestadii: typis J. Lucii [not included in AA VI, 2, sources directory].

[806] Hermann Vulteius (1658), *Jurisprudentia Romana contracta.* Amstelodami.

understanding of a definition by having recourse to well-known and ridiculous from real or imaginary events, if the occasion arises, e. g., as in the example of a testament *inter liberos*[807], which makes the assumption of King Philip arranging a controversy between his son Demetrius and Perseus, and so on. As far as the marks are concerned, the more they are sensitive and considerable, the more they remain strongly impressed in one's memory in §. 14 and 23 General Part. The preceptor will also have taken care to make an appropriate distribution of the terms among the students so that the one can recite the history of this term, the other of a different term, §. 13. General Part; moreover, since discernment is enhanced by interrogating (see the *preface*, where the example of Socrates, from which Jonston in the *Idea of Hygiene* recommends the *Collegia interrogatoria*), it is advisable to instruct students to apply the cases to the words [of the law] and vice versa. Additionally, care should be taken to ensure that a single case is given for many terms so that the connection strongly facilitates the memory. A period of two and half months could be devoted to all these activities.

§. 95. The terms should be followed by the Elementary Precepts, omitting those which are made evident by the terms themselves and also are obvious to any peasant; with such a procedure, only few of the abstruse terms will remain, mainly involving words that are used almost exclusively in solemn legal formalities. It is necessary to omit above all the ancient and repealed laws (as stated *supra*, §. 23). The reason for this omission is as follows. Many will assume, according to the common use, that one should start from the Institutes of Justinian, subse-

---

[807] Berger, see note 19, *ad vocem Testamenti parentum inter liberos*, "A testament by which a father *(pater familias*), disposed of his property in favour of his children alone".

quently continuing with the *Digest* and *Code*. I have never liked such a method. It is a method which has the following consequences: 1) we will have unnecessary duplication; 2) these single books of the old law have their own order, hence the confusion among the students; 3) that order is often very inappropriate; 4) those books contain many rules no longer in force, and, on the other hand, nobody who intends to provide the teaching of the Latin language begins from obsolete fragments of Ennius and Pacuvius; although they were more ancient than the age of Cicero and their style comes in handy for those who, through discernment, can separate the use from the non-use. In effect, some illustrious masters of teaching believe that in instilling the rules of Latin tone one should begin from the most recent works, of which both the phrases and the topics more suitable to our age [are to be used]. In vain, objections are raised, stating that the old laws are the origin of today's laws, which are derived from the previous; for even the origin of pure Latin style of Cicero is obsolete. In learning, on the contrary, it is not always the nature of things, but rather their utility that is to be observed. Once discernment has been strengthened, then students will easily learn the origin; 5) those books are more difficult because of the excessive references to antiquity and because of the state of the republic which moves away from ours; hence 6) this may lead to confusion of exegetic and didactic jurisprudence, and 7) the beginner not only faces the difficulty of the arguments but he is also burdened by the obscurity of the words, 8) among young students, false views on the republic and the current regime of the Roman Empire have crept in, leading to the belief that teaching should focus on subjects of the same kind, namely monarchical; the reading of ancient right and ignorance of present-day right has led many lawyers into this error, which not wrongly has been deplored by the in other respects very bad author Hippolytus a Lapide[808]. On the other hand, I have found no suitable book to be recommended, which in the meantime could be read in the absence of the Elements of Right that has yet to be composed, nor a book which has treated present-day right methodically and concisely: I do not know if this implies great shame on my behalf or dishonour of jurisprudence. Furthermore, in order to hold in the mind the present-day Elementary Precepts more effectively, one should ensure that the preceptor's explanations provide a reason for any maxim of law, even doubtful, though sometimes some playful similarity is invented, stating for example that in the testament seven witnesses are required, because seven are the syllables of these words: *testes in testamento*. Jews use these devices in teaching Hebrew. Subsequently, both in the definitions as also in the precepts, there should be an indication in the margin, referring to the classical places of the law, which should be clarified during the teaching so that, little by little, students become accustomed to the legal style and acquire local memory of them, quickness of expounding and a basic knowledge. Once the terms are known, three months should be employed for the elementary precepts. In this way, the elementary course could be completed in mid-year.

§. 96. There follows the course of exegesis. But not even now should the beginner be led to an orderly and comprehensive examination of the books of right themselves, before he has been imbued with the breviary of the controversies, or has completed the polemical course. For otherwise he will study without any utility, not understanding which thing is connected with another. But if he

---

[808] See note 426.

has acquired a thorough knowledge of the controversies, not only will he see the goal, but also during the course of the study his personal initiative will enable him to observe new things not discovered by others, which concern the decision of the one or of the other controversy. However, as regards the main chapters of the subjects, so that it is as if he had read the *Libri Authentici*, it is possible to propose, 1) the series of the titles, 2) the institutes of the entire law or a compendium of *the Libri Authentici*, 3) the antinomies. The series of the titles can be learnt successfully through tables, by strongly imagining the method of Triboniano; and, as far as possible, by preparing the titles of a single book according to only one common way. To this should be added *supra* §. 52. In any event, we have without doubt summarized the books of the *Code* in 12 lines and in a single line we have included the titles of any book whatsoever, so that whoever holds them in the mind can easily judge through the track which book belongs to any title, even though in the Code there are many titles of a single book. It is very satisfying to note the series of the titles by Jacques Godefroy, and this can be accomplished within a month, provided that an exercise on how to expound a subject is added afterwards.

§. 97. We have expounded in §. 54 the Institutes of the whole of right, namely how a compendium of the *Libri Authentici* should be composed[809]. This compendium is already to be read by an expert of the Law, so that he learn not only what is the right, but also what it was in the past; from these subjects the student will draw up the former from the Elements, the latter from the Institutes. These Institutes should also include the repealed rules, just as the same Justinian himself did not forget them in his *Institutes*. There should also be annotations in the

---

[809] See note 83 and *retro* §. 93.

margin concerning the passages of the laws which are to be explained, not only the Classical passages, such as in the Elements §. 95, at the end, but entirely all the passages concerning the matter in question, in such a way, however, that the Classical passages can be distinguished from the others with a mark or particular book-face. In place of the Institutes of internal Law it is possible to use, for want of something better, *The Roman Jurisprudence* by Vulteius, not the short one, published in Belgium in in book-face 12, see §. 95, but the broader book-face 8, published in Marburg, which fulfills the same purpose, not without advantage. Because, in truth, most of the arguments have been anticipated in the Elements, the Institutes can be completed in three months; the progression will not be conducted in the college, but at home. The preceptor should propose only some of the passages to one or the other student, selecting from the course those which are to be explained in college itself, for the purpose of exercising the attentiveness. The way in which the antinomies are to be collected in a booklet that we called the *Antinomicus Minor* has been explained in §. 51. But the matter must be treated as follows. Firstly, the passages of the law should be expounded, testing the scholar of law to ascertain if he can penetrate on his own initiative to where there is a conflict of laws, and how way they are to be reconciled. Then, the student should consult other authors who solved the antinomy; not because it is necessary to learn by heart the proposed solutions, but in order that he learns through examples the art of solving and becomes accustomed to restoring harmony even in the laws not reconciled by others. However, he should diligently learn by heart those passages which illustrious men have considered irreconcilable. Without difficulty, therefore, the *Antinomicus* can be carried out in a month. But this kind of *Antinomicus* that I am looking for has not been written and can be summarized in four sheets. Therefore, the whole exegetic course will be completed in one semester. Meanwhile, during the same course, the expert of the law can gradually get used to the College of Controversies (*Collegia Disputatoria*), and also attend the courts and the trials, and examine public deeds, thereby becoming familiar with things which form an excellent preparation for genuine practice and real cases.

§. 98. There now follows the polemic course, which requires another year of juridical studies. Now, therefore, students of right can approach the breviary of controversies, not so much as almost in the position of a judge, but at this point only as an attorney. The issue of how a breviary has to be compiled and held distinct from other works was addressed in §. 78 (but, as a similar one has not yet been completed, in the meantime we will make use of Treutler, which we do not like). In contrast, we now propose to show publicly how a particular thing should be used: namely, a mix of College of Controversies and Practical to be experienced through the breviary in this College. Naturally, the disciples should number at least 12, and two the hours of the day should be dedicated to this topic. 12 questions should be dealt with in two hours. 6 disciples can be *respondentes,* 6 *opponentes* or 6 plaintiffs and 6 defendants. Students can defend or contrast at least two questions. The mode of treating should not be completely syllogistic, but should be dealt with according to the practical German mode, as in the trial. Therefore, they should learn *vom Mund aus in die Feder verfahren*, [in German in the text, e. n.], that is, to relate verbally, and respond or reply according to circumstances. The plaintiff should form the case *in seinem Satz* [in German in the text, e. n.] and put forward arguments pro; the defendant should respond and bring arguments con, in very concise terms without a Gregation of useless words: this reciprocal movement should take place twice. The president, such as a judge, passes the sentence, and inserts the grounds of the decision. In this way this compendium will be prepared, because many arguments will be collected in a single book; it should not be proposed in syllogistic mode nor should time be wasted with invitations, or minor premises or pleads of grace (*actiones gratiarum*). And because in the the court, in decisions or public orations, arguments are not proposed with syllogisms, students of right will learn to perceive the force of the arguments and disclose the hidden error, even though it is not syllogistic. Thus this Practical College of Controversies is not considered either for learning logic or the Latin language. And this will be the advantage: moreover, young scholars will become accustomed to this Practical College of Controversies excellently, because when engaging in extemporary replications and replies, expounding his speech in the manner he considers most appropriate, without interruption by others, as is the custom in public orations of the great men, he is required to remember the many arguments and the answers given by other scholars; and this is something that he cannot do without considerable practice. In this context, it should be borne in mind that the common custom of disputing is not frequent in the usual life of the Universities, both because of the Latin, and because of innumerable interruptions. But, in public meetings, deliberations, consultations of senators, ambassadors and lawyers it is not permitted to interrupt the speech of others. For this reason students in the universities gradually have to be prepared to the experience of interaction with others. Subsequently, the plaintiff will communicate the formed case to the defendant and the judge two days before. It is useful, on the other hand, to learn the utmost conciseness, so that 6 questions can be dealt with in one hour. But here one can use a singular expedient; namely several questions related to the same matter can be conveniently combined into a single case, just as in the trials many controversies concur simultaneously. In such a manner [the work] will very easily be completed and the Breviary can be finished in one year, although it contains 3,600 questions. To find the arguments pro and con the disputants will explain the places of the laws quoted in the Breviary, so that each can foresee the reasons of the other.

§. 99. Accordingly, the whole study of the law will be completed in the space of two years, and more [results] perhaps will be achieved than in the common five year period, which the anonymous author of the *Menippus*[810] (or, Johann Valentin Andreae [1586–1654] in the *Magia Christiana*[811]) crammed into such a small space of time that if one also subtracts unnecessary occupations, one may even feel regret for the passing of this ancient time period. Once this period of two years has expired, the student of law ceases to be a disciple and will already arrogate to himself the judgment of the controversies and

tandem custode remoto,
in aprici gramine campi[812]

will hover over the vast spaces of jurisprudence, and slowly read the *Libri Legum Authenticarum*[813], the first time glancing at the titles and especially the indispensable laws, then add the remaining material according to the defined order in that praised book *supra* §. 47; the student will then extract all that is suitable for the decision on the

---

[810] Johann Valentin Andreae (1617) *Menippus sive dialogorum satyricorum centuria*. Cosmopoli.
[811] Not found by Johann Valentin Andreae *Magia Christiana*, but (1618), *Mytologia Christiana*. Argentorati, quoted by L. in by the same (1666) *De casibus perplexis in jure*, in AA VI, 1, [not included in AA VI, 2, sources directory]
[812] Horace [65 BC–27 BC], *Ars poetica*. I, 160, "free of tutor at last, in the sunlit Campus" (e. trans.).
[813] See *retro* §. 93.

various controversies, and invent new rules, new universals neglected by others; use commentaries, penetrate into the purposes of the laws and gradually obtain the competence of a Law-maker, or even the role. Thus, he will advance in the vast sea of the controversies, observe the customs of the ministries, and the opinions handed over by the ancestors, the disputes and the mutual dissensions and notice that changes occur in the right because of the people and the difference of the states: he will also learn to deduce valid demonstrations with continuous concatenation from the immutable principles of natural law and the public interest, and to cut with the sword of invincible science both the inane witticisms of the practitioners of law, and the unimportant allegations, and the twisted knots arising from the arrogant authority of doctors and the application of *Brocardica* off the point. I will call such a scholar the true philosopher of the law, the priest of justice and of the law of nations, and since he will judge according to it, I will call him a jurisconsult of the public and divine law, one to whom the republic can be entrusted, and whom neither frivolous reasons of state, nor the inane fear of certain cavils deters from promoting the public health. This will bring to an end the mockeries of the followers of Machiavelli (they call themselves politicians, and if it pleases God, even Statesmen), who call jurisconsults inexperienced in the law, experts in precautions, inane pettifoggers; and the Princes will no longer undergo the counsels, or better to say, the yoke of some gluttons of the imperial households, when an eminent man, safe in prestige and eloquence, will surround his counsels with fairness no less than with utility (inseparable friends for those who can estimate them in the proper way).

§. 100. With this wish, we would have finished, were it not that some topics scattered in the previous paragraphs should preferably be gathered together in a single statement, firstly the Computation of time; then the Catalogue of the desired things in imitation of Francis Bacon in *Advancement of Learning*[814].

This is the computation of the times:

Years, Months, Weeks A. M. W.

For the History of Law
(inexperienced in Law) . . 2
For Juridical Terms . 2 2
For the Elementary Precepts . 3 .

Sum of the Elementary Course . 6 .

For the Series of the Titles . 1 .
For the General Institutes . 4 .
For the *Antinomicus Minor* . 1 .

Sum of the Elementary Course and
simultaneously Exegetical 1 . .

For the Polemical Course or Exegetical Breviary 1 . .

Sum of the Study of the Law 2 . .

Free Time to be devoted to free lessons, travelling abroad, procedure and businesses of the real life.

---

[814] See note 69.

BE THIS THE CATALOGUE OF THE DESIRED THINGS:

1. *Partitions of Right §. 7*
2. Sciagraphia *in the Art of Collecting Right §.20*
3. *The new Body of Right §.21*
4. *Elements of Right §.21*
5. *Reformation of Brocardica §.24*
6. *Compendium of Menochi and Mascardi on proofs and presumptions §.25*
7. *Legal Theater §.28*
8. *History of the Changes in Law §.28*
9. *Irenical History §.40*
10. *Philology of the Law §.41*
11. *Philosophy of the Law §.42*
12. *Juridical Concordances §.43*
13. *Tropes, Forms, Adages of the Law §.45.46*
14. *Arithmetic of the Law §.49*
15. *Antinomicus Minor §.51*
16. *General Institutes of the Law §.53*
17. *Institutes of Imperial Right §.54*
18. *Institutes of Saxon Right §.54*
19. *Principal Matter of the Titles §.55*
20. *Numbered Laws §.61*
21. *German Translation of the Laws §.64*
22. *Art of Hermeneutics §.65*
23. *Elements of Natural Law expounded in a demonstrative manner §.71 ff.*
24. *Nomothetic Science §.76 [77]*
25. *Breviary of the juridical controversies §.78*
26. *Reformed treaty of the Treaties §.83*
27. *Library of the Law §.84*
28. *Classical Places: determining the appropriate place for each Subject §.84*
29. *Lives of the Jurisconsults §.84*
30. *Repertory of Right §.85*
31. *Pandects of the New Right §.90*

No more comes to my mind, and I have to preserve something for myself; I have, however, revealed more than I established, almost no paragraph comes forth without a new discovery and observation. I did not seek glory, but the public interest, otherwise I would have written my name[815]. If I see I have achieved some results, I will attempt to reduce the proposed catalogue of the desire achievements here: if not, I will free myself from the stigma of envy; ignorance will be enough punishment for the detractors. There will perhaps come another time more worthy of ours, in which, hatred having been eradicated, the truth will triumph. Wish this together with me, reader, goodbye!

---

[815] The first edition of the *NM* was published in Frankfurt in 1667, with only the initials of the Author: *Autore G.*[*ottfredo*] *G.*[*uilielmo*] *L.*[*eibnuzio*] *L.*[*ipsiensi*]; it was not total anonymity.

INDEX

Abelard, Peter, 59
Accursius, the Glossator in Italian, Accursio, Accorso or also Accorso di Bagnolo, 106, 116, 153
Aconcio, Jacopo, 17, 100
Adam of Bremen, 89
Adam, Melchior, 188
Aesop, 6
Albert of Stade, 89
Alciato, Andrea, 11, 154
Alegambe, Phillip, S.J., 88
Alemanni, Niccolò, 77
Alsted, Joh. Heinrich, 14, 33
Althusius, Johann, 49
Ammianus, Marcellinus, 76
Andreae, Johann Valentin, 11, 206
Andronicus of Rhodes, 12
Antognazza, Maria Rosa, 11, 14
Apel, Johann, 41, 53, 54
Aquinas, Thomas, 59
Aristotle, 1, 12, 23, 33, 44, 65, 68, 114, 116, 164, 165, 166, 168, 170, 188
Arngrim (Arngrin), Jonas, 90
Arum, Dominik van, 97, 177
Assmann, Erwin, 89
Augustine of Hippo, St., 85
Augustinus, Antonio, 192
Ausonius, 77

Bachmann, Conrad, 108
Bachoff von Echt, Reinhard, the Younger, 147, 177
Bacon, Francis, 21, 22, 37, 58, 208
Bacon, Roger, 109
Baldo degli Ubaldi, 147
Barbosa, Augustinus, 64
Barclay, William, 85
Barclay, John, son of William, 151
Barillari, Michele, 52
Baronio, Cesare, 80, 82
Barrow, Isaac, 175
Barth, Caspar von, 74, 108, 148
Bartholinus, Bartolus, 74
Bartolo da Sassoferrato, 147, 191
Baudouin, François, 146
Becanus Goropius, Johann, 104
Becanus Martin, S.J., 174
Bede, the Venerable, 82
Bellarmino, Roberto S.J., 83, 85, 86
Bembo, Pietro, 92
Bennett, Jonathan, 16
Berger, Adolf, 34, 38, 39, 40, 44, 59, 66, 70, 71, 74, 76, 79, 103, 110, 111, 112, 121, 124, 133, 134, 135, 136, 137, 140, 141, 144, 148, 150, 152, 164, 168, 169, 170, 199
Berman, Harold J., 41, 53, 54
Bernegger, Matthias, 72
Bertachini, Giovanni, 186
Barthélemy de Gramond, Gabriel, 95
Besold, Christoph, 93, 104, 189
Bèze, Théodore de, 100
Beust, Joachim von, 161
Binns, James W., 109
Birks, Peter, 42, 43, 57, 60
Bisterfeld, Johann H., 15
Bizarri, Pietro, 95
Blume, Fred H., 78, 133, 141
Boddenius, Gerhard, 153
Bodenstein, Liborius von, pseud. of Wawrzyniec Goślicki, 112, 113
Böckler, Johann Heinrich, 172, 173
Bolduan, Paul, 186

Bono, Giovan Battista Agostino, 51
Borkowski, Andrew, 42
Brandes, Johann Marti, 107
Brawen, Justus, 153
Brederode, Pietr Cornelis van, 185
Brett, Annabel S., 59
Brunnemann, Johann, 148
Brunner, Georg Adam, 114
Bucer (Butzer), Martin, 98
Buchanan, George, 90
Bucksulber (Bucksylber, Buxelberg) George, 109
Budé, Guillaume, 74, 106, 113, 147
Bugnyon, Philibert, 112
Bulferetti, Luigi, 51
Burchard of Ursberg (Abbas Urspergensis), 89
Burns, Tony, 166
Burrill, Alexander Mansfield, 176
Butler, Harold. E., 158, 159
Buys, Paul, 115, 187
Bzowski, Abraham, 80

Cairns, John W., 153
Calixtus, Georg, 100
Calov (Calovius), Abraham, 18
Cambden, William, 90
Campbell, Gordon, 42
Cantiuncula, Claudius, 115
Cappellini, Paolo, 68
Carafa, Carlo, 95
Carey Miller, David, 40, 41, 60, 63, 133
Carpzov, Benedict, 177, 181
Carranza, Bartholomaesus, 84
Carve, Thomas, 91
Casali, Giovan Battista, 81
Casaubon, Isaac, 75, 82
Cassander, Georg, 99
Castro, Alfonso de, 85
Castro, Paulus di, 179
Cedrenus, Georgius, 78
Celsus, Aulus Cornelius, 161
Chacoìn, Alfonso, 87
Chalcocondyles, Laonikos, 79
Chambers, Ephraim, 2
Châteillon, Sébastien, 161
Chemnitz, Bogeslaus Philipp von s. Lapide, Hyppolytus a, 96, 98
Cherubini, Laerzio, 69
Chiaramonti, Scipione, 20
Chopius, Franz Julius, 48
Chytraeus, David, 94
Cicero, 4, 31, 38, 74, 105, 154, 155, 156, 160, 164, 165, 170, 171, 198
Claudian (Claudius Claudianus), 77
Clucas, Stephen, 14
Cochlaeus, Johann (pseud. of Johann Dobneck), 94
Codronchi, Giovan Battista, 113
Coler, Christoph, 179
Comenius, John Amos, 28, 101
Conring, Hermann, 93, 98, 172
Cooke, Robert, 83
Coras, Jean de, 48
Coriolano, Franciscus Longo a, 84
Corse, Taylor, 20
Corsetti, Antonio, 183
Corvinus Belderen, Arnold van, 119, 120
Coudert, Allison, 11, 20
Couturat, Louis, 13
Crawford, Matthew R., 35
Creid, Kenneth G., 164
Crespin, Jean, 147, 188
Cromer, Martin, 91
Crusius, Martin, 92
Ctesias, 69
Cucchi, Marco Antonio, 120
Cujas Jacques, 79, 93, 115, 116, 145, 146, 147, 148, 191, 192
Cureus, Joachim, 92
Curtius, Sebastianus, 101
Cuspinian, Johann, 92
Cyprian, bishop of Carthage, 76

Daillé, Jean, 82
D'Alessandro, Alessandro, 191
Daneau, Lambert, 88
Dario, Mario di, 17

Decio, Filippo, 147
Delrio, Martin Antonio, 48, 107, 161
Dempster, Thomas, 73
Descartes, René, 16
Dewar, Michael, 77
Dewey, John, 51
Diaz de Luco, Juan Bernardo, 64
Dieterich, Johann Conrad, 87
Dietherr von Anwanden, Christoph Ludwig, 104
Dio Cassius, 72
Diodorus Siculus, 69
Dionysius of Halicarnassus, 72
Dobneck, Johann, s. Cochlaeus, Johann, 94
Dominis, Marco Antonio de, 85
Doneau, Hugues, 48, 145
Döring, David von, 190
D'Ors, Álvaro, 34
Dorsche, Johann Georg, 36
Draud, Georg, 186, 187
Drechsel, Jerimias, 184, 194
Dreier, Christian, 100
Douaren, François, 116, 147
Dumoulin, Charles, 178, 179
Dubravius, Jan, 91
Duff, John Whight, 72
Durie, John, 101
Dutens, Louis, 51

Eichel von Rautenkron, Johann, 77
Elmacinus, Georgius (or Girgis Al-Makin also known as Ibn al-'Amid), 79
Emili, Paolo, 91
Emmius, Ubbo, 91
Enantiophanes, 111
Epicurus, 165, 166, 168
Erasmus of Rotterdam, 94, 98
Errico, Scipione, 95
Euclid, 19, 34, 36, 46, 109, 175
Eusebius of Caesarea, 76
Evangelical Lutheran Church, 99
Everaerts, Nicolaas, 114
Exea, Andrés de, 182, 183

Fabricius, Georg, 91
Fabrot, Charles Annibal, 79
Fairclough, Henry Rushton, 4
Farinacci, Prospero, 180
Farrell, Alan P., S.J., 4
Favre, Antoine, 178, 179, 182
Fazello, Tommaso, 92
Felden, Johann von, 36, 46, 48, 66, 114, 166, 168, 170
Ferrari, Ottavio, 73
Ferrari, G.R.F. (John), 31, 166
Finckelthaus, Sigismund, 179
Flacius Illyricus, Matthias, 80, 84
Florus, Lucius Annaeus, 71
Fomann, Ortholph, 177
Forbesius, Johann, 84
Forster, Carolus, 198
Forster, Valentin, 70
Forster, Valentin Wilhelm, 177, 198
Foxcroft, Edward, 11
Freher, Marquard, 92, 93
Freige, Johann Thomas, 37, 113, 114
Freinsheim, Johann, 71, 87
Fresne du Cange, Charles, 97, 105, 159
Frey, Janus Caecilius, 14, 15, 191, 195
Freymon von Randeck, Johann Wolfgang, 186

Gail, Andreas von, 179
Gaius, 38, 110, 111
Galen, 33, 161
Gallonio, Antonio, 82
Garuti, Giovanni, 77
Gaudenzi, Paganino, 77
Gellius, 38
Gennep, Jasper (Kaspar) von, 93
Gensini, Stefano, 154
Gentili, Alberico, 27, 109
Gerhard, Johann, 83, 84
Gerhard, Johann Ernest, 84
Giaccone de Angeli, Jolanda, 71
Giasone del Maino, 147, 191
Giffen, Hubert van, 117, 118
Gilmann, Adrian, 179
Glass, Salomon, 101, 102

Godefroy, Denis, 108, 119, 148, 149
Godefroy, Jacques, 70, 79, 112, 113, 118, 161, 187, 198, 202
Goold, G. P., 6
Goldast, Melchior, 87, 93
Goślicki, Wawrzyniec, s. Liborius von Bodenstein, 112
Gossmann, Bernhard, 153
Goudelin, Pierre, 120
Graeculus, 68
Graf, Arturo, 107
Graf Zamoyski, Johann, 72
Gregorius XIII, pope, 183
Gregorius Tolosanus, Petrus, 180
Gribaldi Mofa, Matteo, 51, 160
Griffith, Tom, 31, 166
Gronovius, Johann Friedrich, 74
Grotius, Hugo, 27, 29, 33, 35, 36, 48, 50, 66, 95, 100, 109, 149, 165, 167, 170, 180
Grotius, Willem, brother of Hugo, 178, 179
Gruter, Jan, 73
Guise, Chales de, Cardinal of Lorraine, 100
Gunther of Pairis, 89

Hackelmann, Leopold, 177
Haeften, Benedict van, 11
Haersolte, Arnold van, 67
Hahn, Heinrich, 146
Harmenopoulos, Costantine, 79
Hart, John, S. J., 83
Heilbron, John Lewis, 109
Helmold of Bosau, 92
Helmont, Franciscus Mercurius van, 11, 20, 48
Helwig, Christoph, 108
Hendrickson, George Lincoln, 31
Herburt de Fulstein, Johann, 70
Hering, Johann, 183
Herodian of Alexandria, 75
Hicks, Robert D., 166
Hildebrand, Henricus, 97
Himmel, Johann, 87, 88
Hippocrates, 33
Hobbes, Thomas, 1, 2, 13, 33, 36, 60, 165, 167, 170
Hooke, Robert, 189
Hoppers, Joachim, 48, 172
Horace, 4, 63, 106, 115, 116, 207
Hortleder, Friedrich, 96
Horváth, Jaìnos, 80
Hospinian, Rudolf, 87, 94
Hotman, François, 78, 93, 112, 113, 114, 116, 146, 192
Hotson, Howard, 14
Hottinger, Johann Heinrich, 81
Hubbel, Harry Mortimer, 31
Hülsemann, Johann, 36, 174
Hunnius, Helfrich Ulrich, 177
Hutchinson, Adam, 1
Hutter, Leonhard, 94
Hyamson, Moses, 68

Irenicus Irenicorum, pseud. of Daniel Zwicker?, 101
Irnerius, 152

James I of England, 86
Jansen, Nils, 164
Jerome, St., 10, 83
Johns, Christopher, 50
Jones, Rhidian, 165
Jornandes, 77
Josephus, Titus Flavius, 75
Jowett, Benjamin, 166
Justinus, Marcus Junianus, 72
Juvenal, 3, 34, 173
Justinian I, Flavius Petrus Sabbatius Iustinianus Augustus, Byzantine (East Roman) emperor, 34, 38, 39, 40, 41, 42, 44, 45, 47, 51, 60, 65, 68, 71, 76, 77, 78, 110, 111, 116, 119, 121, 133, 135, 136, 137, 146, 152, 153, 161, 163, 169, 176, 178, 187, 197, 200, 203

Kahl (Calvinus), Johann, 103, 104
Keckermann, Bartholomaeus, 188, 189
Keller, Adam, 112
Kircher, Athanasius, 14
Klock, Caspar, 179, 180

Kouropalates, i.e. George Kodinos, 78
Kyriander, Wilhelm, 90

Labitte, Jacques, 76
Lacoste, Jean Baptiste, 110, 111
Laet, Johannes de, 81
Lagus, Conrad, 53
Lampadius, Jakob, 97
Lampridius, Aelius, 75
Lancelot, Andrewes, 86
Lancelloti, Giampaolo, 120
Lansius, Thomas, 88
Lapide, Hyppolitus a, pseud. of Bogeslaus Philipp von Chemnitz, s., 98, 201
Lausberg, Heinrich, 156, 157, 158, 159
Lavinheta, Bernard de, 193
Lee, A. Dough, 60
Lehmann, Christoph, 90
Leibniz, Gottfried Wilhelm, 4, 5, 11, 12, 13, 14, 15, 16, 17, 22, 25, 26, 33, 34, 48, 49, 50, 51, 52, 63, 68, 106, 113, 122, 126, 154, 163
Lewis, Charlton Thomas, 22
Liceti, Fortunio, 73
Limnaeus, Johann, 88, 97
Linden, Johann Antonides van der, 187
Lindenbrog, Erpold, 93
Lindenbrog, Friedrich, 69
Lipsius, Justus, 2, 73, 105, 172
Liutprand of Cremona, 89
Livy, 71, 72, 95
Locamer, George David, 177, 178
Loemker, Leroy Earl, 5
Ludwell, Wilhelm, 146, 177, 178
Lugioyo, Brian, 98
Lull, Raimond, 15, 193
Lundorp, Michael Caspar, 96

MacChombaich de Colquhoun, Sir Patrick, 40
Magnus, Olaus, 90
Manuzio, Paolo, 72, 73
Marci, Johann Christoph, 149
Maróstica, Ana H., 15
Mariana, Juan de, 91
Marsilius of Padua, 86
Martial, 71, 75
Martone, Arturo, 154
Mascardi, Giovanni, 67, 209
Mathesius, Johann, 94
Matthaeus, Anton, 44, 47, 106, 115
Matthiae, Johann, 101
Mayer, Johann Friedrich, 184
McCain, Paul T., 99
Megiser, Hieronymus, 92
Meibom, Heinrich, 93
Meier, Justus, 44, 146
Meisner, Joachim, rector of Torgau, 187
Meisner, Michael, rector of Meissen, 105
Meteren, Emanuel van, 95
Meyer, Ludwig (anonymous Arminianus), 154
Meyer, Martin, s. Philemerus Irenicus Elisius, 96
Melanchthon, Philip, 94, 98
Menochio, Giacomo, 66, 67, 180
Metzger, Ernest, 40
Meursius, Johannes, 69, 105
Micalori, Biagio, 183
Migliorini, AnnaVittoria, 98
Miller, Walter, 167
Middendorp, Jakob, 88
Modestinus, 110, 11, 148
Modrevius, Andreas Fricius, 100
Molanus, s. Jan Vermeulen, 82
Mommer, Aegidius, 44
Montagu, Richard, 82
Mousourakis, George, 55
Mozambano, Severinus de, pseud. of Samuel Pufendorf, s., 98
Mundig von Rodach, Georg, 179, 180
Müsinger von Frundeck, Joachim, 179

Nadanyi, János, 92
Natta, Marcantonio, 179, 180
Nebrija, Antonio de, 106
Neff, Stephen C., 50, 170

Negusantius, Antonius, 182, 183
Neldel, Johann, 18
Nevizzano Giovanni, 186
Nogent, Guibert de, 79
Nolte, Johann Friedrich, 14
Novarini, Aloisio (Luigi), 107

Oertl, Hieronymus, 92
Oldendorp, Johann, 67, 103, 104, 188
Olinger, Paul, 105, 112
Olivecrona, Karl, 59
Orestano, Riccardo, 51
Orosius, Paulus, 76, 77
Osiander, Lucas the Elder, 81
Osório, Jerónimo, 91
Otto, Daniel, 114
Otto of Freisig, 89
Ovid, 5, 6

Pace, Giulio, 117, 121, 147
Palmer, Lucia M., 17
Panciroli, Guido, 77, 78
Panvinio, Onofrio, 87
Pappus, Johann, 80
Pareus, pseud. of David Wängler, 100
Parks, Gerald, 11
Passeri, Niccolò, 117
Paul (Paulus Iulius), 38, 103, 110, 148
Pausanias, 69
Peregrino, Marco Antonio, 182, 183
Pérez, Antonio, 146
Persona, Gubelinus, 89
Persius, 3
Petau, Denis, S.J., 83
Pflug, Julius von, 98, 99
Phedericis, Stephanus de, 154
Philemerus Irenicus Elisius, pseud. of Martin Meyer, s., 96
Philo of Alexandria, 75
Piro, Francesco, 154
Pisani, Ottavio, 48, 173
Pithou, Pierre, 68
Platina (Bartolomeo Sacchi), 87
Plato, 31, 165, 166, 167, 171
Plessis, Paul J. du, 42, 54, 124, 153
Pliny the Younger, 75
Plutarch, 4, 72
Polanus, Petrus Suavis, pseud. of Paolo Sarpi, s., 94
Pomponius, Sextus, 112, 124, 127, 128
Pontanus (Jakob Spanmüller, S.J.), 78
Pontanus, Johann Isacius, 90, 104, 105
Pozzo, Paride del, 184
Priscianus Caesariensis, 106
Procopius of Caesarea, 77
Puccini, Clemente, 113
Pufendorf, Samuel, 36, 48, 98

Quintilian, 31, 32, 33, 106, 154, 156, 157, 158, 159
Quodvultdeus, St., 85

Rackham, Harris, 31
Rainolds, John, 83
Ramée, Pierre de la, 37
Ramsay, George Gilbert, 3, 34, 173
Rayger, Arnold de, 186
Raynaud, Teofilo, S.J., 33
Rebhan, Johann, 59
Reinesius, Thomas, 73, 74
Remnant, Peter, 16
Richter, Christoph Philipp, 161, 179
Riggsby, Andrew M., 41, 42, 43
Rivet, André, 83, 100
Robortello, Francesco, 72
Roding, Wilhelm, 120
Rous (Roo, Rhoo), Gerhard de (van), 92
Rorario, Girolamo, 2
Rosenkreuts, Franz Christian, pseud. of Johan Valentin Andreae, s., 11
Rossi, Paolo, 14
Rufinus, Licinius, 68
Rulant, Rutger, 112, 113
Ruiz de Moros, Pedro, 178, 179
Russel, Donald Andrew, 33
Ryves, Thomas, 77

Saavedra y Fajardo, Diego de, 11
Sachs von Löwenheim, Philipp Jakob, 189
Sagittarius, Thomas, 185
Salian, Jacques, S.J., 80
Salis, Nicolaus von, 117
Sánchez, Thomas, S.J., 182, 183
Saìnchez de las Brozas, Franciscus, 63
Sande, Frederik van den, 178, 179
Sarpi, Paolo, 94, 95
Saumaise, Claude, 74, 182, 183, 192
Saxo Grammaticus, 89
Scala, Aidée, 2
Scaliger, Joseph Justus, 73, 77
Schädler, Ulrich, 11
Schardius, Simon, 89, 90, 103, 104
Scheplitz, Joachim, 179
Scherzer, Johann Adam, 63
Schickard, Martin, the Elder, 114
Schickard, Wilhelm, 7, 14
Schlüsselburg, Conrad, 85
Schmitt, Carl, 33
Schmuck, Wilhelm, Leibniz's grandfather, 118
Schnobel, Joachim, 178
Schoppe, Caspar, 63, 151
Schorer, Christoph, 29
Schottel, Justus Georg,
Schreiner, Thomas R., 35
Schultes, Jacob, 186
Schultz, Georg, 121
Seckendorf, Veit Ludwig von, 81
Seel, Otto, 72
Selden, John, 90
Serarius, Nicolaus, S.J., 90
Serres, Jean de, 91
Sforza Pallavicino, Pietro, 165, 167, 171
Sharrok, Robert, 166, 168
Short, Charles, 22
Sibiuda, Ramon, 33
Sidonius Apollinaris, 77
Sigonio, Carlo, 72
Sigebert of Gembloux, 89
Simocatta, Theophylact, 78
Siri, Vittorio, 96
Sleidan, Johann, 93
Solari, Gioele, 12, 16
Sole, Brunoro da, 186
Sozzini, Fausto, 35, 36
Sparrow, Tom, 1
Spee, Friedrich, 5
Speidel, Johann Jakob, 104, 186
Spener, Philip Jacob, 5
Sphrantzes, George, 78
Sponde, Henri de, 81
Sprenger, Johann Theodor, 97
Starowolski, Szymon, 90
Statius, 75
Stella, Johannes Venetus, 87
Stephani, Matthias, 48, 114
Strauch, Johann, Leibniz's uncle, 152, 178
Struve, George Adam, 178
Stumpf, Johann, 80
Suarès, Joseph Marie, 80
Suetonius, 75
Summenhart, Conrad, 182
Surius, Laurentius, 83, 93, 94
Sutholt, Bernhard, 177
Sutton, Edward William, 31
Sylburg, Friedrich, 75
Symmachus, Quintus Aurelius, 77

Tabor, Johann Otto, 58, 118
Tacitus, 2, 75, 95, 152
Tertullian, 75, 81
Textor, Johann Wolfgang, 98
Theophrastus, 68
Thomasius, Jakob, 48, 49, 63
Thoming, Jakob, 182
Thou, Jacques Auguste de, 95, 100
Thysius, Anton, the Younger, 91
Tornielli, Agostino, 80
Torto, Matthias, pseud. of
Roberto Bellarmino, s., 86
Toschi, Domenico, 70, 186
Trapezuntius, George, alias of George of Trebizond, 78
Treutler, Hieronymus, 177, 178, 204
Tribonianus, 39, 43, 45, 112

Trogus, Pompeius, 72
Turmair, Johannes, called Aventinus, 92
Turnèbe, Adrien, 73
Turturetus, Vincentius, 112

Ughelli, Ferdinando, 87
Ulpian, 38, 103, 110, 111, 139, 182

Valla, Lorenzo, 106
Varro, Marcus Terentius, 103, 106
Velleius Paterculus, 75
Venezia, Sigismondo da, 149
Vermeulen, Jan (Molanus), 82
Vico, Giovan Battista, 17
Vigel, Nikolaus, 114, 145, 146, 180
Villalobos, Juan Bautista de, 180
Vincenti, Umberto, 52
Vinnius, Arnold, 146, 147
Vittorelli, Andrea, 87
Vivio, Francesco, 180
Voet, Gijsbert, 187
Vossius, Gerhard Johann, 104, 105, 108
Vulteius, Hermann, 49, 120, 199, 203

Waal, Marius J. de, 164
Wagenseil, Johann Chistoph, 11
Walaeus, Antonius, 149
Walenburch, Adrian de, brother of Peter, 36
Walenburch, Peter de brother of Adrian, 36
Wängler, David s. Pareus, 100
Watson, Alan, 65, 122, 125, 128, 129, 138, 140, 145
Wehner, Paul Matthias, 104
Weigel, Erhard, 19
Wesenbeck, Matthaeus, 67, 118, 145, 146
Wesenbeck, Petrus, cousin of Matthaeus Wesenbeck, 179, 180
Westhemer, Bartholomaeus, 107
Whaley, Joachim, 99
Wheeler, Arthur Leslie, 6
William of Ockham, 86
Winckelmann, Johann Justus, 91
Wissenback, Johann Jakob, 152
Witgeest, Simon, 20
Witzel, George, 99
Woldenberg, Christian, 102, 107, 110, 112, 113, 188
Wright, Frederick Adam, 10

Yates, Francis Amelia, 14

Zacchia, Paolo, 113
Zasius, Ulrich, 147
Zehner, Joachim, 107
Zepper, Philipp, 68
Zimmermann, Matthias, 35, 81, 82
Zimmermann, Reinhard, 164
Zonaras, John, 76
Zouchaeus, Richard, 48
Zwicker, Daniel, autor Irenici Irenicorum?s., 101
Zwinger, Theodor, 37

www.ingramcontent.com/pod-product-compliance
Lightning Source LLC
LaVergne TN
LVHW092116300926
849161LV00002B/155
9781616195472